I read *A Life of Miracles* in one sitting because I did not want to put it down. This autobiographical account of one married couple's journey of obedience to God's call on their lives will build your faith and stir your soul. Most of all, it brings glory to God rather than people, and it provides numerous glimpses of the coming Kingdom.

LYLE W. DORSETT, PHD

Billy Graham Professor of Evangelism, Beeson Divinity School, Samford University

A Life of Miracles is a series of engaging stories strung together with the thread of God's faithfulness, love, and supernatural power. Told in an easygoing, conversational style, these stories ring true because they are true. I wholeheartedly recommend this book.

ROBERT WHITLOW

Bestselling author of *Water's Edge* and *The List*

Filled with adventurous stories of faith, *A Life of Miracles* is exciting, inspirational, and hard to put down. This book encourages us to greater faith, and the author's humility reminds us that faith is an adventure in which we can all participate. We can identify with him in his struggles and rejoice with him in his victories, while the real hero who shines through these stories is the same God who regularly shows himself stro~~ng in the lives of~~ his children.

DR. CRAIG S. KEENER

Professor of New Testament, Asbury Theological S~~eminary~~
The Credibility of the New Testament Accounts and ~~...~~

I loved reading *A Life of Miracles* because I love faith-building stories and testimonials of our gracious God's everyday faithfulness. I stayed awake much longer at night than I planned on, while telling myself, *Okay, I'll read just one more quick story, then I have to turn out the light. . . .* Four stories later, I was telling myself the same thing. Whether you have been in ministry for twenty-five years or have known the Lord for just twenty-five days, you will be encouraged, educated, and challenged by this book. You'll learn how to walk deeper with God too.

BRIAN HOWARD
Gold Record Award–winning Christian songwriter; author of *The Butterfly Song*

Don Schulze is a talented natural storyteller, so I could commend his book as a series of well-crafted and engaging accounts of miracles witnessed by ordinary people. And that it is. But it is more than just an uplifting read. The stories will inspire other ordinary people to try out the spiritual life lessons Don teaches. As my wife, Beth, read the book, she was inspired to pray for the healing of a chronic injury in my back. I was healed and am now pain free. This happened for two ordinary people. Be encouraged to become an ordinary person witnessing the power and presence of an extraordinary God.

REV. HENRY ANDREW CORCORAN, PHD
Charlotte, NC

What I especially admire in Don Schulze's writing is this: in everyday life he finds a constant flow of "God sightings." *A Life of Miracles* encourages me to look for the same affirming glimpses in my own life.

JOHN SHERRILL
Roving editor, *Guideposts* magazine; coauthor of *The Hiding Place*, *The Cross and the Switchblade*, and *God's Smuggler*

It was impossible not to stop and smile as I read Don Schulze's book. An infectious joy bubbles forth from story after story of our Lord's astounding power and mercy. Miracles, we learn, are not for special people; they are for anyone who dares to believe that God sees, God cares, and God acts! This book is a powerful and worthy record of God's unending faithfulness to those who will follow him.

GREGORY V. JOHNSON
Associate Pastor, DFW New Beginnings Church, Dallas

From the opening chapters describing Don's life-threatening experiences while serving our nation in Vietnam to his ten years of missionary service in East Africa, the book is an enthralling roller coaster of faith tried and tested in the midst of amazing circumstances.

DR. A. CHRISTIAN VAN GORDER
D.Phil. of Queen's University of Belfast, Ireland, and Professor of Religion at Baylor University, Texas

A Life of Miracles serves as a wonderful reminder that we serve a living God who desires to have an intimate relationship with his people. It encourages, inspires, and challenges each of us to "give more" to the Lord, even during times of great struggle. This is a must-have book for all who hunger and thirst for the truth.

RAYMOND M. THOMANN
Senior pastor and founder of Hope Is Alive; host of *Tough Love* daily radio program

I found it hard to take a break from reading *A Life of Miracles*. I was amazed at the number of miracles Don and Leia experienced, and I was in awe of their obedience to God's call.

DONNA WAREN
Fayetteville, NC

A Life of Miracles is a must-read—saturated with the love of God, filled with truths of God's handiwork. Because of the tears of joy it brought to my eyes, I had to stop reading this book several times.

JAMES CLAYTON
Christian businessman, San Dimas, CA

A Life of Miracles describes an exciting way to live that all people can experience but that very few people do. This book encourages readers to give God the chance to prove that his promises are true. If you want to experience an exciting life full of miracles and answered prayer, follow the example of the Schulze family.

JEAN ROACH
Teacher, York County, South Carolina

Don Schulze expresses himself with clarity, humor, and sensitivity. *A Life of Miracles* is a fascinating read that will challenge and amaze anyone who believes that miracles have ceased and are not for this day and time. The book offers an authentic and candid portrayal of God's miraculous and exciting intervention in the life of a couple who are living by faith.

PATRICIA JOHNSON
Retired educator and administrator, Charlotte-Mecklenburg School District, North Carolina

A LIFE OF MIRACLES

WHAT ONE ORDINARY FAMILY GAINED
WHEN THEY GAVE UP EVERYTHING TO FOLLOW GOD

DON SCHULZE

TYNDALE™
MOMENTUM

An Imprint of
Tyndale House Publishers, Inc.

Visit Tyndale online at www.tyndale.com.

Visit Tyndale Momentum online at www.tyndalemomentum.com.

Tyndale Momentum and the Tyndale Momentum logo are trademarks of Tyndale House Publishers, Inc. Tyndale Momentum is an imprint of Tyndale House Publishers, Inc.

Published in association with the literary agency of Les Stobbe, 300 Doubleday Road, Tryon, NC 28782.

Library of Congress Cataloging-in-Publication Data

Schulze, Don.
  A life of miracles : what one ordinary family gained when they gave up everything to follow God / Don Schulze.
     pages cm
  Includes bibliographical references.
  ISBN 978-1-4143-8321-7 (sc)
  1. Miracles. 2. Healing—Religious aspects—Christianity. 3. Trust in God—Christianity. 4. Missions. I. Title.
  BT97.3.S38 2014
  231.7'3—dc23   2013050889

Printed in the United States of America

20	19	18	17	16	15	14
7	6	5	4	3	2	1

To my wonderful wife, Leia, without whose faith, faithfulness, and sacrifice none of this would have been possible . . . and to our precious Heidi and James, who paid the price and shared the experience.

Contents

Invading the Impossible

April 1995
Uganda, East Africa

Covered by only a stained sheet, Lieutenant John Ssjemba* lay on a bare mattress. His head was propped up on one thin pillow, and his eyes were closed.

As my eyes adjusted to the darkness of his apartment, I took in John's bleak surroundings. Though a member of Uganda's elite Presidential Guard, he lived in a shabby flat set aside for junior military officers. The furniture was simple and un-upholstered. Unspeakably dirty and torn draperies hung in front of filthy windows. The cracked concrete walls were sullied with mold, smoke, and dirt, and the paint was flaking off in places.

The modest furnishings of John's small apartment were in stark contrast to his person. Even though he was weak and lying flat on his back, he seemed to maintain his military bearing and quiet dignity. The enemy he faced now was far more brutal than any he'd encountered in his army career.

John was dying of what the Ugandans ruefully call "slim." We know it as AIDS. When I visited Lieutenant Ssjemba, nearly two million of Uganda's nineteen million people were living with HIV; hundreds of thousands had died, and entire villages had become

---

* This name, and many others throughout the book, have been changed to protect the individuals' privacy.

virtual ghost towns. Seeing John lying there, I was sure he was within twenty-four hours of becoming another statistic.

John attended the church I pastored in Kampala, Uganda's capital. Richard, my Ugandan assistant pastor, and I had been summoned to John's home by Vincent and Mary, church council members. They rose to greet us as we entered the darkened room where John lay.

Vincent whispered, "The doctor says he dies soon. He hasn't taken food for many days; now he cannot keep water down. His family is bringing in a coffin from the village."

I glanced toward John's sleeping form. I hoped he hadn't heard Vincent. "John," Vincent said softly, "Pastor Don is here." He and Mary tried to rouse the dying man. John opened his mouth, trying to say something, but no sound came out. He opened his eyes; they were feverish, red and yellow, and sunken into gaunt cheeks. His breathing was raspy, shallow, and irregular. He tried to smile. I reached down and touched his cheek. His skin felt like very hot, dry, thin rice paper. His skeletal hand gripped my wrist.

From just behind me Mary broke the silence. "Pastor, can you pray for John now? Maybe it's not too late!"

I glanced at Richard; he turned his palms upward in a sign of helplessness. His eyes said, *It's up to you.* They were looking for a miracle, and I was confronting the impossible.

I'd first met John several months before during a Sunday morning church service, not long after my wife and I arrived in Uganda. That morning I felt I should offer to pray for anyone who needed healing. Many of the slum dwellers who came to our church couldn't afford medical care. God was their only hope.

A long line of people came forward and faced the platform. As Pastor Richard and I prayed for each one, I asked them what their need was.

Eventually a well-dressed man reached the front of the line. His neatly tailored gray suit and crisply pressed white shirt indicated that he was a man of some substance.

"What can we do for you, sir?" I asked.

He looked at me through red-rimmed eyes. He cleared his throat several times. "Ah, I have a very, very bad cough. Please pray for me."

Suddenly the man had a severe coughing fit. And before he could retrieve his handkerchief and cover his mouth, he sprayed droplets of saliva all over Richard and me. When his coughing subsided, I spoke a brief but sincere prayer for healing of the cough. When I glanced up, I noticed that Richard was almost grimacing as he continued to pray silently and intensely.

After the crowd was gone, Richard asked, "Pastor, do you remember that man in the suit?"

"Of course," I replied.

"That was John Ssjemba. He has AIDS and is in the last stages of the disease."

I felt the cold hand of fear grab my heart.

Today, antiretroviral drugs enable people to live with AIDS for many years. In 1995, an AIDS diagnosis—especially in Africa—meant death in a few months or, at most, a couple of years. We knew that body fluids contained the virus, though it was unknown whether AIDS could be transmitted by saliva.

"Richard, I wish I had known that. How am I supposed to pray for a guy with AIDS when I think he has a cold?"

It suddenly hit me that I was more concerned for myself than I was for John. I felt ill as I left church that day.

———

A few weeks after praying for John at the front of the church, Vincent and Mary had summoned Richard and me to John's home. They'd gone there regularly to pray with John and comfort his family; now they asked us to join them before it was too late.

As Richard and I bounced down the dirt road in my Land Rover toward John's home, I felt terribly inadequate.

God, what do I say to this man? He wants me to pray for him; his friends want me to pray for him. How do I pray?

I tried to still my racing mind. I'd learned years before that when I wasn't sure how to pray for someone, I needed to ask God, *Lord, give me grace that's sufficient for this situation.* I couldn't help John, but I knew that God's grace—his love and power in action—could overcome anything. After asking the Lord for his grace that day, I simply listened. Suddenly, I knew that God was directing me to tell John about certain verses of Scripture. I didn't understand why, but I knew it was important. I breathed a deep sigh of relief. At least I wasn't going into this situation without direction.

Then I was there, on one knee in John's apartment after Mary's urgent plea. It was time to pray.

"John, I want you to know that God loves you," I began. "He has given me something to share with you. These are his words, not mine. I believe they will have special meaning to you." Then I opened my Bible to the Psalms and began reading:

> For as the heavens are high above the earth,
>   So great is His mercy toward those who fear Him;
> As far as the east is from the west,
>   So far has He removed our transgressions from us.
>   (Psalm 103:11-12, NKJV)

After reading the psalmist's familiar words, I turned to the book of Isaiah:

> I, even I, am He who blots out your transgressions for
>   My own sake;
> And I will not remember your sins. (Isaiah 43:25, NKJV)

By now, John's eyes had closed. I wasn't sure he even heard me. Yet I had one more passage to read to him:

> Indeed it was for my own peace
>   That I had great bitterness;

But You have lovingly delivered my soul from the pit
   of corruption,
For You have cast all my sins behind Your back.
   (Isaiah 38:17, NKJV)

I looked at John when I'd finished reading the final verse. "John, did you hear what I read to you?"

He nodded slowly and smiled weakly.

"John, I don't want to presume what God is doing. But it seems to me that there is a clear message here. Whatever you have done in the past was forgiven when you put your faith in Jesus. God has forgotten all about it."

John smiled again and seemed to doze off.

"Well, Pastor," Mary said insistently, "aren't you going to pray for him?"

I had already done what I felt God wanted me to do, so as we prayed, I simply asked God to help John. Mary gave Vincent a disgusted look and shook her head. I had not raised the dead.

———

The next Sunday morning, I stood in front of our church, which met in a big, green tent, welcoming people as they arrived.

Ugly marabou storks picked at piles of garbage on the street corner. It was not quite ten in the morning, but I was already perspiring heavily. As I squinted in the blazing, equatorial sun, I watched a large group of people approaching.

At the head of the crowd was a tall, thin man in a suit. *I must be seeing things*, I thought. The man looked like John Ssjemba. But it couldn't be—John was supposed to be dead. Yet it *was* him. John came up to me and wrapped his arms around me. His cheek pressed against mine.

John slowly pushed me to arm's-length distance. His white teeth glistened in his wide smile. His eyes were clear and white. He looked radiant.

"Pastor, later I have to tell you my story. . . ."

Sounds of people singing the opening chorus pulled us inside. Throughout the service my eyes were drawn again and again to John's beaming smile.

After the service, John and I sat together on a bench.

"When I got very sick from the slim," John began, "I thought it was my punishment for what I did in the war. You see, I fought in the bush against the Obote government. The Obote army terrorized and punished the villagers who supported us, and we terrorized the ones we thought supported the government troops."

John looked down. "I was a commander. I did terrible things. I beat the brains out of children with a shock absorber right in front of their parents. I led gang rapes and murders of many people. My crimes were so horrible that I felt that even though God had forgiven me in a general way, I still had to pay. My first wife infected me with AIDS. I felt the slim was a just punishment, and I had no hope of being healed. Now my second wife and most of my children are also infected with AIDS.

"After you came and read those Scriptures to me, I realized that God had not only forgiven my sins, but he had forgotten them. After you left, I prayed. I asked God to heal me and give me another chance at life. I wanted to be able to tell people what a wonderful God he is and to raise my family.

"Then I drifted off to sleep. Sometime in the night I had a dream, or a vision. I'm not sure which. I was standing in a great room with blood up to my knees. I was horrified. Then I heard a voice calling me. Some distance away I saw my first wife. She had contracted AIDS from someone while I was away fighting. Like I said, she infected me before she died. Now there she was. She had an evil smile on her face. 'John,' she said, 'today you will be with me!'

"I heard myself say, 'Lord Jesus, save me.' There was something like a bolt of lightning that came and struck my former wife. She disintegrated into many tiny pieces. There was another great flash of light. I looked down, and the blood I had been standing in was now crystal-clear water."

John looked back up at me. I didn't know what to say. It was incredible, but there he was. He continued. "When I woke up in the morning, I felt so good, so happy . . . so full of life. I thought I must have died and gone to heaven. But when I looked around my flat, I realized this was not heaven."

I could certainly understand that.

John began to chuckle. "I got up out of bed. I had not been outside in weeks, so I wanted to see the sun. I went out wrapped in my sheet. My neighbors all started screaming and running away; they thought they were seeing a ghost."

"So, John, how are you?"

"Pastor, look at me. I am as strong as ever. I've been eating and putting on weight. I feel wonderful! I truly believe God has healed me of HIV!" Looking at him, it seemed he might be right.

"The army is going to give me my job back in the Presidential Guard if my blood test comes out negative. I'm very happy!"

John's smile faded a bit as he met my gaze. "Pastor, I hope I haven't gone too far in my faith. Now I have also asked God to heal my wife and children. When I go for my blood tests, I am going to take them with me. Do you think that's okay?"

What could I say? "John, that seems perfectly fine to me. I'll be praying for you and your family. Please let me know what you find out."

The next Sunday John stood before the whole church and testified of his complete healing. There were no HIV antibodies in his blood at all. The blood tests of his infected wife and children also came back negative. It seems they were all healed at the same time.

Skeptics kept waiting for John's AIDS symptoms to reappear. Frankly, I wondered about his prognosis myself. But when my wife and I left Uganda three years later, John was still healthy and telling everyone what God had done for him.

My wife, Leia, and I are ordinary people. Yet over the past thirty-five years, we've seen God show up in extraordinary and miraculous ways. John's story is among the most dramatic, but it's really not all that unusual.

Early on, we agreed to do whatever God asked of us; to go wherever he led. We didn't usually stay in any one place, including Uganda, very long. And as we began living out our adventure of faith, we slammed almost immediately into a disconcerting truth: on our own, our resources were utterly insufficient. Yet when we had nowhere else to turn, God always showed up, pouring his power and grace into one desperate situation after another. I can think of no more adventurous and faith-building approach to life than to walk in step with him!

When I first sat down to retrace our journey, which spanned four continents, I began making a list of each time God answered our cry for help in an unmistakable way. By the time I finished, I'd recorded more than fifty hope-giving, faith-stirring illustrations that showcase God's provision, protection, and direction.

As you read about our experiences, I hope you will be in awe of God's miracles but also keenly aware of the weakness and humanity of Leia and me. I pray you'll also find answers to your questions about the way God works today. Perhaps you've wondered,

Can I really expect to see God work miracles?
Can I trust God to care for me and my family if he calls
    us into uncharted areas?
What should I do when I'm asked to pray in a situation
    that seems hopeless?
How can I even know what God is asking me to do?

I don't claim to have special insight into God's plans for your life. But I do know this: God is good. He performs small miracles and great miracles according to our needs, according to our faith, and always, according to his good purposes.

But what if you are unconvinced, not only that miracles happen, but also that God even exists or cares for you? My story is for you, too, because God's supernatural work in my own life began before I even knew him. When he first showed up, I, like John, was a soldier fighting for my country—and for my very life.

CHAPTER 1

VIETNAM

May 1968
I Corps Area, South Vietnam

Marine Lance Corporal Ken White and I walked across the broad expanse of white sandy soil on the way to our night posts. It was nearly midnight, and the bright moon behind us cast long shadows across the dunes ahead. My attention suddenly shifted from the sand to the sky as I saw bright orange flashes on the distant hills miles from our base. The flashes were followed by a staggered series of muffled explosions.

At eighteen, I was a new guy in Vietnam, less than a month "in country." Ken had been there about ten months. He had been through the Tet Offensive in January 1968, when the Vietcong had launched massive attacks on almost every American base in South Vietnam.

Taking note of the explosions in front of us, Ken calmly said, "Looks like they're getting hit with rockets over at the air base." I had seen no real action yet but tried to sound matter-of-fact as I agreed with his observation.

A moment later a set of brighter orange explosions appeared off to our immediate right. Like thunder following lightning, the reports of the Russian-made 122mm rockets came much faster, much closer. Ken was not so low-key now as he said, "Man, they're getting hit right over there at Hotel Battery [a nearby artillery base]."

My eyes quickly scanned the dark, jagged shapes of the surrounding hills. There were more flashes of light and booms of thunder behind us as another nearby Marine position came under bombardment from the rockets.

In a high-pitched voice, my friend suddenly shouted, "Don, they're hitting all around us!" We stood in a large, open area with no cover available.

I heard something that sounded like the amplified hiss of tires on wet pavement passing overhead. I looked up in the direction of the *whoosh*, and a bright flash lit up the sky behind the building directly across the field from us. Instantly, this was followed by the sharp crump of an explosion. It sounded like the slamming of a car door magnified a hundred times. Flames leaped up now from that direction.

I looked at Ken. I could barely make out his voice over the din caused by more *whooshes*, more explosions, and men shouting and screaming.

"Incoming—those are incoming rockets! Run for cover!" Ken shouted.

I lost sight of him as we both sprinted for a sandbagged bunker. Terror I had never known propelled me across the soft sand. I glanced to my left, looking for Ken. Instead, I saw a newly constructed building disappear in a sheet of white-and-orange flame. The sound of that explosion was indistinguishable from the general chaos. Several other rockets hit almost simultaneously among the enlisted men's tented huts. I could now clearly hear the cries and screams of wounded Marines.

More rockets passed overhead and exploded nearby as I reached the bunker. I dove into a narrow opening. My hands pulled my helmet down tightly over my head and neck, but my legs and feet were well outside the protection of the sandbags. I was too paralyzed with fear to wiggle the rest of the way into the bunker.

I had not prayed in years. As the cries of the wounded grew louder and the salvos of rockets continued to fall, I felt sure I was

DON SCHULZE

about to die. In panic-stricken, hyperventilated breaths, I talked to God: "O God, I'm too young to die! I believe you have some purpose for my life! If you will get me out of Vietnam alive, I will do whatever you want. I'll be whatever you want me to be. I'll serve you the rest of my life!" I was desperate, but I was sincere.

A few minutes later, the attack was over. I slowly crawled out of the bunker, barely able to believe that I was still alive. I jogged over to the enlisted men's area behind the smoky remains of our now-demolished mess hall. The sputtering fire among the ruins provided a little light. On the ground were several bodies. They were small, shriveled, and blackened—barely recognizable as people. The bodies were lying on top of green ponchos with only tatters of clothing sticking to them. They were so small that I was sure they must have been Vietcong soldiers—our enemies. I spoke nervously to a captain standing nearby: "Sir, how did these Vietcong get here, right in the middle of our base?"

He looked up and said, "These aren't their soldiers, son." Pointing to my left, he said, "These are Marines who were caught asleep in that hut right over there. As soon as their ammo finished cooking off, we brought them out here." I looked over at the jumble of smoldering plywood, twisted metal, and charred two-by-fours.

Horror gripped me. I realized these must be the same young men with whom I had drunk my first whiskey just the night before. None of these boys were over twenty-one. Two of them had told me they were due to go home in just a few days. My knees nearly buckled, and bile rose in my throat. I felt dizzy and disconnected. Now, I heard the captain yelling at me, "Don't just stand there, son. Run over to the corpsmen and grab some stretchers so we can get these poor guys out of here."

For several days after that, the slightest sudden sound made me jump. Since I was pulling night duty, I had to try to sleep during the day. My hut was near the perimeter of our base. The senior NCOs (noncommissioned officers) had their huts close to the center of the compound.

Not far from their housing were two tall radio masts. Each mast had a red light on top to keep helicopters from running into them. Unfortunately, the masts also served as something like goal posts for the Vietcong, who aimed their six-foot-long rockets in our direction. As a result, the majority of rockets hit somewhere in the vicinity of the senior NCOs. We called it "Rocket Alley." After a while, the plywood sides of these huts were seriously ventilated with holes made by shrapnel.

As the shelling increased, the commanders made a strategic decision to move some of the enlisted men, including me, into the more dangerous "Rocket Alley" area. The senior NCOs would then move into our huts.

Before going to my post on the night that order came down, I reluctantly dragged my gear over to my new quarters in the central area. The very next afternoon, I was startled by the cracking explosion and concussion of the first of a volley of enemy rockets. The surprise daytime attack was over quickly, and I saw smoke rising from the edge of our base. Men began running in that direction. I followed. I soon realized that we were running in the direction of the hut I had just vacated.

My former residence was a smoking ruin. Behind what was left of a plywood wall, I saw a couple of corpsmen feverishly working on someone. After a few minutes, they stood up and put their hands on their hips. Their dejected posture made it obvious that the bloody, burnt Marine was dead.

A cold chill radiated from my heart and spread outward as I realized that if I had not moved the previous night, I could have been that poor guy.

A few months later, I was recuperating from a minor wound at the US Naval Hospital on the little island of Guam. God had heard my prayer. After sustaining a "million-dollar wound"—serious enough that I had to leave Vietnam but not so serious as to disable me permanently—I was miraculously alive and out of Vietnam in one, only slightly damaged piece.

After surgery, I was able to move around. Days were given to physical therapy and minor hospital chores. Evenings were spent at the enlisted men's club, where I enjoyed the free-flowing alcohol and the island girls who hung on to us. One boring day after another passed as I waited to be sent to a hospital in the "world," as we called the continental United States.

God, who is faithful, had answered my prayer and kept his side of the bargain. As for me, I conveniently forgot the promises I had made to him. I didn't yet know that God keeps good books and doesn't forget a thing. It would be seven years before he came to collect.

Meditation on the Miraculous

God pursues us before we even acknowledge him. His ears are already open to our cries for help.

> I will answer them before they even call to me.
>> While they are still talking about their needs,
>> I will go ahead and answer their prayers!
>
> ISAIAH 65:24

CHAPTER 2

THE VOICE

April 1970
Glendale, California

I was discharged from the Marine Corps in September 1969, just before I turned twenty. Though I came home a disabled veteran, I was not ready for the VFW or the American Legion. I had come close to dying, and now I wanted to *live*.

When I arrived back in Southern California, I felt I deserved a brief hiatus to celebrate my liberation from the "green machine"— Marines' affectionate nickname for the Corps—to make up for the teen years I had given to my country. But what I'd intended to be just a few weeks of hitting the Hollywood clubs, partying, and playing around became months of nonstop carousing. I didn't let the couple of small jobs I took interfere with my pursuit of pleasure.

California's hippie culture had already let go of its original search for transcendent meaning, flower power, beauty, peace, and love. By now it had degenerated into an orgy of drugs, alcohol, and sex, all packaged in a tie-dyed, long-haired, groovy veneer. Feeling that I had somehow missed out, I jumped into this atmosphere with both feet. Wine-soaked, drug-fueled love-ins at Griffith Park in the Hollywood Hills provided a daytime interlude between nightly parties. When no friends were available, I'd sling my guitar on my back and head to the park, where I could indulge my fantasy of being a song-writing standout.

That is where I met Wendy, who was into vodka, tarot cards, magic, and musicians. While I found her fascinating, I'm not sure what she saw in me. I guess she was humoring me while she waited for an opportunity to date a real guitar player. She told me that she had been a Jimi Hendrix groupie and was deeply into magic and witchcraft. I overheard her telling a girlfriend that they were too far into it to ever get out. I didn't know what that meant and had no desire to find out. I didn't believe in any of that "superstition."

Home was just a pit stop between parties and hanging out with Wendy, which may be why I barely noticed Leia Jennings and her friend Alice the day they knocked on the door of the apartment I shared with my mom and my brother, Chuck. Alice had been determined to make a surprise visit to see my brother, who was her boyfriend, even though it meant hitchhiking a few miles from the Eagle Rock area of Los Angeles. Leia had come along to keep her company.

When Alice knocked on our door, I opened it. Leia still recalls how the afternoon sunlight swept across my face. As it revealed my features, she heard a voice. While it was audible, it was not the voice of anyone she knew. She heard it say, "This is the man you will marry."

Leia quickly realized that Alice and I had not heard the voice. The next couple of hours were difficult for her as Chuck and Alice talked and I stayed out of their way, busy with other things. The truth is, I barely noticed the two girls who were there to visit with my brother. Leia sat alone on the couch feeling sorry that she had decided to come in her "hippie" attire: hair ironed straight; wearing little round granny glasses, an old brown herringbone coat, and Levis with a flowered band around the cuff. Her fashionable appearance made her look more mature than her sixteen years, but she felt very unnatural, unfeminine, and unattractive. Yet she kept remembering the voice she'd heard when she first arrived.

After she and Alice left, Leia told her friend, "Alice, you might not believe this, but I know I'm going to marry him!"

Alice looked at her in amazement. "What? Who?"

"Chuck's brother, Don. I just know it."

"How can you say that? You don't even know him."

Leia looked at her friend very seriously and said, "All I can say is that as soon as that door opened and I saw him, a voice said to me, 'This is the man you will marry.'"

Alice shook her head, laughing. "Yeah, sure, you heard a voice. Do you know what happens to people who hear voices?" She laughed again and pushed Leia off the sidewalk. "So what are you going to do about it? Are you going to call him?"

"No," replied Leia, "and don't you tell anybody about this. It's going to happen; somehow it will just happen."

Over the next several days, Leia daydreamed about her wedding and began to practice writing her "married name"—Mrs. Leia Louise Schulze—all over her book covers.

Leia and Alice talked about this every day, in school and after school. For weeks, it was a great mystery to them as to how Leia and I would get together since they had agreed to say nothing to anyone.

Despite the lack of contact between us, Leia was sure that what the voice had told her would indeed come to pass. One day Alice asked her again, "If you're supposed to be with this guy, why don't you just call him up before he forgets who you are?"

"No," Leia replied. "I'm sure of what I heard. Someday he will call me."

About a month after Leia's visit, Wendy and I broke up. I was throwing a birthday party for my best friend just a few days later and didn't want to be the only one there without a date. I asked Chuck, "Do you remember that blonde girl who came over with Alice a few weeks ago? You know, the one with the granny glasses? Could you call Alice and see if she would be interested in coming to the party as my date?"

It wasn't a proper way to ask someone for a date and certainly not a particularly propitious way to start a lifelong relationship. Leia, however, graciously accepted my invitation. After that party, there was hardly a day when we were apart. We had fun together, but what made us inseparable was that we could talk together about anything. Well, except one thing: Leia never spoke about the voice she'd heard the first time she saw me. That was her secret, shared only with Alice. She felt that if God had said it, God would see that it happened.

Thirteen months later, we were married at Verdugo Community Chapel in Eagle Rock. The voice had decreed it, and so it came to pass. This unknown voice later became familiar to us: it was the voice of the Lord.

Meditation on the Miraculous

God may work in ways we don't understand for purposes we don't immediately see.

God's voice thunders in marvelous ways;
he does great things beyond our understanding.
JOB 37:5, NIV

CHAPTER 3

A NEW LIFE

January 1976
Ontario, California

Just before Leia and I married in 1971, I took an entry-level job with a paint manufacturer. The Marine Corps had helped me develop a solid work ethic, and I began my work enjoying the challenge and the opportunity to learn a new field. Five years later, I was considered a rising star at the company. The problem was, while I was rewarded for performing at a level well beyond satisfactory, I no longer got any satisfaction from my work.

Still, I had responsibilities. I was twenty-six; Leia was twenty-two; and we had a beautiful baby girl named Heidi. Not only that, we were living the American dream. We were buying our dream home, my career was on track, and the bills were paid. We should have been happy—but something was seriously wrong.

I was convinced that the next rung on the career ladder would probably prove just as empty and repetitive as the one I was on. The security and predictability of my career were not attractive to me. While I was young and confident enough to consider a career change, another job didn't seem to be the answer. I felt as if there should be something more to life, something else that should provide more meaning than merely trying to provide for my family and get by. I had no idea what that might be, and at times I found myself feeling frustrated or depressed.

At home, too, life was becoming boring and empty, broken up only by evenings spent drinking and smoking marijuana with friends or the occasional waterskiing or gambling trip.

Our marriage was no longer romantic either. Leia and I were just two selfish people trying to tolerate each other. There were no screaming fights, no thrown dishes or ashtrays—just aggravation and frustration. My wife also felt some disgust at my habits of pornography, drinking, and smoking marijuana. Leia did not like marijuana and resented that I insisted she indulge with me. I did all these things with little regard for her feelings or her dignity as a wife.

When we had no plans for the evening, I would sit in my recliner, smoke dope, and watch TV or listen to rock and roll. One evening, in between hits on my joint, I was changing channels on the cable TV console. I stopped when I saw a bearded, long-haired guy who was beating on a guitar. As he sang, I noticed that he looked very happy. I decided to watch to see what he was smoking to make him look that way.

I recognized the man behind the beard. It was Barry McGuire, who had been the lead personality of the sixties folk/rock band The New Christy Minstrels. Soon he put down his guitar and began talking about his music career. He said that money, fame, dope, and even the girls had eventually left him jaded, bored, and depressed. I wasn't quite in his league, but I could relate. I didn't have the money, the fame, or the girls, but I was getting jaded, bored, and depressed.

Then he explained that a young man who helped with the equipment on his tour had told him how Jesus had changed his life. Barry said that he began to read a modern language version of the Bible and eventually invited Jesus Christ to be the Lord of his life. Now, he said, he had a great joy and peace. I thought, *What's wrong with this picture? I'm smoking some really good dope, and he's telling Sunday school stories; but he's really happy, and I'm not.*

I told myself, *Man, it would sure be nice to be able to believe all that and to be that happy. But how do I make myself believe something that I don't know to be true?*

When I was young, my mother had dragged me through a series of churches. After her divorce, she had left the Catholic church and spent years looking for a spiritual home. Not only that, but I was certain I had made several good-faith attempts to find God on my own. After my time in the military, I had studied philosophy, religion, and psychology in college and then done additional reading on my own. As part of my search, I had gone through catechism and been confirmed in the church as a teenager. Later I had visited the Self-Realization Fellowship in Hollywood, founded by a prominent Indian guru. In my opinion, I had tried everything and found nothing. I was disappointed and disillusioned. I felt that no one had any real answers, just personal opinions, so I had decided to be an agnostic.

Still, Barry McGuire's testimony and the life that seemed to shine through him made me curious. The next evening, I told Leia, "You know, there's a little church around the corner. We ought to go there and check it out. Heidi is going to need some moral principles." Our daughter was less than a year old, but I was too embarrassed to admit that maybe I was the one who needed some direction in life.

When Leia walked into the family room wearing a dress the next Sunday morning, I looked up at her from the floor where I had sprawled out with my coffee and the Sunday paper.

"Why are you dressed like that?" I asked. We hadn't been to a church since we got married, and I had forgotten that I'd suggested visiting one.

"You said we were going to church this morning," Leia said. "I'm dressed, so you need to get up and get yourself ready."

"Oh, yeah, that's right," I muttered as I folded my paper and drained my coffee cup.

I was quite amazed at the Neighborhood Church. The church I had gone to as a child was quiet, solemn, and dark. Everyone in this little church was smiling and singing enthusiastically. People used unfamiliar phrases like "amen," "hallelujah," and "praise the

Lord" without a bit of embarrassment. They seemed genuinely happy and friendly. *Strange*, I thought. *Strange—but interesting*.

I assumed that only the simpleminded accepted all the Bible stories as true, so I was surprised that the people I met that morning seemed intelligent and educated. I filled out a visitor's card and dropped it into the offering plate as requested.

Tuesday evening Dick Stepp, the church's pastor, stopped by. His wife sat with Leia in the kitchen while Dick and I talked in the living room. I still assumed that Bible-believing Christians must be either deluded fools who had never questioned their childhood beliefs or ignorant and irrational people. Yet I couldn't deny that Dick was well educated, intelligent, and quite rational. How could he believe all this Jesus stuff? He told me that he had gone to an evangelistic meeting while he was in college and had received Jesus Christ into his life. He had left his secular school and gone to Bible college so he could enter Christian ministry.

One of my college professors had told me that philosophy was once called "the queen of the sciences" because it provided an anchor for the soul. I knew I had no such anchor. What Pastor Stepp believed seemed so real to him. I found myself wishing it could be real to me as well, but I seemed not to have a shred of faith.

Dick Stepp explained that salvation was a gift from God. All I had to do was "accept it." *How*, I wondered again, *do you accept something that you don't believe or know to be true?*

At the end of the evening's discussion, he asked me if I wanted to pray and give my life to God. He was so sincere that I didn't want to hurt his feelings. Rather than tell him I wasn't sure I believed what he was saying, I simply said I needed time to think about it.

"Will it be okay if I pray for you?" he asked.

I told him that would be fine, since I assumed he meant that he'd go home and pray for me. Instead, he put one hand on my shoulder, bowed his head, and began to pray audibly for my salvation.

After I thanked him, Dick stood to say good-bye. "Don, let me know if anything happens, okay?"

Relieved to be ending such an awkward and unfamiliar discussion, I said, "Sure, Dick. I'll do that."

The next morning as I drove to work, I thought, *Why not? What have I got to lose? This God stuff has really been on my mind. I'm going to try praying.* I thought back to how Dick had suggested I pray. I felt ridiculous because I hadn't really prayed since Vietnam. I fumbled with the words and waited for God to do something to show me that he was really there.

I waited, and, as far as I could tell, nothing happened. I was embarrassed, confused, and disappointed, but not really surprised. I was a bit angry with myself for being gullible. If God was there, I was pretty irritated at him for not honoring my little religious experiment. I made up my mind to forget all about it, and I tried. The truth was, however, I really did want to know God. I didn't understand that God was drawing me to him in his own sovereign way.

The following evening, my life insurance agent came to our house. Jeff was an acquaintance with whom I'd once discussed a career in life insurance. He knew of my drinking, dope-smoking, and foul-mouthed ways.

Jeff was surprised to see a Bible on my coffee table. He raised one brow, smiled slightly, and looked to me for an explanation. Nervously clearing my throat, I explained that "a friend" had been over and that we had been having a religious discussion.

"That's Leia's Bible," I added.

"Don, I'm a Christian," he said. "If you have any questions, maybe I can help."

I didn't want to get into another discussion about Christianity. However, I couldn't resist one question: "Do you really know this stuff is true, or is it just something you choose to believe? I mean, has God revealed himself to you?"

Jeff spent some time telling me about his faith in Christ and his personal epiphany. He saw my struggle to understand and, perhaps, my desire to know the truth.

Finally, he said, "Don, I think I understand your problem. You want to make a deal with God. You want to pray a prayer so God will do what you think he should do for you. It doesn't work that way. He will reveal himself to you in his own time and in his own way. What you need is to make a commitment to give your life to God and honor him as God, and he will do the rest."

Just before seven the next morning, I was driving to work, feeling desperate. In the past, I had usually been able to manipulate people and circumstances and eventually get my way. By now I realized that was not going to work with God. If I was going to know him, he would have to reveal himself to me. This was not something I could make happen. God, it seemed, could be known only by revelation.

I was irritated as I considered that my decision to follow God, if I chose to make it, would involve living my life to please someone other than myself! Then again, living to please myself wasn't working out all that well. I made a decision to take a small but momentous step of faith:

I began talking to God.

Here is an abbreviated version of that conversation: "God, I don't know for sure that you are there. But I believe you are, so I'm going to make a commitment. I give you my life today without reservation. I am willing to live life on your terms. I will try to do what pleases you. I'll do whatever you want me to do, go where you want me to go, and all the rest [déjà vu—Vietnam, 1968]. . . . But I don't really know what you want, and I can't promise to change myself. I've tried. . . . I can't . . ."

Suddenly God was there, and I was aware of just how holy and pure he was—and how bad I was. We sometimes hear how people near death have their whole lives flash before their eyes. Likewise, in a moment, all the selfishness, sin, and filth of my life surged through my mind. And God's holy presence seemed to be right in the car with me. What a frightful thing. It was like Judgment Day!

I realized that what separated me from knowing God was not some philosophical or intellectual problem. *I* was the problem— who I was and what I had done.

I just blurted out, "God, I am a sinner. I don't want to be like this anymore. Save me. Change me." I had never used such terminology. It seemed as if the words were just given to me.

Suddenly, the terrifying aspect of God's presence and the humiliating reality of my sinfulness were gone! I still felt his presence, but I felt the joy that comes from experiencing forgiveness. I felt . . . clean, new. It was emotional and subjective, sure; but it was also very, very real. It affected my whole being.

For some time, I was barely able to see the road as tears of joy streamed down my cheeks. When I finally regained some self-control, I knew two things.

First, I knew that God had heard me and forgiven me. Some, I suppose, would attribute that to an overwrought emotional state and a cathartic event. But I knew it was reality. There was no other explanation for the undeniable sense of peace, cleanness, and closeness I felt in God's presence.

Second, even more inexplicably, I suddenly knew that Jesus was God himself and that he was the means by which I'd been made right with God.

As surely as I had been without knowledge and without faith just moments before, now I knew these truths with an undeniable certainty. I can't explain how I "knew" them. I was embarrassingly ignorant of the Bible and the teachings of Christianity. Despite my church experience, my education, and my supposed searching, up to that moment I had never really understood who Jesus is or what he has to do with a person's relationship with God. I had heard the gospel presented, but it had been as if I were both blind and deaf. The claims of Christ had gone over my head. Now they were in my heart.

One great decision, one step of faith, one prayer, and one "act of God"—all of a sudden I was one of those "crazy Christians." I was saved!

At work that day I was like a man in a trance. I didn't want to talk to anyone. I felt God's presence, and the world felt new.

I wanted only to stay in touch with God. I didn't want to do or say anything except enjoy this new reality. I had prayed, and God had heard me! I was amazed. When I finished work that day, I got in my car and talked to God again. He was still there. *So, this is what prayer is all about*, I thought, *just talking to God.*

I couldn't wait to tell Leia what had happened. I arrived home and rushed in the door. "Leia, you'll never guess what happened to me today!"

"Well," she said, "you'll never guess what happened to me either."

I slowed down and looked her. She wore a slightly mischievous smile. I wondered what could have possibly happened to her while she cleaned house and cared for the baby. I swallowed my excitement and tilted my head inquisitively.

"Well?" I asked.

"Remember that pastor who talked to you the other night? He came by this morning. He said he felt badly that he hadn't taken any time with me. So we talked. Don, you know my family was not religious. They only tried going to church for a very short time. But I used to walk to church all by myself when I was just in elementary school. I would lie in bed when I was upset and listen to a religious program called *Prayer Tower* on my mom's transistor radio. I always wanted to know God. And you know what? Today I prayed . . ."

She saw the shock on my face and paused. When I didn't say anything, she continued, "Yes! I prayed, and Jesus came into my life! It's so real!"

I was astounded. I said, "Yes! Me too!"

We embraced in the middle of the kitchen, and then I shared my story.

My wife was amazed as I emptied my booze into the sink, dumped my expensive stash of marijuana in the garbage disposal, and cleared my *Playboy* magazine collection out of the garage. No one told me to do this. These escapes had previously filled some of my emptiness and helped me squeeze a little pleasure out of living. Now, though, I was truly happy—happier than I'd ever been.

I simply didn't need these things anymore. The same God who had brought Leia and me together through his "voice" had now, in his own wonderful way, brought us both to himself. Only God could arrange these two divine appointments on the same day.

Meditation on the Miraculous

What I once perceived as my frustration over life's emptiness and lack of transcendent meaning, I now understand to have been essential to the miracle of God's gracious work of drawing me to his Son.

> [Jesus said,] "No one can come to me unless the Father who sent me draws them to me."
> JOHN 6:44

CHAPTER 4

VISITATIONS OF THE NIGHT

February 1976

I am a sound sleeper, so I was surprised to find myself wide-awake, sitting straight up in bed at 2 a.m., just a few weeks after my encounter with God.

Leia is a light sleeper, so it wasn't long before she was also awake. As she rubbed her eyes, she asked, "Don, what in the world are you doing up?"

I was puzzled too. I was surprised to be awake, but I was even more perplexed by a word that I heard repeated over and over in my head.

I looked over at Leia. "I'm not sure why I'm awake. I feel like God woke me up." Then I spoke that strange word. I whispered it under my breath again, echoing the strange syllables that were resounding in my spirit.

Leia was now fully awake. "Don, what *are* you saying?"

"I keep hearing this word, but I don't know what it is or where it came from."

"What kind of word?"

"That's what's so odd. I'm not even sure it really is a word."

I'd always been a voracious reader with an extensive and wide-ranging vocabulary. I riffled desperately through my memory—it was not there.

"What's the word, Don?"

"It sounds like *suzerain*."

Leia, ever practical, calmly suggested, "Why don't we get up, find a dictionary, and solve this mystery? Then we can go back to sleep. I have a baby to take care of, and you have to get up for work in the morning."

"Good idea."

Out in the family room, we leafed through the large unabridged dictionary. We guessed at the spelling.

"Wow," I said, "here it is! It really is a word: s-u-z-e-r-a-i-n. The dictionary says it is an obsolete word meaning a type of sovereign or feudal lord."

"What's that all about?" asked my wife.

"Well, it means someone having complete control or authority over other persons or over a state. The dictionary says that this term was used to describe the relationship between lords and peasants in feudal times. I have a feeling that God is trying to show me something about who he is and what our relationship is to be with him."

Leia smiled and said, "Well, get back in bed, peasant; you have to go to work in a few hours!"

A few months later, I unexpectedly came across that word again. As I waited in the living room of a friend with whom I was going out to lunch, I noticed an old book lying on a table. Curious, I picked it up and found that it was an encyclopedia of theology. I flipped the volume open, and on that very page I saw an article under the title "Suzerainty Covenants." I discovered that the idea of a suzerain went back to the Old Testament patriarchs. The suzerain or king dictated the terms of the suzerainty covenant. There were no negotiations and no compromises. The suzerain simply said, "These will be the terms of our agreement. This is what you are to do, and this is what I will do; end of discussion."

I realized that God had been telling me that he is the sovereign Lord who had called me to be his servant. Because I had first reached out to him in my car, seemingly as a result of my own will, I might have presumed that it was I who called to God.

Only a week or so after the 2 a.m. suzerain incident, I again found myself wide-awake in the middle of the night. I was careful not to wake Leia this time. I heard no word, no voice, so I prayed, *Lord, why did you wake me?*

I felt a strong impression to get out of bed and go into the living room. I didn't know why I needed to get up, but I understood that I should obey. Once there, my attention was immediately drawn to a Bible lying on the coffee table. The strong impression came again: "Pick up the Bible, and open it in the middle."

So I did. When I opened it as close to the center as I could, I found myself in Psalm 119, the longest chapter in the Bible. Again, an impression: "Read all of this. You should get down on your knees and read it."

I knelt and read all 176 verses with great attention and reverence. I sensed strongly that God was watching me.

Psalm 119 focuses on the Word of God and the relationship we each should have with it. As I read, God emphasized to me that every word in the Bible is his word. No matter what criticisms humans might make, no matter what doubts I might have in difficult times, the Bible is God's revelation of himself, his character, and his ways, and it contains everything necessary for salvation.

These two middle-of-the-night visitations established some unshakable landmarks for my relationship with God. The first, of course, is that he is the sovereign Lord of my life. The second is that the Bible is the ultimate, unquestionable, objective, and authoritative revelation of God and his will for me and for all men. After years of fruitlessly seeking purpose in pleasure, I had finally been directed to a true and unchangeable anchor for my soul!

Meditation on the Miraculous

God sometimes leads his people in a very direct and personal way.

All who are led by the Spirit of God are children of God.
ROMANS 8:14

CHAPTER 5

DISCOVERING THE POWER OF GOD

February–September 1976

Not long after Leia and I had announced our simultaneous conversions to an astounded Pastor Stepp, he assigned a young couple, Tom and Carol, to lead us through a twelve-week series of home Bible studies. One week we'd meet for dinner and the study at their home; the next week they would come to ours. Carol was a busy mom with two little girls; Tom, a Vietnam veteran, had lost his left leg from the knee down. He worked full-time to support his family while also attending college on the GI Bill. I was amazed that they were willing to take time from their busy lives to get together with us.

Leia and I grew quite fond of Tom and Carol, who faithfully met with us and tried to answer my endless questions. Then at a Wednesday evening prayer meeting, our pastor announced that Carol had been diagnosed with ovarian cancer. He placed a chair in the middle of the room and called for her to sit in it. We gathered around and began to pray as Pastor Stepp anointed her forehead with oil and asked God for a miracle. Everyone loved Tom and Carol, so the whole church began praying for her to be healed.

By then I'd learned that A. B. Simpson, the founder of the Christian and Missionary Alliance, taught about divine healing after being healed himself from a life-threatening condition. When I had asked Pastor Stepp more about this, he'd pointed me to Matthew 8, which says that Jesus "healed all the sick" in fulfillment of the prophecy from Isaiah, who said, "He took our sicknesses and removed our diseases" (Matthew 8:16-17).

Three weeks later, at our Wednesday prayer meeting, Carol shocked us with the report from her oncologist. All signs of ovarian cancer and the tumors were gone. The room broke out in a chorus of hallelujahs.

After the meeting, Carol came to me and looked into my eyes. "Don, as I was dealing with the diagnosis, the treatments, and all the fear and depression, I asked God why I was going through this. He told me it was for you. For some reason I don't understand, he wants to show you his power to heal."

I didn't know what to think of this, but I never forgot what she told me or the intense look in her eyes. Carol's suffering and miracle were a seed planted in my soul that bore rich fruit in faith and a ministry of healing by the power of God.

Another seed was planted one Sunday morning when Ping and Lina, a young Filipino couple, came to our church to give a presentation on their proposed missionary work. They had just finished missionary training and were preparing to head back to their native country to do evangelism and church planting.

As they spoke of their missionary calling, I felt an inexplicable certainty that God had also called me to be involved in evangelism, church planting, and foreign missions.

Later that afternoon, I shared that sense of calling with Leia. She loved the Lord, but she also loved her middle-class life. She seemed less than excited about the prospect of becoming a missionary; in fact, she told me that she wanted her family to have a "normal" life.

Though Leia and I didn't talk much more about our future right then, I asked God to fill me with power so I could serve him, and I began to see him doing just that.

An Early "Ministry" Miracle

I wanted everyone in my workplace to know what God had done for me. Max, one of my coworkers, always listened politely, if not attentively, to my nonstop Jesus talk. I got along well with Max, in part because he was also a Vietnam veteran. He was a genuine hero. He had been a member of an A-Team Special Forces (Green Beret) unit. His twelve-man team had lived in small, fortified villages deep in communist-controlled territory. They trained and assisted indigenous South Vietnamese militia or, sometimes, Montagnard tribesmen in these strategic hamlets.

During the twenty-six months Max served in Vietnam, his team's villages were overrun and nearly annihilated by the enemy three times. Max had been the only member of his team not to be killed or seriously injured. Now he was plagued with guilt, depression, and many questions about life and death. I spoke to him daily about the Bible and gave him gospel tracts to read.

Eventually I asked him if he had read the things I had given him. "Don, I can't read right now," he said.

"What do you mean you can't read?" I asked.

Max explained that a tiny sliver of metal had gotten into his eye and lodged behind his eyeball as a result of an industrial accident. Moving his eye from side to side was agonizing, he said, so reading led to intense pain. He mentioned that he was scheduled to have surgery in less than a month to remove the tiny piece of metal.

Later that day, I took my pocket New Testament and went to talk to Max again. "Max," I said, "do you believe the Bible is true?"

"Yeah, sure." Max had a Catholic background. I knew from my childhood that many Catholics revere the Bible and believe in miracles.

I quickly turned to the Gospel of Mark and read these words of Jesus:

These miraculous signs will accompany those who believe:
They will cast out demons in my name, and they will speak
in new languages. . . . They will be able to place their hands
on the sick, and they will be healed. (16:17-18)

"Do you believe that part of the Bible, Max?"

"Well, if it's in there, it must be true," he replied cautiously.

"Okay then. I'll pray for your eye so that God can heal it and you can read what I give you." I was dogged in my determination that he read those tracts and booklets.

I wanted to follow Jesus' command to lay hands on the sick while praying for them, but I thought it would look odd to do that in our workplace. After work, though, I saw Max getting into his car. I called out, and when I caught up to him, I reminded him that I was going to pray for his eye. Before he could answer, I quickly reached out my right hand and covered his eye. I prayed that his eye would be completely healed.

There, I had done it.

Max gave me an incredulous look as he ducked into his vehicle. He quickly closed the door, gave me a curt wave of the hand, and was gone.

I stood in the parking lot, looking around, hoping no one had seen us. I felt pretty foolish. As I climbed into my front seat, I said, "Dear God, please do something for Max or I'm going to look like a total fool tomorrow when he tells all the guys what I did."

The next morning, we were extremely busy at work and I had no opportunity to talk to Max. The pace slowed down in the afternoon. Max seemed to be purposely avoiding me. Then I saw him go into a storeroom—I knew that was my chance! I followed him into the large, dimly lit room. Max leaned against a shelving unit with a look of resignation.

"Hey, Max, I was just wondering if anything happened after I prayed for you."

"Well," he drawled, "I didn't want you to get a big head—"

"What do you mean?" I asked, starting to get excited.

"Well, since you prayed for me last night, I haven't had any pain in my eye."

I could hardly believe it. "No pain? No pain at all, Max? Are you sure?"

"I told you, the pain is gone, Don. I can't explain it, but I can't feel that piece of metal anymore." He shook his head and pushed past me back into the store. All I could wonder was, *Why would anyone be upset about being healed?*

Max never did have any more pain in his eye, nor did he ever have that surgery. Sadly, Max's miracle did not lead to repentance or faith in his life, at least that I know of. But, then, who knows if the last chapter has been written?

Seeing Max healed increased *my* faith exponentially, however. From that time on, I have never hesitated to pray for anyone needing and believing for a miracle of healing. More than that, I have always encouraged *all* believing disciples of Jesus to lay hands on every infirm, injured, sick, or diseased person who wants to be healed. Not everyone in every circumstance is healed, and it is not within the purpose or the scope of this book to address the multitude of opinions as to why that might be. What we *do* need to consider is what a dynamic change it would make in a lost world that needs to see a living God if we would step out in faith and offer to pray for people in Jesus' name.

Meditation on the Miraculous

Be obedient to the Spirit's leading to pray for people, knowing that because of God's power, miracles are waiting to happen!

You will receive power when the Holy Spirit comes upon you.
ACTS 1:8

CHAPTER 6

WE RAN ON EMPTY

1976

Max may not have embraced my newfound faith, but he didn't seem to resent me for it. Unfortunately, the one person who did seem offended was Bob, my boss.

That took some getting used to. After all, I'd been his favorite employee. He and I had regularly headed to a local pub together over our lunch hour. We'd order a pitcher of beer and some peanuts, and play pinball for an hour or so.

That changed the day after I met Jesus and threw out my dirty magazines, marijuana, and booze. I didn't dispose of them to be "religious." No one told me I had to dump them; I simply knew that I no longer needed them. I was free.

Leia was thrilled with my decision. Boss Bob was another story.

From the time I shared my good news with him, I was no longer his friend. Soon I became a target, a marked man. The other employees, once my friends, began to mock me openly. Bob started assigning me jobs that were several levels below my pay grade. He did his best to embarrass me and make me miserable. I had a feeling that he was trying to provoke an angry response from me and discredit my conversion. Any mistake I made, real or imagined, became an opportunity to chastise me. I did my best to maintain a good attitude and do my work cheerfully, silently repeating Colossians 3:23 to myself: "Whatever you do, work at it with all your heart, as working for the Lord" (NIV).

Finances were tight at home, so Leia began to work at a nearby department store for a few hours several afternoons a week. Since we had only one car, I would rush home on my lunch hour, grab a quick bite, and drive her to work. We had little time to spare. More than once, I was just a few minutes late getting back to work. Before I became a Christian, two-hour liquid lunches were just fine with Bob. Now two minutes of tardiness became a major crime. I was warned that being late could cost me my job.

One day when I arrived home over lunch, Leia was not quite ready for work. I became impatient and a bit angry.

"Leia, I've told you before—you've got to be ready to walk out the door when I get home! Do you want to get me fired?"

She shot me an angry look. "Can I help it if Heidi needs to be changed just before I step into the shower?" she said. "It's all I can do to get her breakfast, clean up the house, and get ready before noon!"

We continued our verbal spat on the way out the door. Once in the car, we sat in stony silence as I backed out of our driveway. The peace, joy, and presence of God we had known were gone. Just then, the inner voice I now recognized as the Holy Spirit seemed to say, *I am not happy when you and your wife are not loving each other.*

Like many couples, Leia and I usually cooled off on our own without resolving our arguments. Neither of us said "sorry," and we certainly didn't ask to be forgiven. Now my ego and the need to be right stood in the way of peace. A compromise would not do. I would have to surrender.

Finally, I looked over at Leia and said, "Honey, I'm sorry for yelling at you. Forgive me."

Leia reached over and took my hand. "I'm sorry too. We should ask God to forgive us for getting so angry." So we did. Praying together felt awkward, almost corny—but it worked.

Just then our car shuddered and the engine coughed. I looked in horror at the gas gauge. Oh, no—empty! The engine sputtered one more time and died altogether. The car's momentum carried us slowly forward.

"Leia, we're out of gas. I'm going to be late for sure now. This is a disaster! The nearest station is a mile down the road. I'll never walk there, get gas, and get back in time!"

"Well," she said, "why don't we pray?"

"Good idea. We need a miracle, or I'm going to need a new job."

We reached across the center console again and joined hands. We asked for the impossible: that God would somehow keep the car going until we reached the gas station.

There was nothing to do but sit back and see what God would do. We could hardly believe it. The road was level, but the car continued rolling without slowing down at all. As the vehicle continued its silent journey block after block, we watched in openmouthed amazement. When we had traveled nearly a half mile, we began to cheer, "Thank you, Jesus!"

We continued to pray aloud, even as our excitement built. The only obstacle remaining was a stop sign just as the gas station came into view. I did not plan to stop.

Then another car approached the intersection from the other street. Because we were coasting, that driver would get to the four-way stop first, so we would have to stop to let him through.

I had no choice but to apply the brakes or risk a collision. Our car came to a near-total stop. After the other car went past, I removed my foot from the brake. Leia and I prayed again, and our car began to accelerate ever so slightly. We were exultant about God's goodness and power as we finally approached the entrance to the service station. As our front tires reached the driveway apron, we came to a full stop.

Once I got out of the car, some bystanders helped me push the car up to the pump.

I looked into the window at Leia, laughed with joy, and said, "Next time, we'll have to ask God to get us all the way to the pump!"

I made it back to work right on time.

Sheba Walks

Soon after this, my brother, Chuck, came to visit. Leia and I had not seen him since we had become Christians, and I wanted to explain to him face-to-face how God had changed our lives. I was hopeful that he might also give his life to God. We had a good time catching up on all the family news and talking like brothers do. On Sunday, Chuck attended church with us.

I had arranged for Chuck to work with me on a small house-painting job on Monday. We both had a lot of experience painting as we grew up; in fact, that was how we had earned money during the summers to buy our school clothes. Monday morning we sat in the family room, pulled our work boots on, and reminisced about the "good old days" painting together.

Just then our dog, a collie named Sheba, came into the room.

Chuck immediately noticed that she had a problem. "Don," he asked, "why is your dog walking like that?"

Sheba was walking on three legs, carefully holding her right rear leg several inches off the floor. "Well, Chuck," I answered, "we think Sheba might have been hit by a car when she got out of the yard a week or so ago. When she came back, she was walking like that. It seems to be very painful. She won't let us touch it. She yelps if we try. We were hoping that the leg would heal on its own, but there's been no improvement."

"Really? Why don't you take her to the vet?" he said, looking at Sheba with real concern.

I was a little embarrassed. "We are having a hard time financially right now," I said. "That's why I'm doing these side jobs. We've been afraid that if we take her to the vet, they will either want to put her down or recommend some expensive treatment that we can't afford. So we've just been hoping her leg will heal."

"Well, Don," Chuck said, "you've been telling me about all that God can do, like how he healed that guy at your work. Why don't you just ask God to heal her?"

The truth was that we had been praying that Sheba would get better, but we had not been expecting a miracle—not for a dog.

I looked at Chuck. He was eagerly waiting to see what his big brother was going to do. I looked at Sheba. She stood there on her three legs looking down at the floor with a forlorn expression.

"Okay," I said, "let's see what God will do." What happened next was one of those things that I can't explain or take any credit for. It was just plain inspiration.

I turned to Sheba, lifted my arm, and pointed my finger directly at her. With boldness that surprised even me, I said, "Sheba, in the name of Jesus of Nazareth, put that leg down and walk!"

Sheba lifted up her head instantly and looked right at me. Then, to our amazement, she extended her injured leg, put her foot on the floor, and turned, walking out of the room without a limp. Chuck and I stared at each other in amazement. Though we had seen it, we could hardly believe it. Sheba never limped again.

Meditation on the Miraculous

No need is too small for God to intervene when we call to him.

> The LORD directs the steps of the godly.
> He delights in every detail of their lives.
> PSALM 37:23

CHAPTER 7

CAT WOMAN AND
LEIA'S SPRAINED ANKLE

1977

Though Bob, my boss, was not the only friend I lost after becoming a believer, Leia and I made many new friends as we became more active in our little church. Home Bible studies, prayer meetings, and outings with our new Christian friends took the place of parties and barhopping. In particular, we liked to spend time with Bill Borngrebe, a Los Angeles County deputy sheriff, and his wife, Joyce. On Tuesday evenings they would come over so Bill and I could go out in the neighborhood to talk to people about Jesus. Joyce and Leia would stay at our house and pray for us.

I began to feel that God wanted me to spend more time learning about his Word and praying. He also seemed to be nudging me to find a job that would give me greater liberty to be involved in ministry. I thought perhaps I should be moving in the direction of the missionary calling that our friends Ping and Lina had spoken of.

Ironically, because I spent so much time in worship, fellowship, and study, I now had little contact with non-Christians, except my colleagues and customers at my job. The paint store became my mission field. As on any mission field, it was not long before trouble appeared.

One day Tony, our company's director of human resources, showed up. He approached me from behind as I was finishing some paperwork. As soon as I sensed his presence, I turned and looked up at Tony, who towered over me. He was a large, muscular man, and he looked ready to burst out of his expensive fitted shirt. His deep, gruff voice was not angry but firm as he greeted me. It was obvious that this was not a casual visit. His huge hands were on his hips, and he leaned forward, uncomfortably close to me.

"Don," he began, "you know we really like you. You're advancing rapidly with this company. But your recent conversion is causing trouble. We are getting complaints from many of your coworkers about your preaching to them and to the customers. What do you have to say about that?"

"Tony, how about you?" I asked. "Do you know the Lord Jesus?"

In retrospect, I can see that this was not the best response. Though I may have sounded rebellious and flippant, that was not my intent. I thought that if Tony were a believer, he might understand my enthusiasm and the sense of obligation I felt to share the gospel. Understandably, he did not see my inquiry in that light.

Rage filling his voice, Tony leaned even closer and pointed a meaty finger in my face. "How dare you preach to me!" he said. "This interview is over. If I get one more complaint about your preaching, you *will* be fired." Then he turned and stormed away without another word.

I knew I was in trouble, because I would not be able to contain what was in me.

Fortunately, one of my frequent customers, Fred, came in soon after my confrontation with Tony. I looked forward to Fred's visits because he was a mature, spiritual Christian and a minister. He had begun teaching me Koine Greek, the language of the New Testament.

I told Fred about my dilemma at work. He suggested that I begin taking more freelance painting jobs. That way I could start my own business and be free to preach and follow the Lord's leading. Fred knew what he was talking about. He had been living by faith for years, planting a couple of churches and starting a ministry for alcoholics and addicts. When necessary, he supported himself and his "startup" ministries through painting and wallpapering jobs. Fred's faith and level of sacrifice impressed me. On the other hand, I had a mortgage, a wife, and a baby; I valued my job security.

I spoke to Leia about my conversation with Tony and Fred's advice. I got a very clear revelation of her will in the matter. She was almost as angry as Tony had been.

"Don, you know that my dad was a small business owner," she said. "I saw the struggle, sacrifice, and suffering his business caused us. I want no part of starting a business on a shoestring—especially with someone who has no business experience!"

I kept praying that God would show me what to do. I was going to have to do something; my career with the paint company was certainly in jeopardy.

Over the next few weeks, a number of people contacted me "out of the blue" to see if I would take on various house-painting jobs. Was this a sign or an answer to prayer?

As I worked on one of these jobs, I thought about my situation. On one hand, the whole idea of starting a business with very little capital and limited experience seemed unreasonable, maybe even crazy. On the other, I had already seen God do some very "unreasonable" things in my life. I couldn't shake the feeling that he might want me to be self-employed.

While I stood on an extension ladder painting the eaves of a large, vacant house, I prayed: "Lord, I can't figure this out. If you want me to be free to serve you by quitting my job and doing this painting full-time, I'm asking for a definite sign. Here is my request: *today*, as a direct result of *this* job, give me the opportunity to tell someone about Jesus." That seemed unlikely since the house was vacant, no one was around, and the day was almost half gone. It would take a miracle.

Not more than fifteen minutes later, I heard a voice from the bottom of my ladder. "Hello, how ya doin' up there?" I looked down to see a young man in his early twenties smiling up at me. He had longish, pumpkin-colored hair and freckles. I looked at him and said nothing.

He spoke again, "So, what are you doing?"

Anxious to continue working, I replied, "I'm up here weaving a basket."

The young man laughed. He did not seem offended by my rude answer. In fact, he smiled and said, "Well, do you want some help?"

"Sorry, I'm not hiring."

He said he wasn't looking for a job; he just had some free time and liked to help people. His offer seemed a bit odd, but it didn't make sense to reject free labor.

For the next hour or so, my new friend scraped paint off some badly weathered windowsills. Then he appeared again at the bottom of my ladder.

"Hey, you wanna grab some lunch?" He told me that his apartment was just across the street and that he could make some great sandwiches. Free labor, free lunch—why not?

His two-story apartment building was built around a common area with a swimming pool. As we approached the courtyard, we saw five or six men chasing a disheveled middle-aged woman around the pool. She was screaming, and the men were shouting. I looked at my new friend; he just shrugged. We continued watching as we leaned on the gate leading to the pool area.

The woman was yelling obscenities and threats, and the men were telling her to go back to her apartment before she hurt herself. They eventually surrounded her and forced her into the doorway of her small apartment. My friend and I gave in to curiosity and joined the crowd. The woman continued to scream curses and threats at her neighbors. Now, she crouched on the bed, assuming the posture of a stalking cat; she hissed, spat, and pawed at the air. The men were debating whether it was safe to close the door and leave her alone.

"Yes, do it before she hurts someone."

"No, don't do it—she might hurt herself."

Confusion reigned.

I remembered reading about demon possession in my New

Testament and how easily Jesus had dealt with it. Even though I had been a Christian for less than a year, I saw no reason not to imitate Jesus.

Without really thinking, I stepped toward the "cat woman" on the bed. She clawed the air in front of me. I pointed at her and said in a bold voice, "I command you in the name of Jesus of Nazareth, lay down, be quiet, and go to sleep!" To everyone's amazement, her eyes went wide; she put her hand behind her and grabbed her pillow, and then turned over and lay quiet.

A few minutes later I was in my friend's apartment, where we ate sandwiches in silence. Finally, he asked me, "How in the world did you do that?"

I found myself fully engaged in telling him about Jesus and how I had come to know him. In those days, I didn't know that I should ask him if he wanted to pray or invite him to church. I was content just to share the gospel and my story with him.

As I walked back to my job across the street, I realized that God had given me the sign I had asked for. I had, in a most remarkable way, been given the opportunity to tell someone about Jesus as a direct result of painting an empty house! Now, what to do about my job? I had prayed but . . . could it have just been a coincidence?

Leia's Sign

My wife was in no mood to hear about my miraculous sign. Two days earlier, she had been running through the backyard looking for our two-year-old daughter.

Somehow Heidi had gotten out of the house, and Leia was in a panic trying to find her. While running across the yard, she stepped into a hole in the lawn. Leia heard a crack from her ankle as she fell hard upon the turf. Despite excruciating pain, she pulled herself to her feet and hobbled around until she found Heidi, sitting safely on a neighbor's lawn.

Once back in the house, Leia collapsed into a recliner in our family room and examined her ankle. The entire area was swelling and turning nasty shades of red and purple. Waves of pain left her feeling nauseous. Leia tried to stay in the chair, but a two-year-old will not let you relax for long. She was up and down all day, hopping on one foot to take care of Heidi.

Normally, when I arrived home from work, the house was spotless, dinner was on the stove, and Heidi was neatly dressed. That evening Leia simply sat in the recliner, enduring the pain. I offered to take her to the emergency room, but she didn't want to move.

"I just twisted my ankle. That's all. You can help take care of Heidi tonight. I'll manage somehow tomorrow. If it's not better, then we'll go to the doctor."

The next day, the ankle was not better. At the emergency room, the doctor gave us the bad news.

"Mrs. Schulze," he said, "you have fractured a couple of bones in the ankle. You also have a very severe sprain—one of the worst I've seen. You've injured some tendons and ligaments. The swelling and discoloration are so serious because some blood vessels ruptured. We are going to have to put you in a soft cast for now. You will only be able to walk with crutches, and you need to stay off your feet as much as possible for two weeks. Then we will look at it again."

Leia was devastated. How could she possibly care for our daughter and our home? But the ankle was so painful, so swollen, and so bruised that she had no choice.

The next morning, I went back to work on my painting job on the vacant house. As I painted, I thought about how God seemed to be directing me to quit my job and start my own painting business.

That evening, I finally told Leia about all these signs. Admittedly, I didn't do it with much sensitivity, considering the pain she was in. She looked at me, not believing I had the nerve to bring this up now.

Undeterred, I asked her what she thought of my sign.

"That's good for you, Don," she said angrily, "but God hasn't given me any sign yet!"

Ignoring her frustration, I plowed ahead with my agenda.

"Well, dear," I replied, "you haven't asked him for a sign yet, have you?"

She looked at me incredulously. "Really? Are you kidding?"

"No, I'm not kidding," I said. "You haven't asked for a sign. So how can God give you one?"

Leia looked at me a moment longer, then she looked up at the ceiling. "Okay, here goes." Gritting her teeth, she said, "Lord, if you want Don to do this crazy thing, then heal my ankle completely by tomorrow morning!"

She picked up a magazine and gave me a smug look. With her mangled ankle propped up on the footrest of the recliner, the case seemed settled. She had me. Her sign trumped mine.

I wanted to say, "That's not fair! Why didn't you just ask God to part the Red Sea or something? Look at that ankle!" Instead, I simply collapsed into the other chair.

I would like to say that I really prayed and believed in a miracle for Leia's ankle. Instead, I figured that perhaps Leia's demand for a sign was God's way of saving me from my own fantasy. The truth is, I was still fearful and uncertain about leaving our security behind.

All the next day, I wrestled with these conflicting desires, fears, and circumstances as I wondered why God made knowing his will so difficult.

When I returned from work that evening, I greeted Leia, sitting in her recliner, ankle extended on the footrest. The family room was separated from the kitchen by a long tiled counter. I stood with my back to Leia as I sorted through the stack of mail on the counter.

"How's Heidi?" I asked.

"She's sleeping."

Finally, I decided to get it over with. "How's your ankle today?"

"Well, why don't you turn around and see?" Leia said.

As I turned to face her, Leia stood up on both feet. Then she lifted her "good" foot off the ground, putting her full weight on the injured ankie. Next she began to dance and spin around on her injured foot, which was still encased in the soft cast.

She danced over to me and said, "Don, I think it's completely healed. When I got out of bed this morning, I tried to hop over to where my crutches were. But I stumbled and accidentally put my weight on my bad foot and . . . it didn't seem to hurt. So I tried putting more weight on it, and it still didn't hurt. Then I tried full weight . . . and there was no pain. Then I walked on it. I've been on the foot all day, taking care of Heidi and cleaning the house, and still there's no pain."

It seemed unbelievable, but there she was, bouncing up and down on her "bad" foot.

"Why haven't you taken the cast off yet if you're healed?" I asked.

"Well, the doctor said two weeks. I wasn't sure."

"Let's take a look. If it's still swollen, you need to stay off of it, pain or no pain."

Leia got back into the recliner. I began removing the bandaging that held the cast in place. Two nights before, the ankle had been swollen to nearly the size of a grapefruit and was almost black in places from several inches above the ankle to the toes. As the layers of elastic bandage came off, our eyes widened in amazement. There was no swelling at all. The badly bruised areas had turned the soft yellow of a bruise that is weeks old—a reminder of the damage that had been done and the miracle that had occurred.

This fresh demonstration of God's power and presence filled us with awe and joy. At the same time, we were aware that we now had to step out into the unknown. I wondered then whether James and John, Jesus' disciples, also had mixed feelings when he called them to leave the family fishing business to follow him on the unfamiliar road of preaching the Kingdom.

The reality of Leia's faith in Jesus as Savior and Lord was never in question. However, she has often said that this incident provided a wonderful reference point for her faith as we endeavored to follow the Lord in many difficult decisions in the future. This dramatic answer to prayer for clear direction gave her much confidence to pray in the future.

My strategy was to wait until I got my first big job lined up before I gave notice to my employer. Within two weeks of Leia's miracle, the PTL Painting Company (Praise the Lord Painting— very original) had a large job. The sweet old lady who hired me told me that she decided to give me the work when she saw the name PTL Painting in the paper. So Leia and I were off to a promising start—or so we thought.

Meditation on the Miraculous

God's people feel great joy at the privilege of knowing that they are called; yet that joy is mixed with great trepidation about all they must leave behind and the many unknowns that lie ahead.

> *[Jesus] said to another person, "Come, follow me."*
>
> *The man agreed, but he said, "Lord, first let me return home and bury my father."*
>
> *But Jesus told him, "Let the spiritually dead bury their own dead! Your duty is to go and preach about the Kingdom of God."*
> LUKE 9:59-60

CHAPTER 8

THE PROMISED CHILD

November 1977

Through all the ups and downs Leia and I faced, Heidi was the consistent bright spot in our lives. She was so cheerful and lively; she filled our home with joy. Since we'd never taken any precaution against conception, after five years of marriage, I assumed we would have only one child.

In May 1976, just a few months after we came to Christ, Leia began to pray that God would bless us with a son. Soon she told me about her prayers; she seemed nearly obsessed with the idea that it was her duty to provide me with an "heir." Though I assured her that I was content with her and our little princess, Heidi, Leia bombarded heaven with pleas for a son. Months went by, and she did not become pregnant. She became discouraged.

I tried to comfort my wife by telling her again that I was perfectly happy with just her and Heidi. She was inconsolable. She promised me that she would not give up until God heard her prayers and gave her a son. Late one night, long after Heidi had been tucked in and I was sound asleep, Leia was praying silently while sitting up in our bed. She concluded her prayers with her regular heartfelt plea for a son.

She was sitting in the dark in silent contemplation when, from the corner of the room, she heard an audible voice—the same voice she'd heard years before. "Do not be afraid, my daughter; I will give you a son!" In the awesome silence that followed, Leia began to cry. After thanking and praising God, she drifted off into a peaceful night's sleep.

Leia expected to become pregnant right away. It didn't happen. Again, months passed, each bringing another painful disappointment.

One chilly evening in February 1977, we were at Bill and Joyce's home for a Bible study they hosted for a few Christian couples. Each week we would worship in song and then a guest speaker would teach and minister in prayer.

On this particular night, the guest speaker taught from an obscure passage in Judges 3. We were amazed at how he brought the story of Ehud to life, as well as the timeless biblical principles he drew from the account. Just a few decades after their arrival in the Promised Land, the Israelites had begun to worship false gods. They had abandoned their pledge to only worship the one true God who had delivered them from slavery. As a result of their unfaithfulness, God disciplined them: "Every time Israel went out to battle, the LORD fought against them, causing them to be defeated, just as he had warned. And the people were in great distress" (Judges 2:15).

The teacher then pointed us to Deuteronomy 4, which explains why God continued to have mercy on his wayward people: "The LORD your God is a merciful God; he will not abandon you or destroy you or forget the solemn covenant he made with your ancestors" (verse 31).

When our teacher had finished, he seemed to look almost straight at Leia and said, "If there is one thing we can learn from this lesson tonight, it is that when God has spoken, when he has made a promise, he is not a man that he should lie. You can take his words to the bank."

Leia felt great assurance that God was speaking directly to her and confirming the promise he had made to her months earlier. In her heart, she said, *Lord, I do believe—I will have a son. Now I receive that promise by faith.*

Within weeks, Leia was pregnant!

Our excitement was tempered by the fact that my fledgling painting business was barely surviving. We had almost no income and no insurance to cover prenatal care or the delivery. We applied for a California health assistance program available to low-income families. We prayed as we began our search for a good obstetrician who would accept Leia under that program. In our circumstances, we should have accepted any willing doctor, but we felt that this was a special child, an answer to prayer and a gift from God. We wanted a Christian doctor.

At last we heard about Dr. Richard Eby, a believer who was also one of the founding members of the College of Osteopathic Medicine of the Pacific and a practicing obstetrician. Though he had a full roster of patients already, he graciously accepted Leia as a new patient. Leia and I were very impressed with how God had surpassed our expectations when we had prayed for a Christian obstetrician.

Several months before our baby's birth, we attended a service at the church of our friends Fred and Brenda Conley. We hadn't seen them since before Leia became pregnant. Near the conclusion of the service, Brenda said she wanted to pray for Leia and some difficulties she was having with the pregnancy. After Pastor Fred called Leia and me up front and the congregation prayed for us, Brenda told Leia, "I believe God has shown me something. You will have a son, and this child will grow strong in the things of God. He shall be a man of God and a preacher of the gospel." We had not told Brenda, or anyone in the church, that we believed Leia was carrying a boy.

That November, James D. Schulze III was born—almost exactly nine months from that night when the Bible study speaker reminded us that God always keeps his promises. That was the night Leia made a firm decision to take God at his word, no matter how long he took.

Once James had been placed on his mother's tummy and the umbilical cord had been cut, the delivery room became a sanctuary.

We all sang praises to God around Leia's bed. It felt entirely appropriate for such a wonderful occasion.

Leia and I were not surprised when James came to faith at an early age. He was a "normal" boy, although even in elementary school, he prayed over his lunch and before taking tests. He regularly brought friends to church. At his tenth birthday party, he insisted that I show an evangelistic Christian film to his friends and give a brief salvation message. Once in high school, James led our church's youth group. By the time he was eighteen, he had already preached to large gatherings of youth in Uganda, Kenya, and Holland. After more than ten years in pastoral ministry, James is now serving God and country in the US Air Force.

Meditation on the Miraculous

When God promises, he truly delivers. You can count on it.

> God is not a man, so he does not lie.
> He is not human, so he does not change his mind.
> Has he ever spoken and failed to act?
> Has he ever promised and not carried it through?
> NUMBERS 23:19

CHAPTER 9

LIVING ON MIRACLES

1977–1979

Our son's birth was just one more demonstration of God's outpouring of love on our lives. The Lord had delivered Leia and me from our guilt, as well as many self-destructive attitudes and behaviors. He had blessed us with two beautiful, healthy children. And he had directed me to a career path that would enable me to pursue the work he had for me—although we weren't yet sure exactly what it was.

As a new Christian, I could relate to the way the Israelites must have felt when Moses brought them out of Egypt. God had delivered them from slavery to Pharaoh; he had delivered me from slavery to sin. He freed his people by sending ten plagues as signs to the hard-hearted Pharaoh and then parted the waters so they could safely cross the Red Sea. Though our rescue was not as dramatic, Leia and I were amazed when we discovered God had saved us both on the same day.

So we began PTL Painting with great optimism, assuming that because God had supernaturally led us to take this step, he would certainly bless the business and prosper us. Then we'd have the liberty to pursue whatever ministry he had for us.

Perhaps we should have paid more attention to the story of the Israelites *after* they crossed the Red Sea. Once they'd watched the collapsing walls of water destroy the pursuing army, no doubt these former slaves expected that their journey to the Promised Land would be an anticlimactic pleasure trip. Not so.

Because of their innate rebelliousness, the immaturity of their faith, their lack of understanding of God's love, and their desire for worldly security, what should have been an eleven-day dash to the borders of Canaan turned into a difficult forty-year learning experience. For many of the same reasons, God allowed Leia and me to go through some long and difficult learning experiences as well.

In fact, PTL Painting was not a roaring success; for a couple of years, it appeared to be a roaring disaster. We went weeks—sometimes months—without work. Even after going through the humiliation of applying for food stamps and government-provided medical coverage, we usually had just enough money to keep the lights on and put gas in the car.

Soon we were discouraged, which led to bouts of depression. For months, we wondered why God had encouraged us to take this path, only to "fail" to bless it now. During this dark period, I continued to pursue ministry opportunities. I gave time to personal evangelism and had the privilege of leading a number of people to Jesus. I also wound up leading something of a house church where we saw many people saved, healed, and otherwise helped.

The apparent contradiction between our spiritual blessing and material difficulty was hard for us to reconcile. However, it drove us closer to God and his Word. Jesus had already revealed himself to us far too clearly for us to question his reality and power. That confidence led to a strange dichotomy. At the same time we had boundless faith for some things, we went through bouts of doubts, depression, and fear brought on by disappointments and financial pressures.

While occasional work and government assistance kept us from going hungry, we struggled to make our house payments. At one point, we needed to make two house payments within less than two weeks in order to stay out of foreclosure.

We had two vehicles at the time—a Chevy pickup I used for work and a ten-year-old Cadillac. One day when it seemed like things couldn't get much bleaker, we were invited to dinner at Leia's grandparents' house in San Bernardino. As we started off on the half-hour drive, I heard the old Caddy's engine make the minor tapping sound that I had been noticing for some time. As we passed the halfway mark to Grandma Mary's place, the minor noise suddenly became a major noise. I knew this was serious. We slowed down and prayed the rest of the way there.

Leia's uncle, Jim, had also come for dinner. He was a professional mechanic, so while the family was preparing the meal, Jim and I looked under the hood of the Cadillac. Soon he said, "Don, this car will have to be left here until you can afford to completely rebuild the engine."

I said, "Let's eat. I don't want to think about this."

After dinner, my family and I piled into Jim's car for the ride home, which gave me plenty of time to think.

I knew the Word says, "In everything give thanks" (1 Thessalonians 5:18, NKJV), but my thoughts that evening were not good. Give thanks? Right! My best thought was, *God, how much worse are things going to get? Can't we catch a break?*

Not long after that, my father, James (Jim) Schulze; my stepmother, Louise; and my teenage sister, Susan, flew in from Maryland for a rare visit. Dad had retired from Maryland Shipbuilding and Drydock Company and now traveled all over the western hemisphere as a consultant. A lifetime of hard work had resulted in a comfortable retirement, so money was no problem for Dad.

Despite our financial difficulties, Leia and I put on a good performance. My father was not an atheist or even an agnostic. He just wasn't interested in God or religion, period. Regardless of the reasons behind his antipathy, we didn't want to provide him with any reason for doubting God or his goodness. We did our best to camouflage our circumstances, which was challenging since I didn't have any work lined up during their visit. We smiled outwardly and told them what a wonderful coincidence it was that I happened to be "between jobs" while they were there.

Dad was generous, as always. He would not allow us to pay for anything—not groceries, not gasoline, nothing—during their stay. It was humbling to watch him constantly pull out his wallet, though probably not as embarrassing as it would have been if he'd had to watch us pull out our food stamps!

Dad and Louise enjoyed being with us so much that nothing seemed to bother them. Whenever we went to see the sights of Southern California, they insisted that Heidi and Leia, who was about seven months pregnant at the time, ride in the cab of my pickup while they sat on cushions in the truck bed with Susan. I was humiliated. I felt like Jed Clampett of *The Beverly Hillbillies*. Dad, however, had grown up poor during the Great Depression. The appearance of poverty was nothing new to him. He thought it was all great fun. He laughed as he told us that he had California sunshine and a "convertible"—what could be better?

As Dad's departure date drew near, so did our deadline for avoiding foreclosure on our house. I knew that if I asked for help, Dad would gladly take out his checkbook and solve our problem. But after telling him what a great God we served and talking about all the miraculous things we had seen, I didn't want to tell him that our heavenly Father couldn't help us with our house payments. We waited for a miracle instead.

On the final day of their visit, I helped pack their bags into the truck for one last embarrassing trip, to the airport.

Dad said, "Son, we have really enjoyed our visit with your family. Is there anything you need? Is there anything we can do for you?"

I wanted to say, "Yes, I need two house payments right now!"

Instead, I just said, "Dad, it's been great just having you guys here. You've already done more than enough. Thanks for coming; thanks for everything."

Just as we were about to leave for the airport, Leia appeared at the front door. "Don, telephone! It's for you. It's Grandma Mary; she says it's important."

I went into the house, impatient to get to the airport on time.

"Don, I've got some good news for you and some bad news," Mary said.

"Give me the bad news first please, Mary."

"Okay. You remember that old Cadillac you have parked in my yard? Well, last night a huge branch fell off a tree and landed right on top of it!"

I groaned silently. *Good grief, what next?*

After a pause she continued, "With the leaves and branches and all, we can't tell just how bad the damage is, but it can't be good. It was an awfully big branch—big around as a man!"

I replied, "Thanks for telling me. That car wasn't really going anywhere anyway. I've got to run to the airport. What's the good news?"

"Well, I'm not sure how good this is. Your car was parked in our yard, but that branch was from a tree in our neighbor's yard. Their insurance agent told them over the phone that the damage to your car might be covered under their homeowner's policy. He wants you and Leia to meet him out here tomorrow, just after noon."

"Okay," I said, "we'll be there." I thanked her, hung up, and hurried out to my waiting family.

As we drove, I did the math and realized that the last day to make the two house payments before foreclosure started was just two days away. I decided that the following day we'd go to the mortgage company's office and beg for mercy. First, though, we would go see the crushed Cadillac.

So the next day we drove back to San Bernardino. The insurance agent, Uncle Jim, Grandma, and the neighbors stood to the left of our old Cadillac. Behind them was a pile of leaves and small branches they had cleared away to better observe the damage to the vehicle.

After introductions, the insurance agent pointed to the place of impact on the car's roof; the large tree branch was still lying there. The agent was a bit odd. He wore a gray fedora. No one in Southern California wears a hat except cowboys and baseball players. His pencil-thin tie drew a straight line from his skinny chest to his belt.

"This is too bad," he said. "If this tree had hit a few inches forward from here"—he pointed his bony finger again at the dent in the roof—"or a few inches toward the back, you would have nothing more than a large dent in your roof. And if the car had been parked a foot closer to the fence or a foot farther from it, then, no problem."

"Uhnnn . . . fortunately," he said, clearing his throat theatrically, "the branch landed right here." He jabbed his finger at the roof like a prosecuting attorney pointing at a piece of key evidence. "It landed precisely in the worst possible place, right between the front and rear windows where the doorpost adjoins the roof. The force of the impact drove the doorpost down, bent the frame, and put the entire body out of line. It can't be fixed, no way; this car is totaled!" Having dramatically made the case against his own company, he stood, self-satisfied, with his hands on his hips.

Then suddenly he became the defense attorney. "Now tell me again, how exactly did this happen? Why did this branch fall on the car?"

The neighbor lady said, "Honestly, Mary and I have been trying to figure that out. There was no wind last night. Nothing hit the tree. The branch looked perfectly healthy, and the tree is sound. We really have no idea what made that branch fall."

The agent shook his head. "Can I use your phone?" he asked the neighbor.

In a few moments, he and the neighbor returned. The agent looked me squarely in the eye. "Well, I have authorization to compensate you for the loss of your vehicle, son. What's your value on it?"

I closed my eyes and prayed. I needed to make two mortgage payments, plus late fees, right away. I was nearly out of gas and money. I was out of time. I quickly calculated the amount the mortgage company needed and the price of a tank of gasoline for the pickup. I told him that amount, expecting him to laugh.

He looked up for a moment, then he looked at the old Cadillac, and then he looked at me and raised one eyebrow. After a long minute, he said, "Okay, that seems fair to me, son." He wrote me a check on the spot.

We were awestruck at God's perfect timing and provision. When the insurance agent left, Leia and I nearly danced in the street. We put the check in our pocket and went to make the two house payments. Another miracle!

The next months, however, brought more of the same struggle. I would get enough work to supplement our food stamps and to take care of the small bills, utilities, and gasoline. We couldn't keep up, though, with the house payments. We found ourselves slipping further behind each month.

We were now almost a year into this stressful ordeal, with no end or answer in sight. God's leading, inwardly and outwardly, had seemed so clear. I felt that we had to stay the course we had started. Then again, it seemed impossible. One afternoon I was so overwhelmed with stress, anxiety, and depression that I could not hide it from Leia.

She said, "I'm worried about you."

I didn't say anything, but I thought, *Yeah, I'm worried about me too.*

I went into the living room where I could be alone while she prepared dinner. I tried to pray. What could I say? I had said it all before. How many times and in how many different ways could I say the same thing?

The words I thought and prayed only reminded me how bad things were. I slipped down on my knees in front of the sofa. Then I found myself lying on the floor, crying from frustration and sorrow. I wondered if I was losing it.

Had I led my family into a disaster? Were the "miraculous signs" just coincidences I had interpreted according to my own desires? Yet I had tried so hard to be honest with myself and with God. I had felt so certain that God was calling me to follow this course.

Finally, I simply lay there quietly. My throat was tight and sore from my silent crying, but my breathing gradually became regular.

I started to pull myself up off the floor in resignation. "God," I whispered, "I just don't know what to do." Then I heard the voice; a voice that was audible but at the same time inaudible—a voice that I knew was God's.

"I'm going to take care of it."

That's what he said.

That was all. But it was so clear, so full of assurance and strength. The words resonated and reverberated in the deep recesses of my soul. I immediately leaped to my feet. I felt almost jubilant. I couldn't wait to tell Leia so she could share in my joy.

I must have been glowing as I entered the kitchen.

"What happened to you?" she asked. "You look like someone just gave you a million dollars."

"Well, not quite; not yet, anyway," I replied. "Leia, I don't know how things are going to work out, but we're going to be okay. God is going to take care of things for us."

The problem was that God didn't say *when* he would take care of our situation. For a while, things got worse!

Waiting on God

My mentor and former customer at the paint store, Fred Conley, and I got together as often as possible. Fred had been the academic dean at a leading Bible college. He would help me study the Bible and biblical Greek. During our sessions, he sometimes counseled me in his soft, slow, Mississippi drawl.

He would say, "Don, studyin' and learnin' Greek is good, but don't try to get aholt of the Scriptures; just pray and let the Scriptures get aholt of you."

When I was really depressed and feeling sorry for myself, he would tell me, "Don, why are you wasting all this valuable time? If God wanted you to be working, you'd have work. Now he has given you time to study, pray, and minister to others. Make use of this time."

I knew he was right, of course, but it was often difficult to pull myself out of the pit of depression and do much—especially encourage others.

One day, Fred told me, "Don, I feel the Lord is leading me to start a new church in the city of Baldwin Park. I plan to launch this in a couple of months. I'd like you to pray about coming over there to assist me in this ministry."

Fred and our church's pastor were friends, so Leia and I decided to talk with our pastor about Fred's request. The pastor said he'd be happy to release us to work with the Conleys. In light of this, Leia and I felt we should give prayerful consideration to Fred's offer.

Chief among our concerns, still, was how to make our house payments. Again, we found ourselves flirting with foreclosure. After much prayer and discussion, we felt that since the Lord was providing for everything but the house, perhaps he wanted us to sell it so we could be free to do whatever we might need to do. Leia loved our home and was often tearful, sometimes even angry, about the situation. I felt terrible and responsible for her sadness.

I wanted to contact a good real estate agent, but I didn't know anyone in the business and wasn't sure where to look.

So I did the practical thing. I prayed and got out the Yellow Pages.

"You know, Century 21 is a well-known company with good advertising," I told Leia. "Maybe we should sign with one of their agents."

Leia was still not excited about selling the house. "Call whoever you want," she said.

I looked for a local broker and dialed the number.

"Century 21, Ontario. Tom Gerrod speaking."

Tom showed up at our house the next afternoon. A fit, trim man in his early sixties, he wore business-casual attire.

"Folks, I am an honest man, so let me tell you a couple of things," Tom said. "Until recently, the housing market in Southern California has been hot, so prices have gone up. The good news is that even though you've been in this house a relatively short time, you've got maybe twenty thousand of equity. The bad news is that recently the economy has gone soft and houses are not selling like they were. I will do everything I can, but it could take a while to come up with a qualified buyer."

Since we were already one full house payment behind again, this was not welcome news. "Anything else?" I asked.

"Yes." His voice grew soft and grave. "I told you I am an honest man. That's because I am a committed Christian." Leia and I looked at each other. Could this be *another* "coincidence" as a result of prayer?

"I have to tell you I haven't been at this very long," Tom added. "It's a second career for me. I haven't done too well at it. Many people look at houses on Sundays, and most agents hold open houses on Sundays. I won't do either. I won't compromise on that. Recently, I prayed and said, 'Father, I'm trying to honor you in this business; I'm working hard, but it doesn't seem to be paying off. I'm going to give it to you and ask you to make me prosper.'"

He looked up and smiled. "Since that prayer, things seem to be improving. Now, if you still want to list your house with me, I won't work Sundays, but I'll do everything else possible to sell this property for you."

Leia and I looked at each other for an answer. I thought, *If God doesn't prosper this gentleman's business any better than he's prospered mine, we're in trouble.*

"Tom, we prayed that God would give us a good real estate agent," I said. "I don't know how good you are at real estate, but I can tell you're a good man. We'll sign the listing agreement and see what God does."

For weeks, then months, God didn't seem to be doing much. A few people came to look at the house, but no qualified buyers.

When our ninety-day listing with Tom was about to expire, we received another foreclosure notice. This time, things were even worse. We had taken out a second mortgage to try to stay afloat.

(Remember, we were young and stupid. As the old saying goes, "Life is hard, but it's harder if you're stupid.")

Now our monthly payments were much larger than before, and this time we needed three payments instead of two. It appeared that our house would be foreclosed on before we could sell it. We prayed desperately.

Once again we felt we couldn't ask friends or relatives for help because they wouldn't understand why our God wasn't helping us. While we were willing to worship and serve him without understanding everything, we were afraid our situation would cause other people to doubt God's goodness.

One day I heard a knock at the front door. I looked out the curtain and saw Tom Gerrod's vehicle. My excitement evaporated once I realized he was alone and had no buyers with him.

As soon as I'd welcomed him inside, Tom took some papers out of his briefcase. "Don, Leia, I'm really sorry we haven't been able to come up with a good buyer for you. My listing agreement with you expires in a couple of days. I can certainly understand if you want to try another broker or agent. There will be no hard feelings."

"Tom," I said, "it probably doesn't make any difference. We haven't told you how bad things are because we didn't want to put any more pressure on you. But it looks like we are going to lose the house before we can sell it. We're just days away from foreclosure."

Tom looked down at the carpet and then looked firmly at us. "Look, now, you do not have to relist with me. You can choose any agent you like, even use another company. But I'll tell you this: you kids are not going to lose your home. Tell me how much you need, and I'll write the check this minute. You can repay me from the proceeds when the house sells. I don't believe God will let you down!"

Tom wound up giving us a check for over $2,000 (which would be equal to nearly $10,000 today). He refused to let us give him a promissory note. "Just give me your word," he said. "That's good enough."

We felt that we could not find a better agent. Tom couldn't be blamed for the flagging economy. We signed another ninety-day listing with him. Two weeks later, we had a qualified buyer with a short escrow.

Although the sale of our home did not end all our struggles, it helped Leia and me see that God's purpose in leading us was not to bless us materially at this time; his purposes were much greater.

Jesus taught his disciples some of the same lessons. He told them to go out preaching around the country and take no money, not even a change of clothes or spare tires (that is, sandals). Their trepidation must have turned to joy and grown into faith as they saw God provide for them as they went in obedience.

God is so faithful. As we began learning what it meant to live by faith, God showed his love and faithfulness by providing finances, help, and work in the most unexpected ways and always at just the right moment. We lived on miracles.

Meditation on the Miraculous

God uses hardship to break the hold of "earthly security" on our lives. In fact, we often see his sovereignty, love, wisdom, timing, and faithfulness most clearly during difficulty.

> The Lord now chose seventy-two other disciples and sent them ahead in pairs to all the towns and places he planned to visit. These were his instructions to them: "The harvest is great, but the workers are few. So pray to the Lord who is in charge of the harvest; ask him to send more workers into his fields. Now go, and remember that I am sending you out as lambs among wolves. Don't take any money with you, nor a traveler's bag, nor an extra pair of sandals."
> LUKE 10:1-4

CHAPTER 10

WILDERNESS YEARS

1979–1982

At last God seemed to be showing us a way forward. Once Tom sold our house in Ontario, California, we moved to Baldwin Park so I could take up my responsibilities at the new church as associate pastor and youth pastor. The senior pastor, Fred Conley, was a gracious and caring man who attracted a loyal following and taught me a great deal. PTL Painting Company was finally in the black as well.

For several months, everything seemed to fall into place. I was involved in fulfilling ministry, finances were no longer an issue, and the church was growing. Someone said, "Every silver lining has a cloud." That's not always true; in this case, however, the dark clouds began to reappear before long.

Despite our respect for Pastor Fred, Leia and I took notice when he began teaching on casting out demons. We had no problem with this initially, since my early experience with the "cat woman" and my reading of the Bible confirmed the reality of these dark spirits. Before long, though, most worship services, teaching times, and prayer meetings appeared to be turning into deliverance services. It seemed to me that demons were cast out as the solution to nearly every problem, and the same Christians were often delivered of the same demons. We hoped that this phase of ministry and emphasis at the church would pass, but it didn't.

Leia and I discussed what we should do about our involvement in the church. Our ministry to older teens and young adults was thriving, though they were also troubled about the emphasis on deliverance. Though I knew it could strain or even rupture my relationship with Pastor Fred, I felt I needed to respond to some of their questions by honestly confessing my own doubts and concerns.

About six months after we began our ministry in Baldwin Park, Leia told me, "Don, I didn't understand this when it happened, but God spoke to me when I was unpacking our things here in Baldwin Park. It was funny—I knew it was God, and all he said was, 'Nine months.' I believed he meant we would only be here nine months, so I was selective about what I unpacked. I haven't said anything to you about it because you were so excited about being here. But, if you'll notice, I never did finish unpacking our boxes. I never put many pictures on the walls. I knew we would have to leave for some reason."

There were tears in her eyes as she finished. She loved me and she loved God, and she had committed herself to following me wherever God led. For a young wife and mother along for the ride, it had not been an easy one.

I was confused and not a little angry. Everything we had been through since our salvation seemed to have been preparing us for our ministry in Baldwin Park. I'd assumed that our earlier struggles with PTL Painting and even the sale of our home had been part of God's plan to bring us here. Now, after just a few months, it was all turning into a bad dream.

I talked to Pastor Fred. He was not sympathetic. He seemed defensive about his deliverance ministry and furious that I had "undermined" his teachings among the youth. He suggested that if I could not follow him, I should find another place of ministry. I knew he was right, but I was heartsick. (The good news is that, in later years, he came back to center and now has a wonderful ministry helping many people.)

This was a bad time. I felt that I could not trust Fred's ministry enough at that point to submit to his leadership. I was beginning to wonder if I could even trust God with my life. Or at the very least, I felt that I couldn't trust myself to discern what God's plan was for me. I was hurt, dejected, and confused. I could never turn my back on God or deny what he had done in my life; however, I no longer had any idea how I could serve the Lord within the church or even where we should go to church. I decided to leave Baldwin Park, quit going to any church, and find a real job with a future. Many of my family and friends had felt that the decisions and directions I had taken were foolish. Now I truly felt like a fool.

Fortunately my spiritual temper tantrum did not last too long. Without the accountability, inspiration, and discipline of regular worship and fellowship, I noticed that my relationship with God was beginning to suffer. Temptation was stronger, and I found it difficult to sustain spiritual focus. Though I knew I was still God's child, not being a part of his body made me begin to feel disconnected from him. I realized that "some" church was better than no church. Shortly after we moved to Rialto, California, we began to get involved in the Rialto Bible Fellowship.

I got a great job as a sales executive for a paint manufacturer. Leia and I were able to buy a home in a beautiful suburban neighborhood. I was recruited by a Canadian equipment manufacturer to represent them to their dealers and to corporate customers. Eventually my territory included all of the United States west of the Mississippi. I traveled extensively, did trade shows in convention centers, stayed in upscale hotels, ate at the best restaurants, made very good money—and was absolutely miserable.

Despite our outward success, the next several years were really wilderness years for me. I knew God had a call on my life to do something full-time for him, but each success in the secular world seemed to lead me further away from that purpose.

Leia became agitated with me because whenever we talked about our lives or the future, I got frustrated or depressed—or both. She was quite content with our lifestyle: solid church, good friends, two cars, waterskiing or camping on weekends, nice house, two beautiful children, and all our bills paid. What more could a person want, right?

"What is wrong with you?" she would ask.

"Leia, I just feel like I'm not doing what I should be doing with my life. I can't really explain it, but I feel like I'm headed in the wrong direction and getting further and further from my purpose."

Now it was her turn to be frustrated. "What exactly do you suppose God wants you to be doing?" She felt that we had experimented enough with trying to pursue God's destiny for us. One day, perhaps, we would understand our journey. For now it was over, and we could simply go to church and be "normal" Christians.

"I don't know, sweetheart, I just don't know," I'd say as she poured out her heart. And I really didn't know, and I didn't know how to find out. Secular friends advised me to enjoy the "good life," and my Christian friends said I should be content until God gave me direction. No one understood the misery I felt as I spent endless, pointless hours driving or flying across the country doing business I didn't care about so I could make money that only seemed to bury me deeper into an occupation I didn't want.

I listened to preaching tapes, read the Bible, and prayed a lot, but the heavens were silent. No direction. Those early days when God had seemed so present and real were like a distant dream. I did my best to share my faith with my customers and business acquaintances, but those opportunities were rare and generally fruitless.

I wondered at times whether I should enroll in seminary or Bible college and follow the conventional route into ministry. That would make sense to people. The problem was that path would entail a great deal of sacrifice on the part of my wife and children. I didn't feel that I could ask them to give up everything if I couldn't tell them it was the will of God. Without that assurance, I had no choice but to wait and do nothing.

At the time, I didn't see the value in all the isolated hours I spent listening to great preachers on tape as I was driving or traveling. As I cried out, prayed, searched God's Word, and sought his presence in cars and hotel rooms, God was doing something in me: deepening my relationship with him and his Word, teaching me to submit my impatience to his timing, and helping me understand what it means to "seek him with my whole heart."

When I remember this time, I think of Moses on the backside of the desert, tending Jethro's sheep even as he longed to shepherd God's people. I consider Joseph, languishing in prison when he knew God had revealed a great purpose and leadership role for him. God puts yearnings in our hearts that we cannot always define, and he brings these longings to life in his time. But, to be honest, it can be pretty depressing and miserable as we wait.

Meditation on the Miraculous

In those hidden times, when we try to be faithful to God's call but can no longer sense his direction, he may be doing an imperceptible but absolutely critical work within us, just like the farmer sowing seeds underground.

> Those who plant in tears
> will harvest with shouts of joy.
> They weep as they go to plant their seed,
> but they sing as they return with the harvest.

PSALM 126:5-6

CHAPTER 11

MIRACLES IN THE WILDERNESS

1980–1982

When James was four years old, he was hooked on a certain TV western and was determined to dress up like his favorite character. For Christmas, he told us he had to have a particular blue-denim cowboy hat. The hat in question cost about forty dollars.

One evening when I went into James's bedroom to listen as he said his prayers, he reminded me of the hat. I gently explained that I didn't think a forty-dollar cowboy hat for a four-year-old would be the best way to spend our money. I told him that maybe he should ask God for it. So he did. I heard him.

Several weeks later, Leia's parents came out from Los Angeles for the family's traditional Christmas Eve celebration. After a huge meal, we gathered around the tree to exchange gifts. When James opened his present from Leia's parents, his eyes got big. They'd given him the exact hat he had prayed for. Being a man of great faith, I was stunned.

I looked at Grandma Pat and Harold, whom the kids called Poppy. "Did James tell you guys that he wanted that hat?" I asked.

They shook their heads no, so I looked at Heidi. Maybe his sister had let it slip. Heidi quickly excused herself: "I didn't even know he wanted a cowboy hat!" Only one other person could have told them. My eyes turned to her.

Leia said, "Don, you *know* I wouldn't ask my parents to buy an expensive gift like that!"

Finally, Grandma Pat said, "No, honey, Poppy and I saw that hat when we were shopping, and we both felt something was telling us that James would love it. So we just bought it."

It had to have been God. James's faith grew by leaps and bounds as he saw the evidence of God's attention to a little boy's prayer.

The Divine Surgeon

Since 1971 Leia had been bothered by bouts of unusual pain during her menstrual cycle. For years we prayed that God would relieve her pain, believing he would take care of this problem since we had seen him heal people so often. By 1981, however, the pain had become almost unbearable.

Once Leia's family became aware of how seriously she was suffering, they castigated me for allowing her to endure pain to prove my faith. There was a grain of truth to their accusations since I had encouraged Leia to trust God for healing. Now we decided she should see a specialist.

A pelvic examination, X-rays, and sonograms revealed that she had a serious case of endometriosis—the ovaries and uterus were covered by tissue that should have grown only in the uterus. This caused her severe pelvic pain. In addition, the doctor told us there were cysts on her ovaries. One of the growths was so large that it could be seen from the outside when Leia lay flat on her back.

The doctor told us that if we had come before the one cyst was so large, he probably could have saved that ovary. Now he would definitely have to remove it. If the surgery revealed that the cyst or cysts on the other ovary were beyond a certain size, my wife would have to have a complete hysterectomy. Leia was devastated, and her family was furious.

They said that if I had "allowed" her to see a doctor sooner, she would have been all right. My "faith" and "foolishness" were to blame for her condition.

I joined them in beating myself up. I felt terrible for my wife and wondered, *Have I messed up again trying to believe God and live by faith? Am I just a presumptuous fanatic?*

The day of the surgery arrived. Leia and I, along with her parents, met with the doctor who would perform the operation. He told us that before they began the surgery, they would make a small incision in her abdomen and inflate the cavity with a gas. Then a small camera would be inserted to make a visual confirmation of the diagnosis. The doctor said that if the smaller cysts on the one ovary were not too bad, they would remove only the ovary with the large growth on it. If both ovaries had large cysts, then they would do a complete hysterectomy. He said he would come to the visitors lounge and give us a report before the actual surgery.

Family members and church friends pressed around the gurney as Leia was wheeled from her room for the laparoscopy. Some were praying, some were crying, and some were still talking about me.

I kissed Leia on the forehead, squeezed her hand, and headed for the small chapel in the hospital. At first, I didn't know how to pray. Finally, I simply said, "Dear God, I'm asking you that the doctor will come back with a better report than we think possible. Amen." After a long spell of silence and tears, I headed back to the visitors lounge.

In time I saw the doctor appear at the door of the lounge. He hesitated and then came directly to where I was sitting. He seemed to be at a loss for words. Finally, he spoke. "Mr. Schulze, what we found is better than we hoped for."

I sat up at attention.

He continued, "Actually, the results of the laparoscopy were much, much better than we hoped." Then he stopped and rubbed the back of his neck. He looked very uncomfortable for a man bringing good news. "I'm not quite sure what to tell you. I know I saw and felt the cysts on your wife's ovaries. Even on the sonogram images. . . . And we previously confirmed the endometriosis. But when we actually saw the area, there was no sign of endometriosis at all. All the cysts have disappeared. There was scar tissue on the ovaries as if the cysts had already been surgically removed. I'd have to say it is like a miracle."

It wasn't *like* a miracle; it *was* a miracle. During these wilderness years, God kept us going by showing us his love and power at just the right times.

One wonderful consequence of this miracle was how it affected Leia's parents. Up until this time, they both had only a generic belief in God. They tolerated our Christianity simply because they loved us and felt it was better for me than drugs and alcohol. After this undeniable, medically verified miracle, they began to consider that, perhaps, we were in touch with something very real. Soon they began to regularly make the hour-long drive from their home in Los Angeles to attend church with us. Eventually they both came to faith. Thanks be to God.

Giving and Receiving

When Leia and I first became Christians, we attended a little church in our neighborhood. As we were being vetted for membership, we were asked a series of questions about our faith, our lifestyle, and our willingness to take on the responsibilities of membership. One of these responsibilities was financial stewardship. The church expected all members to give 10 percent of their gross income as the tithe.

In the enthusiasm and joy of our new faith, we didn't question any of the requirements of membership. Among other things, we committed to tithing.

As the years went by and we moved from one church to another, we heard different ideas about tithing. Some said that tithing was an Old Testament law and we were no longer under law. So, it seemed to follow, tithing was legalistic. We were free, in Christ, to give whatever we pleased. Others told us that tithing was not a Christian principle because Jesus had "bought us with a price," so all that we have belongs to him, not just 10 percent.

It is embarrassing, but I must admit that because we often did not have a regular income and finances were so tight, we willingly accepted these arguments and quit disciplined tithing. Even when I had a job with a sizable income, we always seemed to live from paycheck to paycheck. Our needs and obligations consumed almost all of our income, and we no longer followed the thrifty habits we'd picked up while trying to make a go of PTL Painting. We never considered giving 10 percent, because we felt we just couldn't afford it.

In 1982 we were attending Rialto Bible Fellowship. The pastor, Jim Chalupnik, was a big man with a large family. He was a great guy; his heart was as large as his body. His three teenage sons were also big, stocky boys—football players. I thought sometimes of how much money it must take to feed and clothe that family. I knew that the small church didn't pay Pastor Jim much of a salary. I wondered how they managed to make ends meet.

One Saturday I asked Jim about this.

"Jim, it's none of my business, but how do you guys make it financially?"

"Well, brother," Jim said with a disarming smile, "we do our part, and the Lord does his part." He was really a gentle giant. It was obvious he did not want to talk about his personal needs.

I respected that. "Okay, Jim, but what do you mean, his part and your part?"

"Well, I believe the Bible teaches tithing as a spiritual principle."

In my ignorance, I spoke up as if I knew all about it. "Oh, yeah. I've heard of that. Do you mean you actually give 10 percent of your net income?"

"No. I don't normally talk about this, but since you ask, I actually give 10 percent of my *gross* income."

Gross income, wow. I quickly tried to convince myself that the embarrassment I felt over my meager and sporadic offerings was not necessary.

"Well, Jim," I asked, "isn't tithing an Old Testament principle— part of the law?"

A smile played at the corners of his mouth as he picked up on my sudden discomfort.

"Don, I think the God of the Old Testament is also the God of the New Testament. Jesus taught tithing. If you study the story of Melchizedek, you'll see that he received tithes from Abraham. Abraham was a man of faith, and he gave the tithe almost five hundred years before the law."

He was right. He had me.

I saw that I was out of my depth theologically. A man has to know his limitations. I knew that I just could not afford to tithe.

"Okay, Jim, let's let that go for now," I said, feeling magnanimous. "How in the world can you afford to tithe?"

He looked serious now, in a very sincere way. "Don, it's not a question of affording or not affording. The tithe belongs to God. That's what I mean when I say 'we do our part.' We give him what belongs to him. Then he gives us what we need. I can't explain it, but God is always faithful. And we try to be faithful."

I could see that Jim was hoping to teach me something. Most of us are fairly protective when it comes to our personal finances. I wasn't sure that I wanted to pursue this conversation.

"Jim, I have a fair idea of your income. I don't see how you provide food, clothing, and all the other things that go with three teenagers. How do you manage to do all that and make your house payments?"

"I'm glad you asked that," Jim said. "Actually, we were having trouble keeping up on the mortgage. The church owns the house, and the payment is part of our package. But as you know, our income—I mean, the church income—is sometimes not enough. We just kept on trusting God, and the bank kept working with us. It was always a strain."

I thought of my own struggles with house payments.

"I can imagine," I said.

"Anyway, I was shaving early one morning, getting ready to come over to the church for a men's prayer meeting. I was wondering how we would make the mortgage payment. There was a knock at the door. My wife, Sandy, was getting breakfast for the kids, so I went to answer it with shaving cream all over my face. I wondered who could be banging on my door at that early hour."

He told me that he saw a homeless man standing on the porch. The stranger had several days' growth of beard. His old corduroy jacket was wrinkled and soiled. In his hands was a dirty, wrinkled, crumpled paper grocery bag. The man asked whether Jim was the pastor of the church across the street.

Jim wondered how this man had been able to identify his house as the church parsonage. There was purposely no sign to indicate that.

The stranger spoke again, "You are the pastor, aren't you?"

"Yes, sir, I am. Is there something I can do for you this morning?"

"Yes, you can take this bag. It's for you." A dirty hand held up the creased and crumpled package. Jim said he hated to think what could be in it. He ignored the bag and extended an invitation.

"My friend, are you sure you don't need something to eat? Breakfast is on; we'd be happy to share."

The weathered face showed no expression.

"No, Pastor, I've just come to give you this, then I need to get goin'." The man held the bag up again. He seemed determined.

"Okay then, if there's nothing I can do, you have a good day." Jim reached out and took the surprisingly hefty bag. Before he'd finished speaking, the man was already walking away down the sidewalk.

Jim put the bag on the dining room table and went back to finish his shave. Since the family ate breakfast in the kitchen, the bag sat there unnoticed. After eating, Jim passed through the dining room on the way out the front door. When he saw the crinkled brown bag, he thought, *I can't leave that for Sandy to find. Who knows what that poor old man left here?*

Jim hefted the bag again, as if the weight might indicate the contents. He shook it. No revealing noise. He sat the bag on the table and unrolled the top. He peered into the bag in the dim light of the dining room. *No! It couldn't be.* He reached in and pulled out a bundle wrapped in a rubber band. The stack of currency was a couple of inches thick. He removed the rubber bands and saw a mix of hundred-dollar notes, twenties, tens, fives, and ones. There was no telling how much money was there. These were old bills, not from the bank. He pulled out another stack, and another, and another.

He stuffed the loose bills and the bundles back into the bag and went to the church office. When the men's prayer meeting ended and Jim was alone, he sat down and began counting. The bag contained almost the exact amount needed to pay off the mortgage. How did this happen? Where did this money come from? Who was the old "homeless" man? No one had seen him before; no one saw him again!

Pastor Jim finished the story and smiled gently.

"So, Don, you see, that's how we make it," Jim concluded matter-of-factly. "Sometimes we live from day to day on what I make. Other times God provides for us in the most remarkable of ways."

I thought of how Tom Gerrod had provided us with money to pay our mortgage until our home sold, as well as the other times God had met our needs. Jim went on, "When we tithe, it is just our way of acknowledging that God owns everything and that we are dependent upon him for our daily bread. Tithing isn't a matter of what we can afford or what we can't afford. It's a matter of faith and obedience."

What could I say? I had no argument against such sincere convictions supported by such convincing facts.

"No matter how much money I make, it never seems to be enough. You're barely making anything, but your family is doing fine. I guess I need to reconsider this whole thing."

That evening I talked with my wife as she fed James in his high chair.

"Leia, you know that when we first became Christians, we tithed on our income."

She looked at me with an expression that said, *And so . . . ?*

"Well, you know we can't afford to tithe now," I said.

"Don, I've always let you make those decisions. What's on your mind?" She was not making this easy.

"I've been talking with Pastor Jim. I feel like we ought to go ahead and begin tithing again."

"Like I said, that's your decision. I just want to do what's right," Leia said. It was true; she always did want to do right.

"Okay," I said, "when we get paid, we will write our tithe check first. Then we'll write checks for the bills, and we'll live on what's left. That's the right thing to do." It sounded so easy!

She offered James a final spoonful of baby food. "Okay, if that's what you think."

When Friday arrived, I sat down to pay the bills. With a flourish I looked up from my envelopes, stamps, and checkbook register and announced in triumph, "Hey, not too bad."

Leia asked, "What's not too bad?"

"Well, I've paid all the bills that must be paid now, and we still have about $120 left for the week."

"That's great. Even after you wrote the tithe check?"

"The tithe check? Oh no." I was embarrassed. "I forgot all about that." I was tempted to say, "Well, we'll just start next week." But Leia read my mind.

"You said we would start tithing this week. I've been praying about this since you brought it up. I think it is what we need to do. We need to put God first in our finances."

I was trapped between Jim's testimony, my own conscience, and my wife's moral compass. I knew she was right. With all the diverse miracles we had seen over the years, how could I not have faith for finances? This is where the rubber of faith meets the road of reality, and, like many people, I'd been tempted to back down.

"Okay, babe, when Sunday morning comes—I'll write the check."

She looked over her shoulder and said, "I think you'd better write the check now." She was right again. Our tithe was ninety dollars that week. We had spent twenty dollars on groceries already. Leia was the grocery coupon queen when she needed to be. She had assured me that somehow we would make it through the week on the food we had on hand. That left us ten dollars for the week.

That Sunday I took the tithe check and dropped it into the brass plate. I felt a sense of satisfaction and accomplishment for taking the right step.

I put my remaining ten dollars into the gas tank. The next day I had an appointment with the purchasing agent for a paint company and had no choice but to drive the ninety-five miles to San Diego. At about one dollar per gallon, I could purchase just enough gas to get there and back home again. At the end of the month, my company would reimburse me, but for now I had no idea where I would get gas money for the rest of the week. But Jesus said, "Do not worry about tomorrow, for tomorrow will worry about itself. Each day has enough trouble of its own" (Matthew 6:34, NIV). I would take care of today; God would have to take care of tomorrow.

I looked at my watch as I rolled down I-15 toward the Miramar Road exit. I was early. I was supposed to see Joe, the purchasing agent, after lunch. Glancing down at the spare change in the car ashtray, I could see that I had more than a dollar's worth of coins, enough for a cup of coffee.

I exited the freeway and pulled into the coffee shop to wait. The last thing I wanted was to get to Joe's office and find out that he hadn't been to lunch yet. As a sales representative, proper protocol was that I offer to buy my client's lunch.

Since I was only getting coffee, I decided to sit at the counter. I sat on my stool and spun around to face the waitress. She was talking to the gentleman next to me who was—oh, no—Joe, the purchasing agent!

"Hey, Don," Joe's eyes lit up with recognition, "look at this. You probably just missed me at the office. I took lunch a little early. Well, we can visit over lunch." He patted me on the shoulder and reached for the menu. I felt sick. I knew he would expect me to pick up the tab—that was just what a sales rep did. I thought he would also wonder why I was only having coffee.

When lunch drew to a close, the waitress placed the check squarely between us. My mind was racing as I tried to choose between several unlikely excuses as to why I couldn't pay for lunch. This was so humiliating. What was I thinking writing that tithe check? More than that, why had the sovereign God allowed me to be put in this position when I had just been trying to please him?

Joe ignored the check and reached for his cigarettes. In those days, restaurants did not object to customers having a smoke after a meal. He fumbled in his pockets for a light. I couldn't even offer him a match. The waitress whipped out a red plastic lighter.

Joe took a deep drag from his Marlboro. "Don, why don't you come on down to the office and show me again how that new airless paint pump of yours can save our customers money?" I wondered how well that demo would go after I made the man pay for his own lunch. Even my coffee was on the bill.

Joe changed the subject and began to talk excitedly about football. As he was describing a particularly great interception, I saw the long ash drop from his cigarette onto the floor. He continued. I felt something warm behind my knee, but Joe had my full attention. As he talked, I saw his eyes drift down to the check on the counter, then down toward the floor.

"Don," he exclaimed, "there's smoke coming from your leg."

I looked down and saw the smoke. What else could go wrong? I stood up and slapped at my trouser leg. Joe's ash had fallen into a crease in my trousers. Polyester fabric doesn't burn; it melts. I had two quarter-sized holes near the knee of my trousers where the folded fabric had embraced the ember.

Joe stuttered out an apology.

"Joe, don't worry about it. It's okay. The fire's out!" I laughed.

"Look, Don, I feel really bad. That was careless of me. I really need to quit smoking, I tell you."

"Joe, really, it's okay."

"No, it's not." He grabbed the check off the counter. "This one's on me. I can't let you buy lunch today, that's for sure." He had no idea how right he was.

While Joe paid, I was quietly praising the Lord. We walked out to the parking lot.

It turned out that we were also parked next to one another. Joe saw my suit jacket hanging in the rear window of my car.

"Don, those trousers you're wearing go to that suit. I feel terrible—the whole suit is ruined!" I did not want Joe to feel too awkward when he might be on the verge of giving me his first order.

"Joe, it's okay. This is an old suit. I don't even like it. I only wore it today because everything else was at the cleaners."

"Well, let's go to my office. Follow me down there."

Once Joe sat behind his big desk, I went through my demonstration of the airless paint pumping system.

"Well, Don, I know you just sold a bunch of those to our biggest competitor. I will talk to the powers that be. I don't know if that will help you or hurt you. I'll do what I can."

I rose to leave.

"Oh yeah! That reminds me." He reached into his desk and pulled out a personal checkbook. He scribbled out a check and handed it to me.

"Joe," I protested, "is this about the suit? It was an accident; this isn't necessary." The check was for fifty dollars. It was hardly enough to buy a new suit, but it was certainly more than I felt comfortable accepting from a client.

"Don, please. It makes me feel better. Is that okay?"

I tucked the check in my pocket. "Okay, Joe, thanks a lot. I'll be back to see you in two weeks."

I drove back up toward Rialto and wondered about the afternoon's events. I had arrived in San Diego flat broke, only to get in an awkward situation with my customer because I had no money for lunch. Now I had fifty dollars in my pocket and a customer who felt he was in my debt.

When I arrived home that evening, I set my briefcase down and sat back in my recliner. Then it hit me. Normally the smell of Leia's wonderful cooking filled the house when I got home. Tonight there was no aroma, no pots and pans rattling in the kitchen. Leia emerged from the hallway dressed to go somewhere. Had I forgotten a dinner date?

"Don, don't you remember that we're going to Los Angeles this evening?"

I had forgotten. Ernest Soady had invited me to come and speak to a small group of Christians who met at his home. Soady was the director of the Free Tract Society, a nondenominational printing house that provided evangelistic materials to missionaries, evangelists, and churches. When my business took me into his part of Los Angeles, I enjoyed stopping in to discuss spiritual matters with this older man. I considered it a great compliment when he invited me to share with his little group. Leia, the kids, and I headed for LA.

The group was indeed small. No more than eight people had gathered in the cozy living room. Soady, who was old enough to be my father, was the youngest of the group. I broke out my Bible and did my best. The group was polite and appreciative.

Leia's parents lived just a couple of miles away. As we had cake and coffee with the group after the teaching time, Leia whispered in my ear. "Don, I don't want to be rude, but if we leave soon, we can stop by and see my folks for a few minutes. They really want to see the kids."

My cue.

"Brother Soady," I said, taking him by the hand, "I really appreciate you inviting me to speak to your friends. We've had a great time. Our kids are getting a little restless, so I think we'd better get going."

As he took my hand, his smile reached his clear blue eyes. He said warmly, "Of course, Don, I understand. Look . . ." He reached inside his tweed sport coat and pulled out a small envelope. "We want to give you something to pay for your gas. We're so glad you came."

"Brother Soady, I can't take this from you. You didn't take an offering tonight. This is very nice, but—"

"Don, I spoke to the group last week about this. We know you drove all the way from Rialto after work to be with us. We just want to help with your gas. It's not much. It's not good form to refuse a blessing." He smiled again.

I gave the older gentlemen a hug.

As we sat at Leia's parents' home, I pulled out the little envelope. I wasn't expecting much. They had to know that ten dollars' worth of gas would get me there and back. Fifty dollars! It might as well have been a million. I was astounded. I'm not a math major and I'm not superstitious, but the calculation was too obvious.

Yesterday I had paid my tithe, ninety dollars, for the first time in several years. I had done this in faith—not a lot of faith, but it was still by faith. Now just twenty-four hours later, after deducting the ten dollars in gas I'd spent to come to LA, I had my ninety dollars back. God was too good. Since that day, we have always tried to do our part when it comes to finances. And, of course, God has always done his part.

Meditation on the Miraculous

We deserve nothing from God, nor can we ever place him in our debt by anything we do. Nevertheless, there is a mysterious connection between giving and receiving.

> Give, and you will receive. Your gift will return to you in full—pressed down, shaken together to make room for more, running over, and poured into your lap. The amount you give will determine the amount you get back.
>
> LUKE 6:38

CHAPTER 12

THE BREAKTHROUGH

1980

As a marketing executive with a territory spread across the entire western United States, I often traveled four or five days out of the week. When I was home, I spent as much time as I could with my family and was as involved as possible in our church. I also devoted concentrated time to Bible study and prayer. With two small children in the house, our garage became my prayer room.

One hot summer afternoon, I knelt in front of my chair in the windowless garage and tried to ignore the beads of perspiration as I prayed. I cannot remember exactly what I said to God that day, but the words he spoke changed my life forever.

This is what he said: "Ask of Me, and I will give you the nations."

I immediately recognized the words as coming from Scripture. A little digging through my New King James concordance led me to Psalm 2:8. God, through the Holy Spirit, had proclaimed these words to his Son, the Messiah, about a thousand years before Jesus' birth. Now he had unmistakably spoken these words to me. Not that I was a messiah. His words, I felt, simply meant that someday I would have a ministry among the nations of the world.

I would like to say that I was elated at this divine communication, but the truth is, I was mystified. How could this ever come to pass? I was just a salesman with two kids, a wife, and a mortgage. I had no credentials, no support, and no direction. Still, I knew what I had heard and who had spoken.

I decided that all I could do was keep praying, asking God for a little more clarity. I decided to get up forty-five minutes earlier each weekday morning, when I would give equal time to reading the Bible and praying. I determined to do this for a month.

I kept praying and asking, "How, Lord? Where? How do I start?" I didn't know how God would have me begin my ministry to the nations.

After three weeks, the heavens were still silent. I grew discouraged but decided to finish my monthlong commitment. Sometime during the final week, on a very ordinary morning, God finally spoke to me: "Begin to go out and tell people about my Son."

Again his communication was clear and unmistakable. Yet I wondered if God had made some mistake! The first word, concerning the nations, seemed too much; this second word seemed too little.

That's it? I thought.

I had expected that, if God spoke to me at all during my thirty-day vigil, his message would be life changing. I knew he had spoken, but I was disappointed. His only direction was to begin telling people about his Son? But I had been doing that, whenever and wherever possible, for more than four years!

As I spoke to the Lord about this, he seemed to make clear that this was to be the beginning of whatever ministry he might have for me. I could take it or leave it!

Now I was to evangelize purposefully, creating opportunities where I could tell people about Christ. He wasn't asking me to make any dramatic changes in lifestyle or calling me to a seminary or mission agency. I was just to go and tell people about Jesus, the Son of God.

I really had no idea where to begin. So I prayed for guidance. It came to me that Jesus had told the disciples of John the Baptist that they could be sure he was the promised Messiah because "the poor have the gospel preached to them" (Matthew 11:5, NKJV). That was it. I felt God was directing me to take the Good News to the people in the poorest part of our town.

Bonnie and Wayne

This should be easy, I thought as I left home to evangelize door-to-door for the first time. *I'm a professional sales executive; I know how to talk to people.* Minutes later, as I stood in front of a weathered door in a shabby, one-floor apartment complex, I found that it wasn't easy at all. I lifted my hand to knock on the door and realized that I had no prepared script, my mind was blank, and my stomach was full of "butterflies." The whole idea seemed ridiculous. If thirty days in prayer had not led me to this moment, I would have turned around and gone home. But because I was convinced that I was doing what God wanted me to do, I decided to rap on the door and just see what happened.

A tall, shirtless teenage boy answered. He looked sleepy and muttered, "Whaddya want?"

I responded, "Well, if you have a few minutes, I'd like to tell you about Jesus, the Son of God." To my surprise, the young man pulled the door open and said, "Sure, come in."

The apartment was small and poorly furnished, but it was neat and clean. After I introduced myself, the boy told me that his name was Wayne and that he was sixteen. I noticed that his face was sad and that his eyes were lifeless and disinterested. His expression quickly changed, however. As I told Wayne of God's love for him and how Jesus could come into his life to make him new, he seemed to melt.

"Would you like to pray and give your life to Jesus?" I asked.

"Yeah," Wayne said eagerly, "I think that's what I need to do."

After we prayed together, Wayne lifted his head. He was smiling now, and his eyes were bright. "Wow, wow!" he said. He began to weep and to laugh.

"God has heard your prayer, Wayne. Jesus has come into your life." I was thrilled but amazed. Other than in my own conversion experience, I had never seen such a remarkable and sudden transformation.

"I know," he replied. "What do I do now?"

God hadn't told me that part. He had said only, "Go and tell . . ."

Acting as if I knew what I was doing, I said, "Wayne, I will come back tomorrow afternoon and bring you a Bible. We can read together about Jesus, and you can start to follow him. Maybe you can come to church with my family on Sunday."

The next afternoon, I headed for Wayne's apartment. This time, I took a close look at his surroundings and noticed how depressing they really were. The planters were overgrown with weeds, the paint on the trim of the building was flaking off, and some broken windows were actually held together with duct tape. I decided to ignore the run-down conditions and focus on finding the right door.

I knocked and waited . . . and waited. Just when I was about to turn away in disappointment, the door opened a crack. I heard a thin, weak voice. "Can I help you?"

Did I have the wrong door? "I'm looking for a young man named Wayne."

The door opened a little wider. I saw a gray, almost skeletal figure in a worn plaid housecoat. Her eyes, her complexion, and her high cheekbones suggested that she was part Native American. She leaned toward me and rasped, "What do you want with Wayne? What has he done now?"

I replied, "He hasn't done anything wrong. I came yesterday and talked to him and prayed with him. I was hoping to give him this Bible."

The bony hand let go of the door and took hold of the Bible.

She examined the Bible, opening and closing it as if she were looking for something suspicious. "Why don't you come in?"

I introduced myself. "I'm Don, ma'am. May I ask your name?"

She shuffled over to a worn recliner that was covered with a sheet and sat down, breathing heavily. When she had her breath again, she said, "I'm Bonnie, Wayne's momma. What did you do to him yesterday? He seems like a different person. He's almost *too* happy."

I explained that Wayne was not on anything but rather that God had touched him. I told her briefly that Wayne had experienced God's love and forgiveness and was now a "new creation."

Bonnie looked down at the floor and coughed. "Wayne's had a hard life. He don't know his dad. I've tried to take care of him, but it's been hard. I have been on drugs and alcohol since I was his age. I had some men in my life, but no one good. Wayne has seen a lot of so-called stepfathers come and go. Because of my addictions, I've done a lot of bad things. . . ."

Tears appeared and ran quickly down the dry, nearly transparent skin that covered her cheekbones. I had no idea what to say, so I remained silent. I wished I had a handkerchief to offer her.

"My health has been gone for a long time," she went on. "I can't afford the dope anymore; I just drink enough booze now to make life bearable. I feel so bad for Wayne—what he's seen, how he's had to live." She wiped at her eyes with the back of her hand. I couldn't help but notice the deep bruising on her forearm. She shivered slightly and then slumped forward, her arms resting on her thighs and her chin resting on her chest. She spoke softly into her lap.

"I can't blame him for getting into trouble. It's really all my fault. I'm glad you talked to him. I'm glad he's happy now."

We sat in awkward silence for several minutes. I still didn't know what to say.

Bonnie looked up and squinted at me. Her face was pinched with a pain that wasn't physical. "Mister, do you think God could do for me what he did for Wayne?"

"Bonnie, I can tell you this: God loves you in spite of everything you've done. The Bible says, 'Whoever calls on the name of the Lord will be saved.' Would you like to call on him right now?"

"I would like that very much." Bonnie reached out and took my hand and bowed her head. I couldn't help but notice how thin her hair was and how gray her skin was. I figured she couldn't be much beyond fifty, but she looked decades older.

I squeezed her hand gently. We prayed together. When we had finished, she kept her head bowed and her eyes closed for several minutes.

When she lifted her head, she looked as if she were in a trance. She dropped my hand and pointed at me with a bony index finger. "You . . . you are a trumpet!" Then she shook her head and smiled at me. She couldn't have had any idea how much that meant to me.

In the Old Testament, the blowing of trumpets often preceded announcements and action. Bonnie's words made me think of instructions Moses gave to Israel just two years after they fled Egypt.

> When you arrive in your own land and go to war against your enemies who attack you, sound the alarm with the trumpets. Then the LORD your God will remember you and rescue you from your enemies. Blow the trumpets in times of gladness, too, sounding them at your annual festivals and at the beginning of each month. (Numbers 10:9-10)

I truly believed that, in spite of my shortcomings, God had somehow called me to "announce the glad tidings" and call God's people to action. Over the years, Bonnie's words have come back again and again to encourage me.

Like her son, Bonnie seemed to undergo a sudden, visible transformation. There was now life behind her gray eyes, and her skin seemed to glow a little. She sat back in her chair with a peaceful look on her face.

Moved with compassion, I asked her, "Bonnie, is there anything I can do for you, or is there any other need in your life that we could pray about?"

She lifted her arm to show me a long lump under the skin. "This is a shunt where they do dialysis. I go several times every week.

Both of my kidneys have shut down, and the doctors say nothing can be done. Because my health is so poor, they won't put me on a donor list. Now that I know I'm going to heaven, I'm not going to worry about that. But the dialysis is so painful. I just dread every trip there."

My heart went out to Bonnie again. "Let me pray for you, Bonnie. Let's believe that God will help you."

The next day, I came back to see Wayne and Bonnie, as I'd promised. They were still excited about what God was doing in their lives. They told me that God had helped them forgive each other and have peace in their home. We agreed that Leia and I would take them to church a few days later.

When we picked Bonnie and Wayne up for church that first Sunday, she told me, "Don, since you prayed for me, I have not had any pain or even any real discomfort in dialysis. It's truly a miracle." I was grateful, though truthfully I had prayed that God would perform a greater miracle, restoring Bonnie's dead kidneys. That was not to be. But before her death several months later, Bonnie never missed church and had great peace despite her difficult life.

Meditation on the Miraculous

As you pray and study the Bible, listen for God's message to you. If you believe he is calling you to act but you want confirmation or are unsure of the details, wait. Continue to pray to determine whether the sense of certainty about his direction fades or increases.

> [Jesus said,] "I am the good shepherd; I know my own sheep, and they know me, just as my Father knows me and I know the Father. . . . My sheep listen to my voice; I know them, and they follow me. I give them eternal life, and they will never perish."
> JOHN 10:14-15, 27-28

CHAPTER 13

LETTING GO

1982

After Bonnie passed away, Wayne lived with us as our foster child for a year. Our children accepted him and loved him as an older brother. For the most part, Wayne was good with them; however, he didn't realize that what might be funny to a teenager was downright scary to our five-year-old son.

Just before lunch one day, James told Leia that Wayne had sneaked outside, scratched on the window screens, and made animal-sounding noises, frightening him greatly.

"James, Wayne was just playing with you," Leia said. "I will talk to him about it though." Then Leia held out a peanut butter and jelly sandwich to him. "Take this. You may go outside to eat it."

He took his sandwich and shuffled out the front door.

Just minutes later James came bursting back through the door, jelly smeared around his mouth and eyes opened wide. "Mom! Mom! I saw Jesus! I saw Jesus!" He was so excited that he jumped up and down, not even noticing when part of his sandwich crumpled from his hand and onto the floor.

"James, settle down." Leia got up and put her hands on James's shoulders. "Tell me what happened."

James's voice quavered with excitement. "Mom, I saw Jesus."

"Where? How?"

"I was standing in the front yard, and I just looked up and there he was. He had something like a dress on and a gold belt around his waist. He was clear!"

"James, what do you mean 'clear'?"

"I could see through him, but I could see him. He was clear."

"You mean transparent," Leia said. "Okay; then what happened?"

"He just told me something, and then he was gone!"

"What did he say, James?"

"He said, 'James, don't be afraid when you are with Wayne. I am always with you.' Then he was gone!"

From then on, whenever we heard the song "Jesus Loves the Little Children," Leia and I remembered how our Savior had comforted our little boy.

Giving Up My Day Job

I continued my evangelism to people in the poorer sections of Rialto. I was happy that I was able to touch some people's lives, but I felt that God had more for me to do. Without his direction, though, I didn't know what to do next.

Going door-to-door talking to strangers in the rough part of town had been a little frightening. What came next was terrifying.

I was in Phoenix on business. I remember clearly the moment when I approached the I-17 off-ramp for Sky Harbor International Airport in my rental car. A voice spoke to me that blocked out the Christian music from the radio: "Go home and quit your job."

That was all.

I looked around; the voice had seemed to come from everywhere and nowhere. It was almost a whisper, but it was loud at the same time.

I was sure it was God. The words were clear, but what could they really mean? I knew I would have to go home and talk to my wife about it. She'd never believe it. If I hadn't heard the voice myself, I wouldn't believe it.

I had been praying—almost begging, actually—for direction to do something. Now here it was. Quit my job? When? Quit my job, and do what? Why? What if Leia adamantly said no (as I was sure she would)? Who would make my mortgage payments if I quit? How would I explain to my employers, or anyone else for that matter, why I was taking this apparently senseless step? All of our struggles from the last time I'd followed God's leading to quit my job came flooding into my mind. And yet if it really was God speaking to me, how could I not obey?

These questions and many others plagued me as my flight from Phoenix approached the airport near my home. Leia and James met me just outside the gate; Heidi was in school. As I saw their smiles, I felt suddenly guilty. Was my news going to destroy their happy lives and their security?

At home that evening I was quiet and evasive. I was not ready to tell Leia. As long as I didn't give voice to what God had told me, it somehow didn't seem completely real. I wasn't ready to bring revelation into reality yet.

I decided to go to bed early to avoid too much conversation. When I went back to the bedroom, though, Leia was blocking the door.

"Don, something is on your mind. What is it?"

Caught.

She said, "We're not going to bed until you tell me what is on your mind." She stood there, arms crossed, eyes straight and set. There would be no escape, yet I continued to hesitate.

She said, "Are we going to stand here all night?"

"Okay, Leia, I'll tell you, but you're going to wish I hadn't."

"Go ahead." She seemed solemn but at peace.

"Well, while I was in Phoenix, I believe God spoke to me. . . ."

I looked down at the carpet. "He said, 'Go home and quit your job.' That's all." I looked up, expecting her to be crying or getting ready to flip out completely. Instead, she continued to look at me with a level gaze.

"Don, I can't explain it, and I don't like it, but I know God spoke those words to you. Somehow, in my spirit I just knew that you were going to come home and tell me this. He prepared me, so I have God's peace about it."

I took her into my arms. "Leia, honestly, I'm afraid."

"Me, too."

I had an agreement with my employers that I would give them three months' notice if I were to leave them. Because they were based in Canada, it could take that long for them to recruit and prepare someone to take my place. The fact that I had those three months was a comfort to me. I could obey God immediately, quit my job, and still have a paycheck for a while.

My boss, Terry, was a self-made millionaire. When I called him in British Columbia to give him the news, he was incredulous. He shouted, "Don, what in the world are you talking about? Quitting? That's crazy. You're making more money than you've ever made in your life. In fact, last month was your best month ever! What's the problem?"

I said nothing.

"Listen," his voice softened, "has someone offered you more money? I'll meet their offer. No, better, I will double the difference! C'mon, Don, you know how difficult this will be for us."

"Terry, I'm sorry. Believe me, if I didn't have to make this decision, I wouldn't."

"Okay, tell me what the deal is. What's the offer? I'll beat it!"

"Terry, you can't beat this offer; you can't match this offer. I'm afraid no one can."

I heard the tone of resignation in his voice. "Oh, no. It's that religious stuff, isn't it? I told you this fanaticism would ruin your life."

When my boss had been convinced of my inevitable departure, I hung up the phone with some relief but with great trepidation. I hadn't heard anything from God since Phoenix. Surely, any day now, he would tell me what was next.

The days before my termination slipped by quickly. Everyone who knew about my decision to leave my job constantly asked me,

"Now what? What are you going to do when your job is finished?" Even those who had seemed to believe me when I first told them of God's direction began to look at me skeptically as time moved on and I had no answers.

Then a sunny Monday morning came, and I was technically unemployed. Since I didn't have to go to work, I went to a morning meeting of local ministers. Most were pastors, but evangelists like me were also invited. Each Monday they gathered at Jim's Burgers in Rialto to share, rejoice, or commiserate with one another concerning their respective Sunday services. I dreaded the questions that would inevitably come, but I didn't feel like being alone.

Randall looked up from his coffee as I entered the restaurant. He had been the first and so far the only one of the group to arrive. Randall was principal of the Christian school my daughter attended and pastor of a local church. For some reason I'd always felt a negative chemistry between us. I was surprised to see him there; he was supposed to be on vacation.

To avoid questions, I struck first. "Hello, Randall. I thought you were in Oregon."

Randall remained silent as I took my seat and ordered my coffee. Finally he spoke.

"Well, Don, you're right. I was on vacation, but you ruined that."

I was taken aback. "Randall, I have no idea what you are talking about. How could I ruin your vacation?"

"Well," he drawled, "at night when I was trying to rest, God kept speaking to me about you."

"About me?"

"Yep, God kept telling me to ask you to come on staff at my church, and I kept saying no. It was a restless time." He smiled. I grimaced.

I couldn't believe my ears. I tried to maintain my composure, but inside I was screaming, *No, no, no! This can't be. God would not have me leave my job to stay here in Rialto and work with Randall.*

"Randall, I'm flattered," I dissembled. "Of course, I would certainly need some time to pray about that. We'll talk later."

Much later, I thought.

"No problem," he said. "I'll be in my office all day."

After breakfast, I began driving toward the headquarters of Youth With A Mission, an evangelism, training, and mercy ministry. Leia and I had been impressed by their ministry philosophy and their work. I thought maybe that's where God wanted me.

YWAM was an hour and a half away in the San Fernando Valley. Though it was a bright, sunny morning, I felt as if I were driving into deeper darkness each mile that I drove. There seemed to be a heavy atmosphere in my car that the cheery Christian music coming from the radio could not dispel. The farther I got away from Rialto, the more convicted I felt that, despite my disappointment and displeasure, God really had spoken to Randall. It seemed like a bad dream. Eventually, I forced myself to get off the freeway and head back to Rialto.

My afternoon meeting with Randall was even more unsettling than the breakfast meeting. He assured me that God had indeed made it clear that I was to come on staff at his church to help them reach the city of Rialto with the gospel. I knew Randall's small church and school likely couldn't support my family in the style to which we were accustomed.

"Randall, I realize we would have to make some sacrifices to take this position. Exactly what kind of compensation could we expect?"

Then I learned that, actually, they couldn't provide any support at all.

"Well, Don, we don't have a salary to offer you. I don't take a salary myself. I pay the bills, we do God's business, and I live on what is left. Somehow God always provides. If this is God's will, I believe he will provide for you, too."

I knew immediately that Randall couldn't make my mortgage payments if he had to. How in the world would we live on what was left after *he* lived on what was left? I was jobless, and here was a job with no salary. I was afraid to say yes, but more afraid to say no. Somehow I knew God was in this.

"Okay, I'll start tomorrow," I said, before turning to go break this news to Leia. She, like me, was reluctant but resigned. God had spoken once again.

Meditation on the Miraculous

When making a major decision or move, we would prefer that God show us the entire picture upfront. Often, however, he reveals only what we need to know in the moment. The good news is that he is always trustworthy and right on time—as the apostle Paul (formerly Saul) discovered after his dramatic conversion.

> As [Saul] was approaching Damascus on this mission, a light from heaven suddenly shone down around him. He fell to the ground and heard a voice saying to him, "Saul! Saul! Why are you persecuting me?"
>
> "Who are you, lord?" Saul asked.
>
> And the voice replied, "I am Jesus, the one you are persecuting! Now get up and go into the city, and you will be told what you must do."
>
> ACTS 9:3-6

CHAPTER 14

MOBILE MISSIONARIES

1982
Rialto, California

I was finally "in the ministry." I continued to evangelize our community while also instructing every willing church member in the fine art of fishing for men.

By this time, I had nearly covered the low-income areas of our city in methodical, door-to-door canvassing. Now that I was formally working with Randall, he and I prayed and felt the Lord leading us to attempt to share the gospel at every door in Rialto, starting in the neighborhood immediately adjacent to the church and then working outward.

During the week, I went out by myself for about four to six hours a day, doing my best to find an open ear and an open heart with whom to share the Good News.

I developed a simple, reproducible method of starting meaningful conversations at our neighbors' doorsteps. I started by asking them to take part in a survey of religious attitudes. That led into a discussion of the person's experiences and beliefs. Whenever possible, I followed up with a simple presentation of the Good News and prayer.[1]

The survey was an effective way to initiate conversations and enabled me to listen as much as I spoke. Over time, I also picked up a consistent, if concerning statistic: less than three in ten of the people I spoke with had ever heard the gospel presented in a way they could understand and respond to. This included longtime active church members. Regardless of whether my "contacts" prayed during our visit or if they ever turned up in our church, I was overjoyed at each opportunity to share the salvation that had made God so real and powerful in my life.

On the weekends, I took our nervous but enthusiastic church members out to practice what I had been teaching them. They, too, found that the survey was a helpful tool. Just having that clipboard in their hands, which gave them a reason for being at the door and a definite place to start, made evangelism doable. Even the most timid people seemed to enjoy going out on a two-person team to pray while the braver, bolder believer did the verbal work. There was an innocent excitement in what we were doing. As we met together afterward and shared our exploits, failures, foibles, and successes, we could feel the presence of God in us and among us.

I tried not to think about money. Leia and I were rapidly burning through my severance pay and savings, and the bills kept coming. Randall gave me five dollars a week as a token and a down payment against the salary he was sure God would eventually provide as a result of our obedience. Because of my service in Vietnam, the government sent me a monthly disability check of about fifty dollars. It wasn't much. I would have to generate some income, at least by working part-time.

I found work painting houses. One day I was on a ladder with a paintbrush in my hand when I prayed, "Dear God, why did I quit my good job just to go back to painting again? I really don't have much more time now to do your work than when I was on that job making good money! I thought you said, 'Ask, and I will give you the nations.' I really believed that you were calling me to be a missionary."

I didn't hear an audible voice this time, but I had a very clear, unmistakable impression of what God was speaking to my spirit by his Spirit. He told me that he *had* called me to be a missionary and that I should start where I was. Like missionaries who leave their homes to live on their mission field, I had to be willing to give up my home. The city of Rialto must be my mission field and my training ground.

As I climbed down the ladder, I began to consider the implications. I knew that, in Luke 14, Jesus essentially said, "Unless you say good-bye to all your possessions, you cannot be my disciple" (see verse 33). He also spoke of "counting the cost" of true discipleship (see verse 28). He said, "Everyone who has left houses or brothers or sisters or father or mother or wife or children or lands, for My name's sake, shall receive a hundredfold, and inherit eternal life" (Matthew 19:29, NKJV). It had been easy to read these verses and even to talk about them in a Bible study. It had been exciting to read the biographies of missionaries like William Carey and Hudson Taylor, who had left everything to reach the people of India and China.

Was I really ready to go all the way as well? Could I ask my wife to join me in this? Leia had no desire to be a missionary wife or to leave her comfortable home. Where in the world *would* we live? Was I "hearing voices" like a lunatic, or was God really leading me to take these bold steps?

No one was around the house I was painting, so I took time again to pray. I told the Lord that I was willing to do whatever he wanted and to pay any price—willing, I confessed, but not necessarily able.

Having made that commitment, I began to think about what we would do. Where would we live if we no longer had our comfortable middle-class home? As I considered this problem in prayer, a plan came together. I wasn't sure exactly where it originated, but I believed that God was giving me some direction and inspiration. It was a crazy plan, but *that* was nothing new.

First, I needed a travel trailer that we could put on the church property. If we connected such a trailer to the electricity, water, and sewer at the church, we would have no bills at all. My VW camper van was paid for and got good mileage. I received the small Veterans Administration disability check every month, along with a little cash that Randall gave me from time to time when "the Lord led him" to do so. Perhaps we could just trust God for groceries and other daily needs. After all, he seemed to be leading us, and I'd heard somewhere that "where God guides, God provides."

I prayed again: "Father God, is this really what you want me to do?"

I felt that he was very precise in his direction: Get rid of your house, sell all your large possessions, and move into a travel trailer on the church property.

Next, I would have to convince Randall that this wasn't an absurd idea. Finally, I would have to hope that Leia wouldn't go back to her mother when I told her.

Randall's reaction completely surprised me.

"Don, 'missionaries to Rialto'—that's a great idea. You'll be really close to work, and your sacrifice will inspire everyone. The property here is plenty large enough to accommodate a small travel trailer." He paused. "Where will you get the trailer anyway?"

I had no idea where the travel trailer would come from, no idea at all. I wanted to obey God and sell the house, but the California real estate bubble had burst, houses were not selling, and we were almost upside down in our mortgage. How was I supposed to sell our home under these conditions?

I spoke to a friend who had some rental property. I had led Wayne T. to the Lord soon after Leia and I became Christians. We had remained friends for about six years now. I needed to get out of our mortgage but had almost no equity. I asked Wayne if he would be willing to just take over our mortgage.

Again, I was surprised.

Wayne said, "Don, I will do this to help you follow God's will. We'll go to the bank and take care of it as soon as you're ready."

The obstacles were falling. It looked like God was knocking them down, but it was still scary!

Soon after these two conversations, Leia and I went to visit some friends we hadn't seen in a long time. Cliff and Wendy lived in La Quinta near Palm Springs. Leia and Wendy went out shopping while Cliff told me about his construction business and his ministry in a local church.

"So, Don, enough about us," he said. "What are you guys doing now?"

I hesitated to tell him about the strange decisions I had made over the past several months. Few people understood—very few. I finally blurted out the whole truth, even my latest idea about the travel trailer. "Cliff, I know it sounds nuts, but I'm convinced that this is what God wants us to do."

He looked concerned. "Have you told Leia about this?"

"No, there's no point in doing that yet. I have no idea where to get a travel trailer. I don't have any money right now to buy one." I looked at the ceiling. When I looked back at Cliff, he wore a mischievous smile.

"This is very interesting. You know, Wendy and I lived in a twenty-eight-foot travel trailer while I attended Multnomah Bible College."

"I had no idea." I waited.

"Yep. We still have it. We've been renting it to a lady from our church. She's moving out at the end of this month. I believe in what you're doing, Don. It's an unusual path to ministry and missions, but you're not the first person God has led in an unconventional way. If you and Leia can get a truck to pull that trailer up to Rialto, you can use it for as long as you need." He folded his hands on the table and looked at me—calling my bluff, it seemed.

"But, Cliff, we can't pay you anything for it."

"That's okay. We're still making payments on it, and we have to make those payments whether it sits empty or someone uses it. Just take the trailer, and if you can help with the payments, fine; if not, fine!" Now not only was our house as good as gone, but we had a travel trailer.

I cleared my throat nervously. "Uh, okay, I'll just have to talk to Leia about it." I hadn't mentioned one word about my missionary plans to her. Why should I? It had seemed impossible anyway.

"Great. We'll tell the girls when they get back from shopping!"

"No, no, that wouldn't be a good idea, Cliff. I need to break this idea to Leia gently."

"Well, if God is in it, then it will work out. But I wouldn't want to be you tonight!"

I looked out the window. Our wives were pulling into the driveway.

"Yeah, I wouldn't want to be me either."

Later that evening, I felt as if I were living an instant replay of the time I had to tell Leia that God had instructed me to quit my job. When I walked into our bedroom, she was already in bed, her face to the wall. I tried to get in quickly and quietly. That didn't work. She was not asleep.

"Don, I know you want to tell me something."

She was wrong; I most certainly did not want to tell her. I loved my wife, and I knew how much her home meant to her.

"I know you want to tell me something. God told me."

How could I argue with that?

"Well, honey," I said, trying to sound sleepy, "if God told you something, maybe *you* should be telling *me*." She ignored my joke.

"Don, I sensed God speaking to me earlier today. I told him that I would know for sure that he was speaking and that I would do what he asked—if he told you exactly the same thing, word for word."

I propped myself on the pillow with one elbow. "Okay, here it is: I believe God spoke to me, and he said to get rid of this house, sell all our stuff, and move into a travel trailer on the church property." Now it was out. I waited for the explosion.

Leia turned to look at me. "Don, that is exactly, point by point, what God told me! Without this miracle of confirmation, there is no way I could do this. Now that I know it was God, we need to obey him."

She actually seemed much braver than me. Other than knowing we'd be moving into the travel trailer, our future was so very uncertain. Again.

With almost dizzying swiftness, we turned the house over to Wayne, had a huge yard sale, picked up the trailer from Cliff and Wendy, and made our home behind the church. The travel trailer was small—twenty-eight feet by eight feet. It was cramped from the beginning for a family of four and our small dog.

I was amazed at how good Leia's attitude was about our greatly reduced living space. The whole "house" wasn't as big as our previous master bedroom. Seven-year-old Heidi and five-year-old James saw the move into the trailer as a great adventure. They now "lived" at their school and church and had more opportunity to play with their church friends. Though they were young, they seemed to grasp that we were doing a special work for God and that they were a part of it. To my surprise, I never heard either of them complain about any inconvenience, such as no longer each having their own room.

About this time, Leia began working in the Christian school at the church. This got her out of the trailer during the day, and she was still able to be with the children.

I spent most days out in the city of Rialto talking to people about Jesus. We were missionaries by the miraculous hand of God. To most of our friends and relatives, and many good Christians, we were irresponsible fanatics. We took comfort in the assurance and peace we had, knowing we were in the middle of God's will for our lives. We also remembered that, early in Jesus' ministry, his own family had gone to "lay hold on him," saying, "He is beside himself" (Mark 3:21, KJV). That is a nice way of saying "he's crazy." So we felt we were in good company!

Meditation on the Miraculous

The command to tell others about Christ intimidates many people, but the joy, meaning, and sense of adventure that come from sharing our faith is priceless.

We proclaim to you the one who existed from the beginning, whom we have heard and seen. We saw him with our own eyes and touched him with our own hands. He is the Word of life. . . . Our fellowship is with the Father and with his Son, Jesus Christ. We are writing these things so that you may fully share our joy.
1 JOHN 1:1, 3-4

CHAPTER 15

A VEGGIE TALE AND OTHER UNLIKELY STORIES

1983

As much as we enjoyed our ministry work, Leia and I struggled personally with the realities of our situation. After a number of months, it seemed unlikely that the church would ever be in a position to pay us for our labor.

When we first left behind our home and employment, I had made a deal with God. I told him, "I will do this thing, but you must provide for us. I will not tell anyone of our needs. I will not borrow anything from anyone, I will not ask anyone for anything, and I won't even ask anyone to pray for our needs. You called us to do this. You must provide."

God was indeed faithful. His faithfulness, however, was not always according to our schedule. Very often, he seemed to grow our faith by waiting to meet our needs until the last minute, and sometimes beyond the last minute.

Our "regular" monthly income came to no more than $125, which included my Veterans Administration stipend and payment from Christian Life Center for Leia's work at the school and my job on the church staff. Needless to say, this did not meet even our modest minimum requirements.

Yet time and space would fail if I tried to tell of all the small but miraculous ways God met our needs. From time to time we received totally unsolicited and unexpected gifts of cash. Out of nowhere, people would bring clothes for our rapidly growing children. My van was often low on gasoline because I used it for my evangelistic work. When the tank got too low, someone always seemed to give me a few dollars on impulse, or people would borrow the van to haul kids or cargo. They always returned it with a full tank of gas.

A great treat for our family was dinner from the recently opened Twenty-Five Cent Hamburger Stand. For only one dollar, we could each get a burger. They were small, but we were "going out to eat!" I took my time eating and wondered what my Canadian millionaire former boss would say about this place. Terry had always insisted on taking staff and clients to the best restaurants when we did trade shows and conventions. We ate at places like Ruth's Chris Steak House, the Ritz-Carlton in Chicago, and the best restaurants in Las Vegas. Our first meal with Terry had been at the Beverly Hilton Hotel in Beverly Hills. Now my family struggled just to buy french fries to go with our twenty-five-cent hamburgers.

Once when funds and groceries were particularly scarce, I was feeling a little sorry for myself. I was starting to feel like God wasn't really taking care of my family—or maybe I wasn't taking care of my family. Life was stressful, at times depressing, and always a challenge.

I was reminded of my time in the Marine Corps boot camp. Now my entire family was going through God's boot camp with me. Though I wouldn't want to go through it again, I wouldn't trade the experience for anything. We learned so much about God's sovereignty and goodness during that time.

The Veggie Tale

One morning, Leia began looking for something to make for dinner. There was a little breakfast cereal and milk, but nothing for dinner. Her search through our tiny kitchen produced a couple of pieces of chicken, a couple of onions, a tomato, and the usual condiments. How would she make a meal from this? Though Leia is a creative domestic expert, she was at a loss. She decided to pray. She prayed a simple prayer: "God, I need to make something for my family to eat tonight. We are depending on you. Amen."

She had just finished praying when there was a knock at the door.

When she first opened the door of the trailer, she didn't see anyone. Then she looked down. There was Pastor Randall's little daughter, Robin. She had a cherubic face, but she obviously wasn't an angel with the answer to Leia's desperate prayer. Or was she?

"Miss Leia, I want to go for a walk in the field to look at birds and insects. Daddy says I can't go for a walk by myself. Would you walk with me?"

The church owned a large, overgrown field behind its buildings. Leia looked out at the field and saw nothing but knee-high weeds and grass. Everything was brown in the middle of a very dry Southern California summer. It didn't look interesting or inviting. But Robin was insistent.

"Please, Miss Leia, please. It can be like a little field trip for school." She smiled. Kids can be so creative—and manipulative.

"Okay, Robin, we'll go for a walk."

Leia and Robin held hands and picked their way among the sticker bushes and clinging weeds. Robin was excited about every bug and bird. Leia tried to enjoy God's creation, but she wasn't in the mood. And then she saw it.

"Robin, Robin, don't step on that!" In the midst of the brown weeds was a patch of green vegetation.

Could it be? Out here in the weeds, all by itself, was a large Swiss chard, a plant similar to spinach.

Robin saw Leia's excitement. "Let's pull off the leaves, Miss Leia. Let's just pull it up!" She started to grab at the chard with great enthusiasm.

"No, no, Robin. If we get some scissors, we can cut off the leaves, and the plant will grow new ones. Let's go back to the trailer and get some scissors."

"Yeah! Scissors." Robin was happy, but Leia might have been more so. Swiss chard! They started to walk away when Leia saw more green a few feet away—another chard plant, smaller, but definitely edible.

"Let's go get those scissors."

Their pace quickened. They had only gone a few yards when another small but unmistakable green sprout caught Leia's attention. It seemed impossible, but there, in the midst of that brown field of weeds, a lone carrot top adorned the earth. This time, there was no hesitation.

"Go ahead, Robin. See what's under the green plant. Dig around it and pull it up." Robin pulled the large single carrot out of the earth and held it up proudly.

Leia paused for a moment to give thanks to God. With this carrot, the two chard plants, and the items in the trailer, she could make a good-tasting soup for our family.

Leia's heart felt so much lighter. They skipped together through the brush, dropped off the carrot in the trailer, and came back with the scissors. While Leia performed surgery on the chard, Robin went exploring.

"Miss Leia, what is this?"

Leia couldn't believe her eyes. Here, in a weed-infested field, grew a solitary strawberry plant. It was loaded with luscious fruit.

"Lord," Leia said under her breath, "you've thought of everything, even dessert!"

As she told me the story later, Leia said she realized that God had sent this child to lead her to his provision. She was reminded of the familiar Bible text about the day when God's Kingdom shall fill the earth:

The wolf also shall dwell with the lamb,
The leopard shall lie down with the young goat,
The calf and the young lion and the fatling together;
And a little child shall lead them. (Isaiah 11:6, NKJV)

Though Leia may have pulled that passage out of context a bit, it was a great reminder that God does take care of his followers. We had lived in the travel trailer for many months by then. We had never considered walking in that unsightly field before that day. Then God sent a little "angel" in answer to prayer.

Out of the Fire and into the Frying Pan

Before moving to the trailer, we had gotten rid of almost everything we owned in a huge yard sale. For a capable homemaker like Leia who had almost every possible kitchen accessory, this was a difficult adjustment. One day I came home to the trailer to see what "Wonder Woman" had concocted for lunch. She was quiet, and I could see sadness in her eyes. I hesitated to ask her what was wrong.

"Sweetheart, what's bothering you? What can I do?"

The tears began flowing, but Leia tried to maintain her composure. "Don, I know this sounds silly, but I really need a little frying pan to make eggs in." Leia had sold or given away most of her kitchen utensils because of the lack of space. She did most of her cooking in a large electric skillet and a toaster oven.

She cupped her hands together in front of her face. "I just need a little frying pan for eggs. Just a little stainless steel frying pan." She began to sob. I felt horrible. I couldn't even afford to buy my wife a frying pan. I stood up and patted her shoulder.

"Leia, God knows our needs. Let's pray about this."

"I don't feel like praying." She sniffled.

"Okay, I'll pray."

She nodded and blew her nose.

I went outside and leaned against the travel trailer. Finally, I prayed.

"Dear God, I need your help here. I don't have any money, and I'm not going to ask anyone for help. Do you care about a frying pan? You've promised to meet our needs. I think we really need this."

The very next day, an unfamiliar car pulled into the church parking lot. A well-dressed lady got out. She ignored me and went to the back of her car. I went over to see if she needed help. Perhaps she had a flat tire.

As I approached, she opened the trunk. Inside was a cardboard box. "Are you one of the ministers here?" she asked.

"Yes, ma'am. I am."

"Well, I'm not a churchgoer, but I know churches have rummage sales." She arched her eyebrow at me inquiringly. It was obvious that this "neighbor" had a bunch of junk she just wanted to dump somewhere.

I nodded slowly. Actually, we never had rummage sales, but I said, "Yes, ma'am, most churches do have rummage sales."

She smiled politely. "Well, then, it's all yours."

I took the box from the trunk. "I hope you'll come to visit with us one Sunday soon. You'll find church isn't so bad."

She gave me a pinched smile and drove off without saying anything.

I carried the box to the storage room where we kept other useless junk. After dropping it on a shelf, I started to leave. I knew what was in that box—the typical "junk for Jesus." Then I looked anyway. Sure enough, I pulled out a big, broken candle; unmatched gloves; a particularly hideous sweater; and a couple of Christmas ties. I kept digging and throwing junk out on the floor. There, under a board game that was missing the board, was a small stainless steel frying pan. It looked brand-new with no sign of either scorch or scratch. I immediately took off for our travel trailer! God is good!

The Incredible Hulk

In the midst of our struggles I tried to be faithful to the original mission God had set me on: "Tell people about my Son." I would like to say I did my best, but that would not be accurate. Now I often wish I had not fallen into the pit of despair and self-pity that kept me from making full use of those days and being as fruitful as I might have been.

Sometimes it seemed like my work of telling people about God's Son was an exercise in futility; few were open, fewer were interested.

One morning, I was in my office praying. "God, I need some success today. I don't know how long I can keep doing this with such meager results. Will you please lead me to someone who will actually listen and respond?" As I continued to pray silently, a glimpse of the upper story of an apartment building flashed through my mind. It was a very clear image, but the "vision" seemed to last less than a second. At first, I was tempted to dismiss it as imagination. Then I realized that the distinctive outline of that building was familiar.

I sat back on my heels and tried to remember exactly where I had seen that building. I thought I knew the neighborhood. After finishing my prayers, I headed for my trusty VW van.

Sure enough, there it was. The wood shake roof, the brick facade, and the iron railing were exactly what I had seen in the vision.

I dismounted and went to the first apartment on the ground floor; the lady of the house at that apartment was almost unbelievably rude. I continued—door number 2, number 3—in my methodical way. At the second apartment no one was home; at the third, the occupant slammed the door in my face.

Where was the success I had prayed for? Then I realized that in the vision I hadn't seen the downstairs apartments. I had seen only the apartment on the upstairs corner of the building.

The first upstairs apartment had a screen door. It's difficult to knock on a screen door, so I tried to open it. It was locked. Suddenly the front door opened, startling me.

In the darkness of the apartment, I saw a large shape. A deep voice rasped, "What you want?"

"Good morning," I said to a man who didn't sound like he was having a good morning.

"Like I said, what you want?" The man was standing close to the screen now and looked bigger, darker, and more threatening. I decided that honesty was the best policy.

"Well, sir, I just came by to tell you about God's Son."

There was an incredulous look on the face of my new acquaintance. He wrinkled up his nose as if he found me repulsive. Silence.

Silence also seemed my most reasonable course of action.

Finally the big guy spoke. "Man, you need to come back when my old lady's here. She's into that stuff." He started to close the door. I was relieved.

Then I heard myself saying, "Hold on just a minute. I didn't come to talk to your wife. What's your name?"

He reached down and unlocked the screen door and silently pushed it open. Had I irritated this monster? I waited and stood my ground.

"Okay, man. I ain't doin' nothin'. I'll listen to ya for a minute. Make it quick."

I put out my hand; he ignored it. I noticed that one of his eyes was almost swollen shut. There was a small butterfly bandage not quite concealing stitches on his forehead.

Desperate to establish any kind of rapport I asked, "Well, anyway, what's your name?"

"Name's Lewis."

"Well, Lewis, I have to tell you that God knows about everything you've ever done. He knows your heart. He knows your anger and your fear."

What was I saying?

"Go on, dude."

"Lewis, you may have done many things wrong. You may not care about God. But God cares about you. He loves you and sent me here today to tell you about it."

Was I seeing things? Tears appeared at the corners of Lewis's eyes. "Go on, man. Go *on*."

"Okay, look, Lewis. Before you were ever born, God loved you and sent his Son, Jesus, to pay the price for what you've done and what you are. When Jesus died on that cross, he took your place and he suffered your punishment. The wages of sin is death, and he died in your place."

Lewis was now wiping the tears away. "That sounds too good to be true, man. What am I supposed to do about it?"

"Lewis, God did all that for you because he loves you and wants to give you a new life as his own child." I quickly explained a little more of the gospel. Lewis was solemn.

"I think I'm ready, man. I need a change."

"We should pray then."

"Yeah."

We prayed and then talked a while longer. I promised to come back and bring him a Bible. I practically skipped down the stairs. The vision at prayer that morning had been legitimate. In these difficult times, it was very encouraging to see God lead me in such a clear way.

The weekend came and went before I got a chance to get an extra Bible and visit Lewis again. I passed by the rude lady I'd encountered at the first apartment, but she ignored me. I climbed the stairs and pulled open the now-unlocked screen door. I knocked. I waited and then banged on the door. The woman from downstairs appeared at the bottom of the stairs.

"You looking for Lewis? He's not here. He's moved. I don't know where." I was very disappointed and felt a little guilty for not coming back sooner. I prayed and committed him to God's grace and left.

About six months later, I stood in a supermarket parking lot on Thanksgiving Eve. I had made hundreds of copies of a simple gospel tract with a Thanksgiving theme. I stood there cheerily handing out my Thanksgiving message to the shoppers streaming in and out of the store. I was having a good time.

Suddenly it looked like things were about to go bad. I saw a huge African American man, bundled up against the cold, striding purposefully toward me. He had a beard, but I could see that he wasn't smiling. Had he been offended by my Thanksgiving message? Maybe his wife told him there was a man down at the market who had harassed her about religion.

I braced myself and tried to give the man a sincere smile. I said, "Hi. Happy Thanksgiving."

He just stood there, staring.

Finally he said, "Hey, man, don't you recognize me?"

With the beanie, the bulky plaid wool jacket, and the beard, I really didn't recognize him. But I had heard that voice before. "Lewis? Lewis!"

He chuckled and grabbed me in a big bear hug and told me how happy he was to find me still doing "the Lord's work." Lewis told me that he had spent time in jail for assaulting his wife. She was so happy that he had come to the Lord that she had taken him back. Lewis now worked part-time; the rest of his time he volunteered at a halfway house for ex-cons and recovering drug addicts. Instead of getting men and women hooked on drugs, he was now helping them find freedom through the power of the Holy Spirit.

"I'm doing the Lord's work too," he said cheerily. "Thanksgiving Eve, them turkeys are real cheap. I'm gonna get some for the guys at the halfway house. God's blessed me. I'm changed. I gotta bless others." He smiled and chuckled through the beard.

"Lewis," I said, "you have no idea what a blessing it is just to see you and to see what God is doing in your life!"

Meditation on the Miraculous

When our heart beats with the same passion for the lost as God's, he will miraculously provide us opportunities to share his love with others.

> "Everyone who calls on the name of the LORD will be saved."
> But how can they call on him to save them unless they believe in him? And how can they believe in him if they have never heard about him? And how can they hear about him unless someone tells them? And how can they hear about him unless someone tells them? And how will anyone go and tell them without being sent? That is why the Scriptures say, "How beautiful are the feet of messengers who bring good news!"
> ROMANS 10:13-15

CHAPTER 16

MINDY'S MIRACLE

1983

One hot afternoon I was visiting homes in the neighborhood near our church. I knocked politely at the door of a neat ranch-style home.

A lady opened the door a crack. "Can I help you?"

She had a very pronounced Texas drawl. She was thin and stooped, and she appeared to be in her fifties. For a moment, she reminded me of Bonnie.

"Hi, I'm Don. I'm from Christian Life Center. I'd like to speak to you for a moment if I may."

"Yes, I'm Mindy. Why don't you come in? I can't stand here long."

When we were seated in her formal living room, she adjusted herself on the chair in obvious discomfort. "Well, I'm glad you're a Christian! I thought for a moment you were one of those two-by-twos."

"Two-by-twos, ma'am?"

"You know, those Jehovah's Witnesses and Mormons. They're always coming around. Two-by-twos!"

I wondered for a moment if she had read how Jesus had sent his disciples out "two by two" to preach in the towns of Judea. Instead, I said, "No, ma'am, I'm not one of those two-by-twos. I'm all by myself, just meeting people in the neighborhood."

"Well, you're a nice young man. It's hot out there. I'd offer you water, but it's hard for me to make it out into the kitchen. I have so much pain in my back that I can hardly move. I can't sleep at night without heavy medication. I can't sit in any one position for more than a few moments. I can't clean my house. I can't take care of my husband. . . ." She began to weep.

It was obvious that she was in great discomfort physically and emotionally.

"My fourteen-year-old granddaughter came to live with us because I can't do anything for myself," she said. "I'm so miserable. I'm sorry. . . . I shouldn't be saying all of this to a person I've just met."

"No need to be sorry, ma'am," I said. Here I was the "great missionary to Rialto," and I was at a total loss for words or an answer.

"I don't know what I did to deserve this," she added. "I had an auto accident several years ago. My back was seriously injured. I've had operations, therapy, and medication. I was in pain for years. A year or so ago, I was feeling a little better. Then one day I went to the grocery store. I wasn't paying attention and stepped on some dry beans on the floor. My feet went out from under me, and I landed flat on my back. Now I'm in worse shape than ever!"

She walked slowly across the room to the sofa. I couldn't help but notice that she limped badly and seemed to have limited use of one arm. I felt intense sympathy for her but still had no idea what to say. I told her that I could see she was in a great deal of discomfort and asked her if I had chosen a bad time to visit. She said she would probably feel no better tomorrow and was happy to entertain my questions. So I decided to dispense with the lengthy survey and get to the point of my visit: "Mindy, I won't take much of your time, but are you a Christian?"

"Well," she sighed deeply, "I was born again when I was a young girl in Texas. I used to be close to God, a long time ago. I still believe, but it's been years since I've been to church or even really prayed. I don't think he hears me. Listen, I'm sorry, but I'm in so much pain right now and my pills are taking effect. I'm going to have to go lie down."

"That's fine, Mindy. Can I come see you again sometime?"

"Yes, yes, sometime. Thanks for coming. Would you mind letting yourself out? I don't want to walk to the door."

Mindy was on my mind the rest of the day. It bothered me that I hadn't known what to do to help her. I could have offered to pray with her, but she didn't seem open to that and I wasn't sure how to pray for her anyway.

That evening Bobbie, one of Leia's friends from church, came by to pick up her son, who'd been playing with James. I knew Bobbie often prayed for the needs of others. While Leia went to find the boys, I told Bobbie all about Mindy. She promised to pray for her. I knew this was a promise she would keep.

The next morning, I got up early to read my Bible to prepare myself for the day. I read the thirteenth chapter of Luke's Gospel. There, Jesus enters a synagogue and finds a woman who has been "bent over" for nearly eighteen years. Jesus spoke to her and laid his hand on her, and immediately she was healed and made straight!

"Man," I thought, "I wish that could happen for Mindy!" I closed my Bible and began to pray. There came that infrequent, but now familiar voice.

"If you will pray for her, I will heal her."

My heart leaped with surprise, joy, and excitement.

Just then the phone rang. It was Bobbie. "Don, I'm sorry to be disturbing you so early, but I had to tell you!"

"Tell me what?"

"Well, I was out praying and jogging through the park early this morning. I had something like a vision. I say something like a vision because it was in my mind and not actually before my eyes. But it was very clear."

"And then?"

"Well, I saw the face of an older woman. I didn't recognize her, but somehow I felt it was the woman you told me about yesterday. I had been praying for her just shortly before I saw the vision. I saw her face and then some writing appeared under her. It became clear, and I saw 'Matthew 18:34-35.'"

"Really?"

"Yeah, really! I was so excited that I ran home and called you. I haven't even looked up those Scriptures yet to see what they say."

"Hold on. I have my Bible right here." I found the reference. After skimming the passage, I said, "Bobbie, okay, I think I understand. This Scripture says that if someone who has experienced God's forgiveness fails to forgive someone else, then God cannot forgive their sins and they will be turned over to tormenters. I know this is spiritual, but it seems to be very real in Mindy's case. Could you go with me to see her this afternoon?"

I told her about what I had seen in Luke 13 and what I believed God had told me. "I don't want to go alone," I told Bobbie. "It would help if you could tell her what you saw as well."

We quickly agreed to a time that afternoon.

A surprised Mindy opened the door. "Mindy," I said, "I'm sorry to stop by unannounced, but I didn't have any way to get in touch with you. This is Bobbie. We've been praying for you, and we have some news we'd like to share."

Mindy was apprehensive but polite. "Of course. I appreciate your prayers. Come in."

We stood awkwardly in the middle of the room. "Mindy, we've been praying for you, and I believe God has shown us some things."

"What kind of things? Good things, I hope." She forced a smile.

"Well, yes, really good things, actually. Before we leave today, God is going to heal you and restore your relationship with him."

She gave me a strange look, and I wondered if I appeared as crazy as I sounded. "Don, this isn't funny. I've been suffering for years. How can you say these things?"

"Mindy, I'm very serious. We believe that God has shown us what the problem is. Someone important in your life has hurt you, and you refuse to forgive this person. God's Word says that if you do not forgive, then neither will he forgive your sins. I believe your condition is somehow related to unforgiveness."

Mindy's face became hard and quizzical. Her defenses were up. "How do you know anything about me?"

"I told you; it's not us—it's God." I told her what I'd sensed as I read about the woman in Luke 13, and I told her about Bobbie's vision. I also did my best to explain those Scriptures that Bobbie saw.

Suddenly Mindy began to shake and to wail. "My God, my God. It's my mother. She always rejected me and mistreated me. She always favored my older sister. I could never do anything right; Sis could never do anything wrong. It was like that our whole lives. Do you know what it's like to be rejected like that? She never loved me.

"When Mother grew very old and ill, my sister claimed to be too busy to help her. So I nursed my mother. She spent the whole time criticizing me and criticizing everything I've ever done. She kept telling me how wonderful my sister was. My mother is gone now, but I can't forgive her. I can't!"

"Mindy, listen. I understand, but if you want to experience God's forgiveness and healing, you have to let go of the hatred and bitterness and forgive your mother."

"I just don't feel I can do that!"

"I'm not talking about feelings, Mindy. I'm talking about obedience. You don't have to feel anything. Pray a prayer of forgiveness as an act of obedience. I'll help you, if you like."

During several minutes of uncomfortable silence that followed, Mindy choked on her sobs and choked even more on what God was requiring of her. Finally she looked up with great resolution.

"No, no, that's okay. It's hard. But I know you're right, of course. That's what I need to do." Still crying, she began to pray out loud: "Father God, you know how I feel. But in obedience to you, I forgive my mother."

She began to cry harder. I felt bad.

Through her tears, Mindy continued, "Oh God, oh God, I do forgive her. I forgive her from my heart. Help me to feel the forgiveness."

Almost immediately, the crying stopped. A great peace seemed to come over her. There was a great silence in the room for a few more minutes. No one moved. Then Mindy looked up. "He's here! He's here! I feel his presence." She smiled from ear to ear. "Oh my, I'm going to need to sit down now—my back, my back."

"Wait, Mindy," I said. "Remember? I told you God would heal you today? Let's pray." Bobbie and I laid our hands on Mindy and began to pray. At last I said, "Mindy, I want you to reach right down and touch your toes. I believe God has healed you."

She looked at me with fear in her eyes. "It may hurt. I don't think I can do that."

"Do it by faith," I said, "just like when you forgave your mom."

At that, she pointed her hands toward her toes and bent right over. She stood upright with a look of shock. There was a question in her eyes, but she did not speak.

"Again," I said firmly.

She did it again. Now she smiled. She bent over again and again, each time with a bigger smile! I took her by the hands. "Mindy, do you remember doing squats in P.E. at school?"

She nodded.

"Okay, hold on to my hands and go all the way down in a squat position." This time, she obeyed immediately. Now she was laughing. She did it again and again. The three of us did not notice when her fourteen-year-old granddaughter returned home from school. As we worked with Mindy, we heard a gasp. I turned and saw the granddaughter.

"Grandma, Grandma, you, you . . . you can't do that!"

"I know, I know," Mindy said, laughing. She began twirling around the living room like a ballerina. Now the granddaughter was crying. Then they embraced.

Bobbie and I encouraged them to come visit our church on

Sunday. We went out of the house exhilarated. Mindy was healed and remained healed for the entire time we knew her. We eventually lost touch with her.

Meditation on the Miraculous

Hatred and bitterness bind people in many different ways. Healing and freedom are possible through the miracle of forgiveness, which we are able to give when we recognize the grace that God himself has given us.

> Get rid of all bitterness, rage, anger, harsh words, and slander. . . . Instead, be kind to each other, tenderhearted, forgiving one another, just as God through Christ has forgiven you.
> EPHESIANS 4:31-32

CHAPTER 17

IN OLD MEXICO

1983
Rialto and Tecate, Mexico

Witnessing a miracle like the one Mindy experienced made my position as "missionary to Rialto" thrilling, yet I still dreamed of someday serving God in a foreign country. Since the Mexican border was just a two-hour drive from our city, I suggested to Randall that perhaps our church should reach out to that country.

I was given permission to launch a mission team that would take used clothing, food, and other supplies to Baja California, Mexico, one weekend a month. The team included Steve Ramirez (a carpenter and father of five), Ruben Arriola (who liked to put ketchup on pancakes), and Tony Gonzales (who built houses and repaired VWs). All three were solid Christian men who spoke fluent Spanish. Though I had taken several years of Spanish in school, I knew I would need these men to interpret for me in Mexico.

That first Saturday we crossed into Mexico at Tecate, southeast of San Diego. We stopped there to purchase seventy-pound bags of frijoles (dried beans), large cans of vegetable shortening, and sacks of corn flour. These were staple foods that would keep for some time without refrigeration.

My vision was to reach some needy community in the area just south of the border. We did not know where we would go exactly. We just believed that the Lord would lead us.

We drove along the border due east of Tecate on Mexico's perilous Federal Highway 2, a two-lane, pebble-and-tar road with no shoulder. Dusty dirt roads branched south from the highway, leading to cattle ranches, farms, and mountain villages. Whenever we saw someone walking along the highway, we asked if any of the side roads led to a small town or village. The answers were uniformly negative until one man pointed down a rutted dirt track between two barbed-wire fences. He told us there was a small town down that road.

We followed that dirt track for about eight miles. Because of the bumps, ruts, mud holes, rocks, and perilous stretches of very soft sand, those eight miles seemed like eighty. Eventually some primitive homes and small farms came into view. The houses had no real windows—just holes in the adobe-brick walls. Their roofs were made from rusty, corrugated galvanized tin. A few crude fences with weathered tree branches for posts separated some of the properties. Barefoot children ran silently alongside our vehicle, their necks craned, eyes inquiring. We kept driving slowly and never saw anything that looked like an actual town. At long last, we saw an adult.

"*Hola.* Hello. What is the name of this place?" we asked. The man pushed a straw cowboy hat back on his head and peered into my old VW van. There he slowly surveyed the one gringo and three Mexican-Americans.

"Guadalajara Dos." He laughed a bitter laugh and shook his head. We did not quite understand his joke, but we could see that this place was far from being a second Guadalajara, which is a large city and the capital of the Mexican state of Jalisco. It is called the "technology" capital of Mexico, as well as the nation's cultural center.

We introduced ourselves to Anastasio, our new friend. We explained that God had sent us to share both spiritual and material sustenance with his village. Having heard many promises before, he was incredulous. Our obvious goodwill and naïveté soon convinced him that we had no evil designs.

He told us a little about his town. The residents of Guadalajara

Dos were among Mexico's poorest. The government had relocated them from the slums of Guadalajara nearly two thousand miles to the south. The authorities had promised them land, equipment, irrigation, and schools if they settled in one of the remote valleys in a dry, barren area of Baja California.

The government's promises were largely unfulfilled. A few hundred families were unceremoniously dumped in the inhospitable, undeveloped, and unpromising desert to fend for themselves. These former slum dwellers had been moved far enough from glamorous Guadalajara that they would not be likely to return.

A few bags of seeds, a crude water reservoir, and barren plots of poor, sandy soil were about all the government gave them. After telling us about their precarious existence, Anastasio offered to serve as our guide and liaison with the other villagers. Impressed with his sincerity, we gratefully accepted. We went to his home and met his lovely wife, Michaela. Because it was lunchtime, they shared their meager rations with us.

My team and I looked around their simple one-room house. A wood-burning oven made of clay stood in one corner. Above it, the walls were black with the smoke that had failed to flow through the ceiling vent. In another corner was a stack of small, recently picked tomatoes. Mud still clung to their red skins. Four simple stools surrounded an equally simple homemade table. A blue kerosene lamp and a stubby candle sitting on a white plastic saucer decorated the table.

An old blanket strung across a wire at the back of the room served as the wall dividing the living quarters from the bedroom. The beds consisted of thick layers of straw covered by coarse woolen blankets.

From time to time as we ate, I saw a small figure appear at the door, look in at the strangers, and then dart away. Finally I asked Anastasio, "How many children do you have?"

Anastasio looked down at his calloused hands; dark curls of hair, streaked with gray, fell on his forehead. Slowly, one by one, he began to put up fingers. Then a broad, white smile cracked his dark, weathered features. "Six children. Six, señor." He looked over at Michaela. She smiled a gentle, contented smile at her husband. Six children—living in these conditions!

I tried to imagine the eight of them living in this small house, all of them sleeping in that tiny back area. There was no refrigerator. On second thought, there was no electricity. Where did they keep the food for a family like this? All I could see was the stack of tomatoes! How could these people be smiling?

I thought of the typical American, suburban lifestyle and found it hard to believe that people lived in these conditions less than three hours from my house. Even my modern, twenty-eight-foot travel trailer seemed luxurious in comparison.

"Anastasio, in our van we have some food—flour, beans, and cans of lard, or *manteca*. We also have good, used clothing, especially for the children. We want to share these things with the people of your village. We also hope we can have an opportunity to share a message from the Bible that will help your people. What do you suggest?"

Anastasio looked over at Michaela and rattled off a string of rapid Spanish. They conferred briefly.

"Sir," Anastasio began, "you know I was a little suspicious when I met you. The people of this village have been abused, lied to, and very disappointed. They don't trust anyone who says that they want to help them. I'm sorry."

I nodded.

"It may have been God who directed you to me. I am a kind of leader in this village. I have the people's confidence. Now, if you will trust my wife and me, we will take these things and see that they are distributed fairly, especially to the most needy. We know who they are."

I couldn't imagine anyone more needy than Anastasio, Michaela, and their family.

"Please go on," I said.

"As far as preaching to these people, I think that will have to wait. Give me some time to explain your purpose and how you brought these things for the people. If I gather them to hear you now, they may feel that you have purchased the opportunity. Be patient, señor, trust me."

I thought about this. I was being asked to leave all the food and clothing with a man we had just met. On the face of it, that did not sound right. As I looked into Anastasio's warm, brown eyes, however, something told me to trust him. Even more, perhaps I should trust God, who had brought us here.

"Anastasio, like you, I must also consider my people. Excuse me a moment." I motioned for my team to follow me outside. These good brothers said they felt sure that we should trust this family and do as Anastasio suggested.

"Brother Don," said Tony Gonzales, "I know Mexicans. I would especially know a crooked man. I believe that in this man we have struck gold. I think we should do exactly what he says. We can come back next month. Then, I believe, we will find an open door for our work here." Tony was a tough, bearded carpenter and auto mechanic. I was surprised to see tears in his eyes.

That was it; we would do what Anastasio suggested. Two of his older children helped us to unload the food and clothing from the van. We talked a while longer, making plans to return in about three weeks. It was beginning to get dark, and we were far from home. Back in the van, we waved at our new friends as they stood by the stacks of provision.

A few weeks later we headed back to Guadalajara Dos. This time I took my wife and children, along with Steve, Tony, and Ruben. The people in our church loaded our two vehicles with gifts for the people of Guadalajara Dos. We took more clothes and money to buy food in Tecate. I had also prepared a message to preach.

As we neared the border at Tecate, I was thinking and directing my thoughts toward God. I suppose you could call it praying.

Dear God, how can I preach to these people and tell them they are sinners? [You must remember, I was a very green missionary.] *Lord, these are such nice people, such good people. How can I say things that will sound like I am better than them or more righteous than they are? Honestly, that Anastasio fellow seems like a much better man than me.*

I felt God's displeasure immediately. I could say he also communicated to me on the same level, conscious but silent. It was as if he said, *Stop right there. That is the problem. You are comparing the people of Guadalajara Dos to yourself and to other people you know. Their problem is not whether they are as good as you are. You need to compare them with me. Then you will understand that they also need to repent and trust in my Son.*

I was chastened. These people in Guadalajara Dos were "good" on a human level. But I also knew enough about human nature, the temptations of flesh, and the weaknesses of men to understand that each and every one of them was a sinner who needed a Savior. Silently I responded, *Okay, thank you, God. I've got that straight.*

In Guadalajara Dos we discovered that Anastasio had done his work well. The people of his village came out of their houses at the sound of my rattling, roaring VW van. Children smiled, waved, and ran after us, cheering. Once we were at Anastasio's home, he told us that he had arranged a meeting under an oak tree. We would gather all the people to distribute food and clothing. Then I would have an opportunity to preach.

The soft beams of the late-afternoon sun were shining through the tree branches, lighting the faces of the Mexican farmers and *rancheros*. They were overjoyed with the food and things we brought. It felt like Christmas as they looked through the piles of clothing. Women and children laughed, joked, and poked one another as they held up chosen garments. The men were more reserved but clearly pleased and grateful for the additions to their wardrobes. Shoes for the children seemed to be the biggest blessing. The people of Guadalajara Dos were respectful, attentive, and curious as I opened the Bible and gave them a simple gospel message.

Soon the meeting was breaking up and the villagers were drifting away toward their modest homes. Long shadows were cast as the sun descended behind the mountains to the west. It was time for us to go home again too. Our team wanted to be back across the border before dark.

Anastasio approached with a thin, wiry, Mexican ranchero. It was obvious that we gringos intimidated this tough man, whose sun-dried, wrinkled features made it hard to estimate his age. He held his straw cowboy hat respectfully in two hands near his belt and smiled as he came up to us.

Anastasio began, "Brother Don, Brother Tony, this is Joaquin. He works on a nearby ranch. He is one of us. Somehow, he learned to ride the horse and do all those things. He's a good man—a hard worker. He's almost rich! He owns his own horse and some land!" Joaquin looked up briefly and smiled. His jeans were torn and threadbare. He didn't look rich.

"He's married to a girl from a tribe in the hills," Anastasio continued.

Now Joaquin looked steadily at the ground. He was himself a *mestizo* (of mixed European and Native American descent), and he had married below his "station" by taking a tribal girl from the hills of northern Mexico.

Anastasio continued, "His wife doesn't speak much Spanish yet, but she's very bright, and they know how to communicate. They recently had twins!" Anastasio raised one eyebrow and smiled slyly. He laughed and punched Joaquin in the shoulder. I was amazed to learn that some native Mexicans didn't speak Spanish!

I was further astonished to discover that whole tribes of indigenous natives lived far back in the mountains. To them, Guadalajara Dos, with its small trading center, is "the big city." These people, I learned, rode through the mountains for the better part of a day to get here. They came to trade for things they couldn't grow. And all of this was only three hours from Beverly Hills! I wondered why no missionaries had come here before.

"Brother Don, Joaquin wants you and your wife to come to his house," said Anastasio.

"That's great. It's nice to meet you, Joaquin. Next time we'd love to see your house and meet your wife." As I spoke, I had one eye on the slight sliver of the sun that was quickly dropping below the horizon.

"No, no," interjected Anastasio. "You don't understand. He wants you to come now. He wants you to come and pray! *Es una emergencia!*" Anastasio's normal, mellow manner was now conveying real urgency. It was clear that there was a real cause for concern.

Forgetting about the time, I asked, "What is the problem?"

Anastasio told us that Joaquin's bride had given birth to fraternal twins about ten weeks before. The little girl was healthy; the other infant, a boy, was at the point of death. There was no doctor, and they had no money anyway. Was it possible that we could pray for the child?

My family piled into the van and bumped and jolted over to the ranch where Joaquin and Maria had their small home. The rest of my team filled the other vehicle and headed for the border.

Goats and chickens impeded our progress as we walked to the front door of Joaquin's house. His wife came out and began to shoo the animals away. Squawking noises and dust filled the air. She was obviously a native: straight black hair, round face, and almond-shaped eyes. She was quite pretty without makeup and was obviously younger than Joaquin.

After wading through the swarm of squawking chickens, we ducked through the opening in the adobe walls. The house was dim, illuminated only by candlelight. After some awkward introductions, the sad-faced young mother led us to a small, elevated pallet in a corner. A blanket formed a makeshift tent over the primitive little bed. Maria looked at us and tried to smile as she pulled the blanket aside. Her chin trembled as she fought to hold back her tears.

I heard Leia suck in her breath sharply. Two infants lay together uncovered on what appeared to be a horse blanket. On the left was an obviously healthy baby girl. Her bright eyes immediately acknowledged our presence, and she began to excitedly wave her hands above her face and move her head from side to side.

Words fail to describe her brother. He appeared nearly dead. His skin was ashen. His eyes were half open, rolled up, and unmoving. His arms and legs were pitifully thin. His nostrils were clogged with dried mucus. Flies buzzed around his eyes and mouth, but he gave no sign of being aware of them. He lay there, silent and suffering. Only the slow, up-and-down movement of his stomach, along with an occasional moan that escaped his cracked, dry lips, indicated life.

Now Joaquin joined us at the bed. Anastasio stood behind us.

"Señor, what can be done? We are afraid it is too late. We hoped he would get well, but he just gets worse. He won't eat anything. It's . . . it's so terrible."

I had once watched my own four-year-old son nearly die during a severe asthma bout. Struggling to breathe, James had turned blue as his eyes widened with fear. I understood the anxiety in Joaquin's face. My mind raced. This child's breathing was so shallow and so infrequent, it seemed it would stop at any moment. I considered driving him to a hospital, but the nearest one in Tecate was nearly an hour-and-a-half drive. It would be impossible to take them across the border. I had little money; they had almost none. God was certainly our only hope.

"Joaquin, let Leia and me pray for this child in the name of Jesus. Let's see what God will do."

"*Si, señor.* That's why I asked you to come."

"Okay, Leia, let's pray." We placed our hands on the boy's hot little head. We prayed a prayer of faith for healing. He never noticed; he never moved.

As we prepared to leave, we noticed that the home of Joaquin and Maria was just as poor and ill equipped as that of Anastasio and Michaela. So we were surprised when Joaquin handed us a small package through the window of the van. It was homemade cheese.

"A gift," he said, smiling. "*Muchas gracias. Hasta la vista.*"

He stood with his arm around his wife's shoulders as we drove away. I watched them in the mirror. As I saw them turn slowly to go back into the house, I felt as if my own heart was breaking for them. *Dear God*, I prayed, *please . . .*

Three weeks later, my family and I bumped back down the dirt road toward Guadalajara Dos. Leia said, "Don, let's not go directly to the village. Let's go to Joaquin's place. I want to see those babies."

I wasn't sure I wanted to see the babies, however. What if the little boy had died?

"Leia, whatever you want. I'm not sure I can find the place again though."

"See that big tree there and that small burned-out building? Just turn left there. That's the road, I'm sure." It had been nearly dark the last time, but she seemed quite certain.

We pulled up in front of the small ranch house a few minutes later, and Maria immediately came to the door. Unlike our last visit, this time she was smiling, almost laughing. She waved to us, motioning for us to come in. She went back in to get Joaquin.

Joaquin seemed equally happy and excited when he met us at the door.

"Oh, Brother Don. A miracle, a miracle of God!"

He was not shy or awkward anymore. He took me firmly by the elbow and nearly dragged me into the house. He looked back over his shoulder and waved excitedly for Leia to come quickly.

In a moment we were standing over the two babies. It was hard to believe our eyes. Both children were alert, strong, nearly the same size, and very much alive. In fact, it was difficult to tell them apart.

"What happened, Joaquin?"

"Nothing happened the night you were here, but the next day . . ." his voice trailed off as he seemed caught up in wonder at the memory.

Then he focused his attention back on us. "The next morning, it was incredible. Little Juan was crying, crying loud. Where did he get the strength to cry like that? He was hungry. Maria fed him and fed him. He couldn't seem to get enough. Look at him, señor!" Standing next to Joaquin, Maria was literally beaming.

"So, Joaquin, now he's not sick at all?"

"No, no, not since that night you were here."

Joaquin was weeping now and kept pumping my hand in a powerful handshake. "*Gracias, muchas gracias. Gracias a Dios!*"

After talking for a few more moments about what God had done, we told Joaquin that we had to get to the village. We had work to do—more clothes, more food, and more gospel to share.

Joaquin accompanied us back to the car.

"Brother Don, I want to give you part of my land to build a church here. I want to do this as a way of giving thanks to God."

I choked up. I nodded and expressed my gratitude for Joaquin's willingness to relinquish some of his valuable land. I didn't know how to tell him that a visit to Guadalajara Dos once a month was probably the best we would ever be able to do.

Someday Leia and I would become foreign missionaries, though not to the Mexican village that will always be dear to us. Still we were able to make a few more visits to Guadalajara Dos before our time in Rialto came to an abrupt—and unexpected—end.

Meditation on the Miraculous

If you have a general idea of what God wants you to do, take whatever steps you can in that direction. Then trust God to lead you, open doors, and make things happen. After all, God can't lead you if you're not moving!

> "Praise the LORD, the God of my master, Abraham," [Eleazer, Abraham's servant] said. "The LORD has shown unfailing love and faithfulness to my master, for he has led me straight to my master's relatives."
>
> GENESIS 24:27

CHAPTER 18

DELIVERANCE AND DISASTER!

September 1982–May 1983

After living for many months in an eight-foot by twenty-eight-foot travel trailer, Leia was getting close to the breaking point. The walls seemed to be crushing her in many ways. She did not complain to me, but the tension and stress were palpable. We both knew God had called us to this, but how long did he expect us to live this way?

One morning as I was leaving the trailer, Leia stopped me. "Don, I don't know how much longer I can do this. I'm trying to submit to God's plan with a good attitude, but it's so hard. I realized last night that we moved into this box exactly seven months ago today. Please pray for me. I got very frustrated and angry. I cried out to God last night and told him I just can't take anymore!"

I was speechless. I had no answers. My heart felt like a stone in my chest, and I had a lump in my throat. "Okay, honey, I will certainly pray for you." My words sounded anemic and insincere. I tried again. "I'm going over to the office to pray right now. You're first on my list."

I walked into the foyer of the church offices. The door to the pastor's office was directly in front of me. Normally it was closed, but today it was open. Randall caught my eye and motioned for me to come into his office. I stood in front of his desk.

"Don, I meant to tell you this yesterday. I got busy and forgot. I received a phone call from a lady who used to go to this church before you and Leia came. She and her husband have moved to

Arizona. They have a nice double-wide mobile home here in Rialto that had been rented out. The tenants moved without giving notice. The place is empty except for some furniture. The owners want to sell it now. They don't want to rent it while it's for sale because they want to be able to close escrow quickly and it can sometimes be difficult to get tenants out."

I nodded. "And so?"

"Well, the lady asked me if I knew anyone who is responsible and could house-sit the mobile home until it sells. I thought of you guys. That travel trailer must be getting a little cramped by now."

"That would be great, I suppose. What do you mean by house-sitting? Reduced rent?"

"No, no. No rent at all. She'll even pay the water and electricity if I can guarantee you'll take good care of the place and show it to prospective buyers."

I was stunned. It seemed too good to be true.

"How soon could we move in, Randall?"

"Today, if you want. I just have to call her and pick up the keys from her friend."

Needless to say, Leia was ecstatic. Later that day, we got the keys and the address from Randall and drove over to take a look at our new home. It was situated in an attractive community. Almost all the mobile homes were on more or less permanent foundations. Most of the homes had neatly manicured lawns and fenced yards. The park itself had a recreation center with a swimming pool.

When we walked into "our" new home, we were thrilled. After the travel trailer, it looked immense. The mobile home was very modern with a large sunken tub for two in the spacious master bath. The kids would each have their own room again. We gave thanks to God and began moving in. We knew it was a temporary situation, as the home was for sale, but we decided to enjoy life day by day as Jesus had commanded.

Our move came during the late months of a warm fall season, so the kids enjoyed the pool tremendously. Leia enjoyed having a kitchen to cook in and a living room in which to entertain. I enjoyed coming home to a happy family after a day doing the Lord's work. It was a great time, but storm clouds began to gather toward the end of the year.

One Sunday morning, only a half hour before the morning service, Randall caught me just outside of the room where we gathered to pray. He appeared distraught.

"Don, do you think you could preach this morning?"

I was taken aback. I usually preached ten or more times a day, but those were short salvation sermons delivered on a doorstep. Preaching to a congregation without the time to pray or prepare was different. Looking at Randall's expression, however, I realized that refusing was not an option. Ready or not, I would have to do my best.

"Sure, Randall, I could do that."

I headed back to the prayer room. To my amazement, God gave me some real inspiration. After the sermon Randall said to me, "Don, that was a great sermon. You have a true gift for communicating God's Word. One day, you'll preach all over the world."

I was happy to hear that, but I hoped future opportunities would be under different circumstances.

As it turned out, I didn't have to wait long for my next opportunity to preach. The next Sunday, the same thing happened. Randall was having serious marriage problems. He was so distracted by the conflict that he just couldn't focus on the ministry. I kept this information to myself. Randall and his wife, Elizabeth, were careful not to air their grievances with each other at church.

Still, people did begin to notice that the pastor was distracted and distant, so they began to gravitate toward me for leadership and counsel. I thought that I was helping Randall by responding to these needs. The pastor did not see it that way. While he continued to push off some of his responsibilities onto me, I could sense his growing distrust and resentment.

Ironically, at the same time that Randall was questioning my motives, I was thinking about our family's next ministry assignment.

Although we knew that God had used our ministry at this church as a kind of "missionary boot camp," I sensed that this phase of our preparation was nearly over. I can't explain how I knew that, but I felt as if the Holy Spirit was leading me to seek his guidance on our next step. One day, in fact, I was in the sanctuary praying over a map of the world, wondering where the Lord would have us go among the nations.

Poking her head into the doors to the sanctuary, Shirley, a leader on the church's intercessory team, said, "Don, Pastor wants to see you in his office."

Randall sat at his desk, looking very deflated. "Don, how is your burden for Rialto?"

"Well, really, I don't have a 'burden' for Rialto in particular. This is your city. I'm just a missionary in training. I appreciate the opportunity to evangelize and work in the ministry here, but I'm praying about serving in foreign missions as soon as possible."

Randall looked even more discouraged.

"Why do you ask?" I said.

"Don, I will probably need to resign from my position here soon. This church is going to need a pastor, and I want to see the evangelistic work of the church continue. I thought that might be why God brought you here."

"Do you mean I might be needed to pastor this church?" I asked.

Randall rested his forearms on the desk in front of him and nodded.

I had no idea how to respond.

"Randall, I hope you're wrong about resigning. If it comes to that, I will certainly do whatever I can to help you. Let me pray about this, and we'll talk again."

It was still early in the day, and I had not yet eaten. I decided to return to the sanctuary to fast and pray the rest of the day. My prayers for several weeks had centered on somehow leaving Rialto to move in the direction of foreign missions. As evening approached, I felt I should put my missionary plans on hold and help the pastor and the church we had been serving.

Later that evening, I shared my impressions with Leia, and we talked and prayed some more. We felt God wanted us to make ourselves available to the church and relieve some of the pressure on Randall.

The next day, I told him that if he felt he had to leave, we would step up and try to do the job.

I thought he would be grateful. Instead, his eyes narrowed with suspicion. "You're really hoping I'll leave, aren't you?"

I was shocked. To Randall, this meant that his suspicions were now confirmed. He really did think I was out to "steal" his church.

Back at the mobile home, I had a feeling we were about to get a lot more mobile. "Leia, I hate to tell you this, but I don't think we'll be able to stay here much longer."

She looked surprised and scared. "Don, we've only been in this home for a few months. What's happened? Did they sell the mobile home? I don't really want to move again. Not yet."

"No." I told her of Randall's suspicions and accusations. I told her that with what he was going through, the situation would probably only get worse. "I believe we are soon going to find ourselves being marginalized and eventually asked to leave."

Over the next three weeks, my relationship with Randall did continue to deteriorate. I was told that he warned others in the church not to trust me, that I was only helping them because I was trying to "win them over to my side." I was hurt and confused. I couldn't understand why God would have led us into this situation. His direction had been so clear; how could the situation have gone so terribly wrong?

Randall did his best to be subtle, but subtlety was not his forte. "Don, I think this season of our relationship may be coming to an end. You should pray about what you're going to do next. We really appreciate the help you've given us in leading and teaching our people in evangelism."

There it was. I was being asked to leave. For a moment I considered appealing to the friendship I thought we shared and the fact that we had only begun to accomplish our original goals. But I realized it would pointless to fight him on this.

"Randall, thank you for being honest with me. I will certainly pray about it."

Once I was home, I shared this devastating news with Leia. We had no doubt that God had led us into this venture. We had risked so much to follow this path. It seemed we had given up almost everything. We had willingly suffered every indignity and done our best to do all that was asked of us. How could this happen? Why? We couldn't seem to find any answers.

Leia was not accusatory or bitter, but she was ever practical.

"Don, what in the world are we going to do now? Is there any chance Terry Douglas will give you your job back?"

It was desperation speaking. I could see the fear and panic in her eyes; she was nearly hyperventilating. Yet, in truth, we both knew there *was* no going back.

"Leia, I don't have any answers right now. We need to pray. We got into this situation by praying; now we need to find our way through by praying." These were brave words, but to be honest, I didn't feel brave and I didn't feel like praying. Along with the confusion and fear, I found that I was too angry to pray. Could things possibly get any worse? No job, no future, no direction, no ministry, and no dignity.

I found out that things could still get worse. A few days later, the phone rang.

"Don, this is Louise."

Louise was now my stepmother of about ten years. She and Dad lived in Baltimore. Though Leia and I loved her and got along well with her, Louise rarely called.

"Your dad has had a serious heart attack," she told me. "We didn't want to worry you since there was nothing you could do, and he's home from the hospital now. The doctor said he's very lucky to have survived, but he's not really doing well. We don't know what the future holds, but I'm concerned that if you don't see him soon, you may not see him again."

I did not want to burden her with our problems or tell her that we didn't have enough money to drive across town, let alone across the country. I knew she was calling only because she felt my dad needed to see me. I also knew that if I asked for money to make the trip, they would provide it without question. The problem was my deal with God to never beg, borrow, or let anyone know about our needs.

"Louise, let me talk to Dad. It's the best I can do right now. We will be praying about making a trip. I'll let you know."

I spoke to Dad. He was normally jolly and enthusiastic. Now he sounded very weak. A great heaviness came upon me.

I told Leia about the phone call.

"Don, that's terrible. But I got more bad news while you were out. The lady who owns this mobile home just told me that it has sold, and we'll have to be out in a couple of weeks."

In one day, bad circumstances had gotten much worse. I looked at my wife and then at my children playing in the living room, blissfully ignorant of our desperate situation. What had I done to my family? Was it as Terry, the millionaire, had said: "Don, your fanaticism is going to destroy you"?

Where was God?

I tried to pray but got nowhere. What could I say besides: why, what, how? It was depressing. Over the next few days, I tried to figure out some kind of plan. We could humble ourselves, break our rules, and ask our parents for money to rent a small apartment. I could find some kind of job and try to get back to a "normal life." It would be difficult but doable. That seemed the most reasonable course to follow. That is what most people would recommend.

But what, then, had been the purpose of quitting my job in the first place? Why had we gotten rid of our house and possessions? That had been God's direction. He had supernaturally confirmed that, by speaking the same thing to both Leia and me. And what about his promise to me, "Ask and I will give you the nations"? What about all of the miracles and the people like Mindy, Wayne, and Joaquin who had been touched through our ministry? I had questions—but no answers. Was everything just to come to a horrible, unexplainable end?

As the days passed, I decided that, since I didn't know what to do, I just had to try to take care of my family. As depressing as it was, I decided to make the calls that would end the dream that had become a nightmare.

One day I walked across the lawn of the church, dejected, hands in pockets. Though I was still technically on staff, I had no responsibilities now. I sat down and took out my pocket-size New Testament. I opened the little book at random and began to read. I felt bad because it seemed like a mechanical exercise. The words seemed to hold little promise or meaning for me at the moment. In fact, the more I read, the more anxious, confused, and bitter I became.

Suddenly, my eyes fell on these words from Hebrews 10: "Now the just shall live by faith; But if anyone draws back, My soul has no pleasure in him" (verse 38, NKJV). These were familiar words. The apostle had used this paraphrase of an Old Testament passage to challenge the Hebrews, who were being persecuted for their faith, not to draw back in fear, but to press on in faith. They were to go forward, not draw backward.

God himself seemed to be speaking these words to me. "Do not draw back in fear. Go forward in faith. *I take no pleasure in those who draw back.*"

I was stunned. This was unexpected. I had been hoping for words of comfort and promise. I had been looking for another miracle like the provision of the mobile home. Yet God seemed to be putting everything on me. He was challenging me by telling me to go forward! But go forward where? I walked out of the church and looked at our van. It seemed that God was telling me to take what I had, take what I was, take my faith in him and all I had learned, and do the best I could.

I told Leia of my plan to "go forward." It sounded as crazy as quitting my job or moving into the travel trailer. I expected her to explode in anger or to laugh in ridicule. Instead, she just listened.

"Leia, God has called me to tell people about Jesus and to encourage others to do so. We've spent the last year or so learning how to do that. Now we have no place to live. We have only the van. I really need to see my dad. I've never had the opportunity to share the gospel with him, and he could die any day. Between here and Baltimore there are millions of people who have never heard of Jesus. We are going to get in the van and drive across the country, preaching and teaching wherever God opens up opportunities."

She looked at me soberly. "And . . . are there any such opportunities?"

"Well, not exactly . . . well, not yet . . . I don't know of any right now. . . . But let's just plan on doing this and trust God to provide as he always has. We have to go forward. But I can't do it without you." She was either going to come along with me or call the men in the white coats to come and get me.

"Don, I believe you're trying to follow God, so I will do my best to follow along."

I printed up business cards that said "Lord of the Harvest Ministries." I told the people in the church, our friends, and our family of our plans. I didn't mention that the tires on the van were nearly bald, that the engine was acting up, and that we had no money and no real plan other than to move forward. We decided we would stay in Rialto for another month. We would leave just after Christmas.

Just days before we had to leave the mobile home, we received an unexpected offer from our good friend, Gerardo, to stay with him until after Christmas. His wife was in the hospital, and he hoped Leia could help take care of their son. God's provision!

God is faithful. Before we left, people gave us small, unsolicited gifts that eventually totaled exactly $700. Someone else borrowed our van and brought it back with a new set of tires. A mechanic in the church insisted on doing a partial rebuild of our Volkswagen engine. Last but not least, we were invited to stay for a night or two in Phoenix and to visit and stay with some folks in El Paso. These two stops would get us started on our new journey of faith.

To recount all the events that transpired on the long journey across America would tax my memory and your patience. Let me mention just a couple of things. Probably one of the most remarkable is that, according to our ethic, we never asked anyone for anything, nor did we let our needs be known—except when they were impossible to hide. It certainly is biblical for believers in a Christian community (i.e., the church) to make their needs known to one another. Yet from the time God called us to move into the travel trailer and live on a "faith" income, we felt that, for us, faith meant looking to God alone to meet our needs. After five months of traveling across America, we eventually returned to California with the same $700 we started with. Along the way, God opened doors of ministry, saved and healed people, and miraculously provided for us and replenished our small treasury.

Unfortunately, my father did not respond to the message of salvation on this trip. I was disappointed, since that had been the primary reason for our journey east. A seed was planted, however, that would bear fruit just a few years later.

After visiting my dad and Louise, we headed back to Southern California. On the way, I was keenly aware that I wasn't any closer to knowing our next destination—the place where God would have us live and serve when we returned.

Meditation on the Miraculous

When God's plan is for us to move on, he sometimes has to "tear up our nest" so it is impossible to stay where we are.

> At that time a great persecution arose against the church which was at Jerusalem; and they were all scattered throughout the regions of Judea and Samaria, except the apostles.
> ACTS 8:1, NKJV

CHAPTER 19

THE VAN AND THE CROSS

1983
Lordsburg, New Mexico; and Los Angeles

On our trip back from the East Coast, along Interstate 10, our van's engine blew up. I led my little family off the highway and onto the very modest main street of Lordsburg, New Mexico. We were out of harm's way, but now what? We needed a phone. We had promised to let Leia's mom know if we had any real trouble. Well, we were definitely in trouble.

First Baptist Church was not far from the freeway entrance. Transients, homeless people, those with car problems, and people seeking help or handouts regularly inconvenienced the young pastor there. After I knocked on the church door, he opened it just a crack. I explained that we just needed to use the phone. Perhaps it was our kids who broke the ice. Pastor Jesse began to ask us questions. As our story emerged, he softened.

"Would y'all like to stay with us tonight, just till you figure out what to do?"

That seemed like a good idea; we had few other options. We called Leia's mom. She listened and sounded worried.

"What are you going to do?"

"Not sure, Mom. We need an engine, but we're in the middle of nowhere."

"What's that going to cost?" she asked.

"I have no idea. A bunch, I guess."

"Okay," she said, "keep me posted."

"Sure."

We went to Jesse's home. His wife, Gayla, was very sweet and made us feel welcome.

"Don," Jesse said over dinner, "we don't have much experience with the kind of miracles and spiritual things that seem so natural to you all. But Gayla and I are open-minded and hungry for more of the Lord. There's a group that meets in a home near here. Some of the people are like you. I guess you'd call them charismatics. They are all looking for more of God. Would you like to go over there tonight and meet them? Maybe you could share a little of what God has done in your life."

James was complaining of an earache. I hesitated. Then I thought, *Well, it won't hurt him any less if we stay here.* I agreed. So I decided to pray for James and give the situation a day or so to clear up.

Just before the meeting ended that evening, the host spoke.

"Don, we want to welcome you and your family. Could you tell us a little of your ministry and how you wound up here in Lordsburg?"

After I told the tale, a man who had been quiet all evening spoke up.

"Don, I build experimental private aircraft. I just got done putting together a Volkswagen engine for one of my projects. I feel like God wants you to have that engine."

What was this? A guy was building "experimental airplanes" in the middle of the desert? He continued, "This would slow me down on my project because I'll have to get another engine somewhere, but I want to help you. Of course, I can't just give the engine away. I'd need about $700 for it. Me and my boys would do the labor for free."

That was quite a bit more money than we had at that point.

"That's very kind," I said. "Let me pray about that."

Leia's mom, Pat, had a wealthy friend whom she had told about our crazy exploit of driving across America during the coldest winter in recent history. The friend had asked Pat to let her know if we needed anything along the way. I decided that I could at least give Pat permission to tell her friend of our situation, but not ask for anything. The wealthy friend was sympathetic but offered nothing.

Leia's parents were not wealthy, but they were wonderful.

"Don, my friend didn't offer to help. But Harold and I have discussed this. I don't know how much you need, but we want to give you $700." Who had told her that amount? Not me. This was very humbling, but it was God. I thanked her profusely. She would send the money by Western Union. We would stay with Jesse and Gayla until the engine was installed.

Meanwhile, James's ear got worse. One morning, he woke in serious pain. When we looked in his ear, we saw what looked like a small, puss-filled sack protruding from the inside of his ear.

"Don, that looks serious," said Pastor Jesse. "I understand your situation, but I think we better get him to a doctor."

I knew that was the sensible and responsible thing to do. Certainly Leia and I planned to take James to a pediatrician if the infection persisted. On the other hand, for several days we had been telling Jesse and Gayla about the reality of God's power. Jesse seemed eager to move into a greater life of faith and power. Going to the doctor sounded more than reasonable, but I hesitated. Inspiration came.

"Jesse, you know how we've discussed Mark 16, where Jesus said that those who believed in him would lay their hands on the sick and they would recover?" Jesse nodded. "Do you remember how I told you about the time I laid my hand on a guy with a sliver of metal in his eye and he was healed?" Jesse nodded again. "Well, Jesse, why don't we try that first? You know, pray in faith for a miracle."

Jesse looked up from James's ear and into my eyes. "Yeah. Great idea. Why don't you do that? I mean, I really would love to see God heal someone like that."

"No, Jesse, you don't understand. I want *you* to lay your hands on James's ear and pray for a miracle of healing. This experience will teach you more than a hundred books or testimonies."

He drew back and looked quite doubtful. He glanced at Gayla, who smiled encouragingly.

"Me? I've never . . . I mean, I don't know. Could I?"

It was almost humorous to watch him wrestle with his sincere desire to see God move and the natural barriers of doctrine and doubt that stood in his way.

I pressed on.

"Jesse, you said you're hungry for more reality of God in your life. Here's your chance. Jesus said that these signs would follow those who believe—that they would lay their hands on the sick and they would recover. You believe him, don't you? Well, go ahead then."

Hesitantly, Jesse laid his hand upon James's ear and put his other hand on top of his head. I believe he surprised himself when he began to pray. "In the name of Jesus, we ask—we believe—for a miracle of healing. We pray that this little boy be healed right now. Let it be so, in Jesus' name. Amen!"

I reached up and pulled Jesse's hand away. Whatever it was that had been protruding from James's ear was completely gone.

Jesse was stunned. He asked, "James, how do you feel?"

James jumped down off the chair. "I'm okay now. Can I go play with Heidi?"

Just three days later, we left Jesse and Gayla's and continued on our return trek to California. Though we never spent much time with this couple after our Lordsburg "layover," we will always remember the way God worked through them to provide for us at a desperate time. Thirty years later, they are pastoring a large, healthy church in their denomination. They have experienced much of God's reality and power since Lordsburg. We thank God that our van broke down there. God's timing, providence, and wisdom are amazing!

As I mentioned previously, we arrived back in Southern California with $700. Now, here we were, back where we started. No job, no house, no ministry, and no direction.

Leia's parents invited us to stay in their home in Los Angeles for a while as we tried to discern what we should do next. Here was more unavoidable humbling; we were moving in with the in-laws. How low could I go? But we had no choice.

The days at Pat and Harold's house stretched into weeks and then a couple of months. We went out from time to time, preaching and sharing the gospel in various public venues. I began to feel like a freeloader, though we did what we could do to help out. Leia's father was kind and much more sympathetic to what we were doing than I expected. He was and always had been a very hard worker: first as a simple laborer, then as the operator of his own masonry business, and now as an inspector for the City of Los Angeles. Yet I knew he probably wondered why a thirty-three-year-old man who had never before been unemployed was not out looking for a job. There was no real pressure, but I felt pressured nonetheless.

I prayed fervently, "God, I want to please you. I want to go forward. I really must have some direction. I have to do something. I can't just sit here." The heavens were silent.

I remember standing at their large picture window, looking out over the city of Glendale. Based on my experience in Rialto, I thought that probably 80 percent of the people in Glendale had never really heard the gospel in a way they could understand and respond to. Maybe I could start a church there. Of course, I had no idea how to start a church. I had no money, no friends, and no connections in the area. Maybe that wasn't such a great idea, but what should I do then?

One evening after dinner, I was feeling more depressed than usual about the impasse. I made a decision. I would have it out with God. It was unfair for him to place this calling in my heart, to lead me into these crazy situations, and then just to leave me without any direction or promise of a future. I was either going to get some answers from him, or I was going to start making some calls, find a job, and put this gospel ministry/missionary idea behind me.

I knew there was a small park on the top of a hill near Leia's parents' place. I decided that would be a good place for a showdown.

"I'm going for a walk," I announced.

"Are you okay?"

"Where are you going?"

"What are you going to do?"

Everyone had a question.

I half joked, "I'm going to the O.K. Corral. Time for a showdown."

Then I headed up the hill.

I sat on a small bench and talked to God. I told him how tired I was and how I felt foolish and useless, like an absolute loser. And, I claimed, it was his responsibility to get me out of this situation. He was the one who had encouraged me, led me, and even challenged me to "go forward." Now there was nowhere to go. I wanted an answer, and I needed it now or I could not go on.

I ran out of words. My heart was heavy, and my mind was too tired to think anymore. I was exhausted and anxious.

It seemed, as I feared, that there was no answer, no response whatsoever.

Where was God?

After a while, I lifted my head. It was dark now. I looked across the valley to a hilltop several miles away. On top of that hill, I noticed a large lighted cross that I'd never seen before. My attention seemed drawn to that cross.

Now God spoke:

I am the one who wants an answer, I heard him say in my spirit. *I carried that cross for you. I saved you. I called you to myself. I have proved myself over and over. Now I want to know, will you follow the Cross? Will you go forward when there doesn't seem to be a way? Will you die to yourself and trust me with your life?*

Rather than just dropping to my knees and saying, "Yes, sir;

whatever you say, sir," I sat there in the darkness, staring at the cross. Somehow I understood what he was asking. There were no guarantees; there was no "deal." To answer yes would mean going back to Pat and Harold's without any answers except to wait until God told me what to do, or perhaps eventually going back to work somewhere, without any satisfactory understanding of what the past few years had meant. I simply had to trust him and commit my life to him, even if it felt as if it might kill me.

Finally, I got up my courage.

Yes, Lord. I will go back down this hill with nothing more than a commitment to trust you, to follow you, and to obey you.

There was no joy, no excitement. There was no sense of awe at having heard from God. I knew it was unlikely that anyone would ever understand. This was between him and me.

Meditation on the Miraculous

Someone said to Jesus, "I will follow you wherever you go."

But Jesus replied, "Foxes have dens to live in, and birds have nests, but the Son of Man has no place even to lay his head."

He said to another person, "Come, follow me."

The man agreed, but he said, "Lord, first let me return home and bury my father."

But Jesus told him, "Let the spiritually dead bury their own dead! Your duty is to go and preach about the Kingdom of God."

Another said, "Yes, Lord, I will follow you, but first let me say good-bye to my family."

But Jesus told him, "Anyone who puts a hand to the plow and then looks back is not fit for the Kingdom of God."

LUKE 9:57-62

CHAPTER 20

A NEW BEGINNING

May 1983

We were still at the in-laws, still waiting on God, when Pat called me to the phone.

"Don," said the gravelly voice on the other end of the phone, "this is Earl Weaver."

Earl was a Christian who owned a large commercial printing operation in Victorville, an hour northeast of Los Angeles. When his presses were not engaged for profit, he ran off thousands of pieces of gospel literature and evangelistic tracts. He gave them to missionaries and churches he knew would use them. I had met Earl through Ernest Soady of the Free Tract Society. I had recently called Earl to see if he could give me a few thousand gospel tracts that we liked to use in our work.

"Yes, Earl," I said. "Great to hear from you. How are you?"

Earl was nearly crippled by a degenerative form of arthritis. He moved around with crutches or a wheelchair.

"Yeah, yeah, I'm okay. I wanted to let you know I have some of those tracts you wanted. Will about ten thousand copies be enough?"

"That would be enough to keep us going a long time, Earl."

"Great. Why don't you all come up for dinner? I want to give you these tracts and make a little cash donation to your ministry. We'll have a nice evening together."

I was thrilled at this blessing. "Earl, that sounds great. Can we come on Tuesday?"

After we finished eating dinner at Earl's place, he pushed his wheelchair back from the table. "Don, here's a check to help your ministry. Your tracts are in that box over there by the front door."

I looked over and saw *two* boxes of tracts.

Earl noticed my confusion. "Don, one box is yours; the other is for a church. Do you think you could take that other box down the hill with you? I need to get it to a church in Rancho Cucamonga. I hate to ask, but . . ."

"Earl, no problem at all. I'd be more than happy to do that for you. But this is Tuesday; there won't be anyone at the church tonight."

With a raspy laugh, he said, "No problem! Who's gonna steal a box of gospel tracts? Just leave them by the door. Someone will find them."

After thanking Earl for dinner and the tracts, we headed out of the high desert and down Interstate 15. A few minutes after arriving in Rancho Cucamonga, we pulled up in front of an old winery that had become Victory Chapel. To our surprise, the parking lot was full of cars. We got out of the van. I grabbed the box of tracts. A neatly dressed young man wearing a tie approached. He wore an usher's badge that said "Ron Ives."

"Can I help you?" he asked.

"Well, I have this box of tracts for the church. Can I just give them to you?"

"Just wait here please." He ran off toward the building before I could say anything.

A few minutes later, I saw Pastor Vic Eason emerge from the church. Our eyes met. His face nearly split with a huge smile.

"Don, I can't believe it. You're actually here."

I wondered what he meant. I had met Vic three or four years earlier when I was still at the Rialto Bible Fellowship and he had come over to speak to a gathering of local ministers. Vic had been pioneering a new church in Upland, California. Our paths had crossed a few times after that, and we had struck up a friendship.

Vic told me that his church was in the middle of a five-night revival. He invited us inside, and out of curiosity, we followed him into the church. I was amazed to see the sanctuary packed on a Tuesday night. Most churches I knew had trouble getting much of a turnout for any midweek service.

The crowd included mostly young couples and singles. That also seemed unusual. Their faces beamed with excitement. The atmosphere was electric with a sense of expectancy.

When the enthusiastic, fast-paced worship music came to an end, Pastor Vic introduced the evangelist, Bill Lampson. This was no polished, professional celebrity. Bill wore a simple plaid shirt, a brown corduroy sport coat, and a pair of chinos. He appeared to be in his fifties, but his face told the story of a man who'd lived a rough life. Bill commanded the platform with high energy.

His sermon was a simple presentation of how the gospel had delivered him from lifelong depression and alcoholism. Bill said that he had not been part of a family intervention or a twelve-step program. Instead he described it as a two-step program: he took one step toward Jesus, and Jesus took one step toward him. At that moment, he was healed and set free from his addictions. It was a simple story, but inspiring and manifestly true. At the end, Lampson invited all those who needed forgiveness, healing, and freedom to come to the altar.

As the building was emptying later that evening, Vic Eason approached me.

"Don, I would love to get together with you and your wife, but I have to take Bill out for dinner and back to his hotel. Let's talk for just a minute. I know what you've been doing, but what are you going to do now?"

I was surprised. How did he know what we had been doing? I hadn't spoken to him in two or three years.

Unsure of what to say, I hesitated.

Vic persisted, "So, Don, what are your plans? What do you want to do?"

Since I didn't have any real plans, I still hesitated to respond. Finally, I blurted out the best answer I had.

"Well, Vic, I want to start a new evangelistic church."

He started to smile, and I thought I saw a twinkle in his eyes.

"Really? Great! Do you know how you are going to do that?"

"I'm praying about it, but I've got to admit, I don't have a plan yet."

Vic chuckled. "Don, look, if it's possible, I want you to meet me here in the morning for breakfast. I want to talk to you about that. I believe I can help you."

Knowing it would be late when we got back to Los Angeles, I didn't relish the idea of getting up early to drive an hour back to Cucamonga. I had, however, heard that word *help*. I didn't know what he meant, but I was intrigued. I needed help.

"Okay, Vic, I'll be here tomorrow morning."

Wednesday morning I drove east from Los Angeles toward the rising sun. This new day seemed auspicious. *God knows*, I thought, *we need a new beginning*.

We met at a McDonald's, where Vic told me an amazing story. Throughout the last few years, I had sent occasional reports about our "progress" as itinerant evangelists to a pastor in San Bernardino who was a friend of mine and Vic's. In turn, this pastor had kept Vic informed of our travels and troubles.

"Don, I've seen your heart to evangelize, and I understand your desire to do a work for God. I am now affiliated with a fellowship of churches that is planting new churches at a rapid pace. I have learned some principles and methods from them that have helped us make hundreds of new believers. We've been able to keep most of them involved in a real process of discipleship."

My interest level jumped up a few notches. "Tell me more."

Vic laughed a little. "I intend to. Three months ago, I told my wife and Marcia, a young lady in our church, that we should make a commitment to pray for you and your wife. We would pray a very specific prayer and ask God to bring you here without us contacting you. I believed that God showed us he would have you be a part of what we are involved in. So we were convinced that if that really was God's plan for you, he would answer our prayers and bring you here somehow. Now maybe you understand why I was so happy to see you last night."

I was stunned. "Do you mean you had no idea that I was coming with that box of tracts? Are you saying that Earl Weaver never told you I'd be bringing them?"

"The answer is no, on all counts. I was happy to see you last night, but I was not surprised, because we believed God would answer our prayer." He leaned forward and placed his hand on mine. "But it was exciting to see the answer to our prayer when you showed up!"

I considered this and was overshadowed by a tremendous sense of awe. For nearly three months, I had been sitting at Pat's praying, fretting, and wondering what to do next. Over those same three months, Vic and the ladies had been praying for us as God arranged this meeting.

"Wow. That's quite a story, Vic."

"Our fellowship is having a weeklong conference of pastors, church planters, and disciple makers in Arizona in a few weeks. I think you should go and see what's going on."

"Vic, I appreciate the invitation, but I don't have the finances to go anywhere for a week."

"Don't worry about that; you'll be our guests. We will take care of hotels, meals, transportation—whatever. All you need is the free time to go."

I laughed. "Well, I certainly have free time. Count me in."

At the conference, Leia and I were deeply touched by the spirit and the work of this fellowship. During the week, we heard constant challenges to go into the cities and nations of the world with the gospel. "Pioneer" pastors, both foreign and domestic, told us of successful evangelism and church planting. I stood in front of a world map and looked at the colored pins that represented the several hundred new churches that had been planted over the past dozen or so years.

On the last night, fresh-faced young couples were called to the platform in front of the assembled multitude, which had gathered from all over the world. They were the new workers to be launched out to preach the gospel. In that moment, I truly believed we had found our place.

The next two years were a whirlwind of learning, training, and working as we prepared to launch into church planting from the Rancho Cucamonga congregation. I got a good job with one of my former employers, and we rented a small house in, of all places, Rialto. Now, however, I didn't see our move as a step backward but as a definite step forward.

Meditation on the Miraculous

When God seems silent, don't be too quick to assume that he doesn't hear you or isn't already working far beyond what you could ever imagine.

> *Take delight in the LORD, and he will give you your heart's desires. Commit everything you do to the LORD. Trust him, and he will help you. . . . Be still in the presence of the LORD, and wait patiently for him to act.*
> PSALM 37:4-5, 7

CHAPTER 21

THE CLOUDS PART

1986

Moreno Valley, Southern California

Two years, almost to the day, after we first visited Vic Eason's church, Leia and I attended a Bible conference where we were launched as church planters in Moreno Valley, California. The long process that had begun when we'd obeyed God's call to take the gospel to the poor of Rialto had led to this long-desired opportunity.

I planned an outreach to our new community. We would take a couple of dozen people from our mother church in Rancho Cucamonga to talk to people in Moreno Valley. We would hand out flyers inviting them to a series of movies based on end-times Bible prophecy.

When the Saturday of the outreach arrived, the skies looked threatening. Heavy black clouds hung over Rancho Cucamonga and the surrounding area. The team gathered in the church to pray, both that the outreach would be successful and that the unusually strong winds would blow the morning clouds away.

As we looked outside, we saw the wind blowing dust and trash across the parking lot. Then the rain began to come down with an intensity rarely seen in sunny Southern California.

Ron Ives, the usher who had first met me in the parking lot two years earlier, said, "Don, sorry, bro. Looks like no outreach today."

I thought of the thousands of flyers announcing the movie out-reach, which was just several days away. If we didn't get these flyers out today, when would we? And if we postponed the event, we'd have to throw away hundreds of dollars' worth of flyers. There was no other time to do this.

I turned to face Ron and the people who had gathered around us. They were sympathetic. They understood how anxious I was to get started.

These were faithful and committed people. I knew they would do whatever I asked. As I prayed silently about what to do, I felt a sudden inspiration.

"Look, guys, Moreno Valley is half an hour from here. How do we know that it's raining there, or that it won't quit by the time we get there?"

I watched as my team made numerous glances out the door, where the deluge was only getting worse. A big gust of wind rattled the double doors. Then we saw a bright flash, followed immediately by a crash of thunder. No one said anything. They just stared at me.

It was my call and I made it.

"Okay, let's get in our vehicles and drive to Moreno Valley. I believe God wants us to do this outreach. So I believe we will be able to do it."

Raised eyebrows and barely suppressed chuckles confirmed their doubts, but they got into the vehicles anyway.

As we drove toward Moreno Valley, the rain was so heavy at times that the windshield wipers could barely keep up. I heard whis-pers and giggles behind me in the van. The off-ramp for Moreno Valley finally appeared.

"Don, should we turn around here and go back?"

"No," I replied. "Let's find a parking lot and pray for a few minutes."

I was buying time. As we got off the freeway and headed down the city street, the heavy rain continued.

We pulled into the first relatively empty parking lot that we saw. As the last vehicle came to a stop, so did the rain. At first the sky above us was foggy with a fine mist. Then it turned a pale blue and finally a bright blue.

We got out of the vehicles and formed a prayer circle in the parking lot. When we finished, we saw that the dark rain clouds surrounded Moreno Valley in what looked like a perfect circle. It was raining all around us, but not on us. A few minutes ago it had seemed that I was a desperate fanatic leading my troops in a doomed effort. Now I was a hero of faith.

It was an auspicious beginning for a new church.

The outreach was a great success. More than one hundred people came out to the movies each of the three nights. Many responded to the gospel at the end of each film's showing. We announced to the visitors that the new church would begin Sunday morning.

That Sunday morning, my wife, my children, and I were alone and setting up metal folding chairs and doing a sound check on our equipment. I whistled nervously, wondering if anyone would actually show up. The hour approached. A visitor came in. He had been at one of the movies. Then came a young couple, then another, and another.

We began with about twenty-five people and never looked back. God blessed that work. Within a year, the hundred or so people who made up our church were thinking about acquiring a new building. Now, when I wonder what would have happened if I had called off that first rainy-day outreach, I am reminded of this Scripture:

Farmers who wait for perfect weather never plant.
If they watch every cloud, they never harvest.
(Ecclesiastes 11:4)

Gangsters and Grandparents

We named our church in Moreno Valley The Potter's House, inspired by Jeremiah 18:2: "Arise, and go down to the potter's house, and there I will cause thee to hear my words" (KJV). In fact, a number of servicemen and women from the nearby Air Force base came to Christ after visiting our church. Many other people first heard about God's grace at our storefront church—sometimes after being drawn there in very unexpected ways.

As I stood up to speak one Sunday evening, I saw a woman enter at the back of the church and then stand there, looking a little confused. She appeared to be in her forties or fifties, and though she was dressed casually, she carried herself with a certain dignity and elegance. One of the Air Force policemen was an usher that evening. He politely but firmly took this matron by the arm and led her to a seat. As I preached that evening, I noticed that she seemed unsettled and uncomfortable. She kept looking around as if she was struggling to see and understand what was going on. At the end of the sermon, which contained a clear presentation of the gospel, I asked everyone to bow their heads while I again recapped the Good News and God's invitation to sinners. I asked those who wanted to repent and receive a new and eternal life in Jesus Christ to raise their hands.

The woman lifted her head and looked around quickly. She bowed her head again and timidly raised her right hand. When I invited those who had raised their hands to come forward and pray, the timidity was gone; the woman strode purposefully to the front and knelt down to await further instructions. Only small tears at the corner of each eye revealed any emotion. One of the ladies of the church came and knelt beside her, draped an arm over her shoulder, and prayed a prayer for salvation with her.

Once the service ended, I went to meet our new convert. She was now bubbling with excitement; her eyes were bright and radiated joy. She reached out quickly to shake my outstretched hand.

She told me that her name was Karen. Then she said, laughing, "Pastor, God does truly work in mysterious ways!"

I nodded, waiting to see what she found so amusing.

"I had no intention of going to church this evening! In fact, I haven't been to church since I was young. I was on my way to the Mexican fast-food restaurant across the way to get dinner for my husband, Phil, and me. I saw your sign—The Potter's House—and because I left home without my glasses, I thought your sign said 'The Potato House.' I don't know what's wrong with me."

She laughed out loud again, greatly amused by her own story. "So I thought this was a new place that had stuffed baked potatoes. We love those. Anyway I came in, and without my glasses on, I really had trouble figuring out what kind of place this was or what was going on. So I let Todd here," she poked our militant usher in the chest with a brightly painted fingernail, "take me to a seat because I was confused and didn't know what else to do. Then it dawned on me, *Oh my, this is a church.* I was too embarrassed to get up and leave, but I was worried about Phil at home waiting for dinner."

She had to stop to laugh again. She regained her composure and continued, now serious, "I am so glad I stayed. Your message . . . Oh! It was like God was speaking right to me . . . about me and what is going on in my life. Phil and I moved here not long ago with the idea of kind of getting a fresh start in our lives in a new place. It wasn't working very well. We had moved, but we weren't changed. Now I know what I was missing. I needed God to change me! I can't wait to tell Phil what has happened! I'm born again! I'm changed!"

The following Wednesday evening, Karen returned, pulling her husband, Phil, through the door. Phil looked as uncomfortable and out of place as Karen had the previous Sunday. Phil was older but very virile and muscular. His hands seemed to swallow and crush mine as I greeted him. He was a good-looking guy in a rough way, and he tried to put me at ease with an awkward smile.

"Hi, Reverend! Karen told me you changed her life. I came to check it out." Then the smile vanished. "She really is different. I want to see what you've done to her." I had Todd show Phil and Karen to their seats.

During our service, the congregation would often stand for prayer and singing. Phil never stood; he just sat there expressionless, looking at whatever was going on in the front. I tried to avoid staring at him and was grateful that God gave me a message that I was passionate about. But it didn't appear to move Phil.

Phil didn't respond to the invitation at the end of the service. However, a number of people gathered around Phil and Karen to welcome them as I went to the back to shake hands with those who were leaving. When almost everyone was gone, I went back into the sanctuary and saw Phil and Karen still talking to some folks.

"Pastor!" It was Karen, laughing again. "I hope you didn't think Phil was being rude because he didn't stand up during the service. He has bone spurs on the bottoms of his feet. He can only stand for a few minutes before he has really bad pain. If he wasn't his own boss, he couldn't even go to work. He is going to have surgery on the bottoms of his feet next week. Would you pray that the surgery goes well?"

Feeling that now-familiar inspiration, I said, "Karen, why don't we do better than that? Why don't we ask God to heal Phil's feet so he doesn't have to have that surgery?"

They agreed. We had Phil stand as we prayed and asked God for a miracle of healing. It was great to watch Karen, a new believer, laying hands on her husband and praying so earnestly and so sincerely.

After we prayed, we asked Phil to walk around the church. He had no pain! Then we asked him to jump up and down. Still no pain. Phil was excited and smiled broadly.

"I can hardly believe it," he said. "This is the first time in months I haven't had any pain." Phil agreed that he, too, needed Jesus to change his life. Todd, Leia, Karen, and I prayed with Phil, who was now in tears.

When Phil and Karen returned to church the following Sunday morning, they told me that new X-rays showed there were no bone spurs on his feet and the surgery had been canceled. They also told me a little about how wonderfully God was changing their hearts, lives, and home. I asked them if they would share some of their story with the church in the evening service.

Phil and Karen stood on the platform together that evening

looking like the happy Christian grandparents they were. Phil, now joyful, no longer looked threatening. Karen held his hand and beamed like a schoolgirl. Phil told us how God had healed his feet and more importantly healed his heart.

Karen told the whole church The Potato House story. As the laughter died down, Karen revealed something unexpected. She said that she and Phil had moved to Moreno Valley in their early fifties to start over again. Phil had bought a concrete pump and started what she called an honest business. We soon understood what she meant. Influenced by drug and alcohol addiction, as well as the bad company they kept, they had supported themselves for a time by robbing rich people at gunpoint. The way Karen put it was, "Phil would hold them from behind, and I'd put a gun under their noses and threaten to shoot them if they didn't give us everything."

There was a collective gasp from the congregation. I was amazed, and it was my turn to be confused. Phil and Karen? The smiling, clean-cut, outgoing grandparents—armed robbers? Phil and Karen laughed good-naturedly at our reaction.

Phil put his arm around his wife's shoulders and said, "We have Jesus now; that's all behind us." We—the church, that is—recovered from our shock and clapped and cheered.

In the weeks to come, Phil and Karen realized that, as Christ followers, they needed to return to the cities and counties where they had committed their crimes and confess. Amazingly, the sheriffs' offices and police departments they contacted were unable to find any victims or criminal complaints. God seemed to have erased their trail as he had erased their sins.

Obviously, not everyone who comes to Christ is so easily relieved of the consequences of their past lives. In truth, the severe repercussions and desperation that resulted from Phil and Karen's crimes had led them to move to Moreno Valley in the first place. For our young church, no sermon or Bible study could have provided a better illustration of God's sovereign grace than the mercy the Lord extended to Phil and Karen, which enabled them to rebuild their lives with their children, their grandchildren, and, of course, their new church family!

It's Me—Jesus

Our son, James, was nine years old when we moved to Moreno Valley.

During school breaks, he developed the habit of waking up early, coming into our room, and climbing into bed with Leia and me.

One such morning after he ate his cereal, he told Leia a wonderful story. He had seen Jesus again. He mentioned the experience as if it were the most normal thing in the world.

It didn't seem normal to Leia. "James, you saw Jesus. When? Where?"

"I was in your room. Dad had already left for work, and you were still sleeping. I was sitting on the end of your bed, and I saw him."

"What did he look like?"

"Just like he did last time I saw him, Mom," James said impatiently.

"Did he say anything?"

"Not at first. He was just showing me something, but I don't really know what it was. He had it in his right hand. Two angels were standing on top of this thing. One of them was holding up a metal thing, and the other one was getting ready to blow a trumpet. Jesus just held this thing in front of me and looked at me. Then he said, 'James, it is almost time for me to return, and there are still nations that haven't heard about me.' Then he was gone, just like that."

James knew what he'd seen Jesus and the angels hold up, but Leia wasn't sure because James had no words or names to describe what he had seen.

Leia, as practical as ever, got a pencil and paper. "Here, James. Draw a picture of what you saw."

James was a budding artist. He took the paper into the other room. After a short while, he came back with a picture of Jesus holding an hourglass in his right hand. A perfectionist and stickler for detail, James had drawn an intricate picture, which even showed the grains of sand in the hourglass. The bottom was almost full; the top was almost empty. Standing on top of the hourglass were two angels. As James had already mentioned, one of the angels had a trumpet almost to his lips. The other angel held up the scales and balances of judgment.

Leia took a deep breath. "What did he say again, James? Don't leave anything out."

Our son repeated, "Jesus told me, 'James, it is almost time for me to return, and there are still nations that haven't heard about me.' That's all, really."

Since then, we have served in four nations on four continents, and James has had the opportunity to preach in Africa and Europe. Whenever I wonder about the crazy lifestyle we've had to maintain to live and serve in so many places, I think about Jesus' visit to James on what was otherwise a very ordinary morning.

Meditation on the Miraculous

God—who never changes—still has command over all of nature.

Jesus got into the boat and started across the lake with his disciples. Suddenly, a fierce storm struck the lake, with waves breaking into the boat. But Jesus was sleeping. The disciples went and woke him up, shouting, "Lord, save us! We're going to drown!"

Jesus responded, "Why are you afraid? You have so little faith!" Then he got up and rebuked the wind and waves, and suddenly there was a great calm.

The disciples were amazed. "Who is this man?" they asked. "Even the winds and waves obey him!"

MATTHEW 8:23-27

CHAPTER 22

MIRACLES IN MANILA

1986–1988

Jesus' reminder to James that many people still need to hear the Good News rekindled my desire to be part of foreign missions. So when I was invited to join a team of pastors for a crusade and revival meetings in the Philippines, I jumped at the chance. This would be my first opportunity for international ministry since our trips to Mexico.

The Intercontinental Hotel, where the team stayed, and the Makati business district of Manila stood in stark contrast to the overwhelming, grinding poverty in which the majority of Filipinos lived.

Despite their hardships, the Christians in Caloocan City—a poor, crowded community at the end of Manila's elevated train line—had a genuine, infectious joy. Although I had gone there to encourage them, they encouraged me.

I had been invited to preach during several evening services, which were held in their simple sanctuary. The church's windows had no glass. Planks sitting on top of crates served as seats. Bare fluorescent bulbs buzzed and flickered, providing unsteady light. The crude platform gave way under my feet and creaked and cracked loudly as I delivered the sermon. The Filipino congregation, however, sang with unbounded enthusiasm and responded heartily to everything I said about God or Jesus. Despite their hard, uncomfortable seats, they seemed oblivious to time. Young men from the church walked in and out of the service pulling visitors in from the busy sidewalks.

One such visitor came in the first night. After my sermon I invited anyone who needed healing to come to the front of the church. A middle-aged Filipino woman, well dressed compared to most of the people, stood stiffly at the crude altar and stared at the ceiling.

"Good evening, ma'am," I greeted her as the Filipino pastor translated. Most of the poor people in this church spoke only Tagalog.

"I speak English, sir," she said. "You don't need a translator."

"Good," I said, smiling. "Do you attend this church?"

"No, I was waiting for a bus, and one of the young men invited me to come in. When I saw that you were an American and would be praying for the sick, I decided to catch a later bus."

"Great. What would you like God to do for you tonight?"

She unwrapped a red silk scarf from around her neck, revealing a huge goiter. I tried not to stare. The Filipinos on either side of her looked away. It was large and ugly.

"This thing," she said, "is choking me. I feel like I can't swallow or breathe properly. The doctors want to operate soon, but I'm too afraid. I would like you to pray for me."

I did my best and prayed fervently. There were no immediate results. However, I had learned from experience that when people hear testimonies of healing or see others healed, they often find it easier to reach out to God for their own needs. So I told her, "Please just stay here and pray by yourself for a few minutes. As you watch God heal other people, your faith will increase."

Then I began to move down the line of patiently waiting people. We saw a number of people healed of injuries and pains of various kinds. After I had finished, I saw her still standing there.

"Has there been any change?" I asked. She felt the scarf around her neck. Looking very disappointed, she shook her head no.

"Look, I forgot to ask you. Are you a believer in Christ? Do you know him?" She confessed that she was, in fact, a nominal, nonpracticing Catholic. I shared the gospel with her, and she gladly prayed to give her life to God and receive his Son as her Savior.

"Okay, that's the most important thing that could have happened tonight," I said. "You have entered into eternal life." She smiled at that. The look on her face told me that she knew already that what I was saying was true. My heart went out to her.

"Ma'am, can you come back again tomorrow?"

"Yes, I take the same bus home every night. It picks me up just across the street. I can always get a later bus."

"Okay, then, come tomorrow and we'll pray again." I watched her small figure go out into the rain.

The next night she was there. Nothing happened. The next night she was there again. Tuesday through Saturday—five nights she came. On the final evening, I prayed quickly for her and moved to the others in line. A long line of expectant and hopeful people stretched from one side of the church to the other. I encouraged them not to wait for me, but to pray for themselves and for one another. Men and women from the congregation helped us to pray. It was quite noisy as many enthusiastic, believing people called out to God. Suddenly, there was a commotion at the end of the line, and the shouting there broke through the general din. Jun Evangelio, the Filipino pastor, and I quickly went to see what was going on.

As we approached the far end of the platform, we saw a knot of people jumping, dancing, and shouting. We tried to make out what they were saying. Finally, one man broke away from the group and came to us. He cried excitedly, "She can hear! She can hear!" I noticed the people were gathered around a young lady in a green dress.

Jun and I worked our way into the group. Jun was smiling broadly as if he now understood. I was still puzzled. He spoke in Tagalog to the people around the young lady. Finally, he turned to me.

"Pastor Don, this is too wonderful! She is the daughter of a family in my church. They usually don't bring her. She's twenty-three years old. She was born deaf and mute. She has never heard a sound or spoken a word. She now seems to hear everything. Her family said 'Jesus' to her. And she repeated it back to them. Her first spoken word ever was 'Jesus.' Isn't this truly wonderful?"

It truly was. Still, I was puzzled. "Jun, why is she crying and holding her head?"

"She can't stand all the noise. She's never heard a thing before. It's too much! Too much!" Jun could hardly contain himself.

I had seen some great things before, but this *was* too wonderful. A deaf-mute healed right before my eyes, just like in the New Testament!

Out of the corner of my eye, I saw one person who was not caught up in the excitement. It was the lady wearing the red scarf. Leaving Jun and the happy crowd, I went to console her. She looked up at me; her mascara was running down her face.

"Look, Pastor, look!" She held one end of the scarf in each hand, exposing her neck. It was gone; the goiter was completely gone! What a night! It was like heaven on earth. We celebrated, we hugged, and we danced with joy.

I wished the night in the ghetto of Caloocan City would never end. But the people had to go home to their shacks, and I had to go back to the five-star hotel. What a crazy world! Thanks to the hope they'd found in Christ, many of this nation's poorest citizens had an abundance of joy that most of its wealthiest people could only dream about.

Sharla's Miracle

When I returned to my church, I had some exciting stories to tell. Those good people of Moreno Valley had financed the trip to Manila, and they were thrilled to hear how their investment had paid off. The stories of people coming to Christ, along with the healing of the deaf-mute girl and the lady with the goiter, drew cheers from the congregation.

The greatest miracles in Moreno Valley were those of seeing the amazing power that transformed people's hearts and lives as they found Jesus as their Savior and King. The greatest disappointments came when we occasionally saw someone walk away from the truth.

One of them was Sharla, a beautiful nineteen-year-old girl who dreamed of a career in modeling and acting. She came to church regularly until she met Scott, whose dark good looks and fast motorcycles fascinated her.

In her pursuit of Scott and her career, she left the church and avoided her Christian friends and relatives. Her dreams seemed to be coming true even though she'd stepped away from her faith. She got a contract for a modeling job and embraced Scott's reckless lifestyle.

When my wife or Sharla's sister, Chrystle, who attended our church, would visit Sharla, she would tell them, "I know you don't approve of what I'm doing, but it looks like God is blessing me anyway!" I remember telling Sharla very pointedly one day that I believed her relationship with Scott would destroy her life. I had no idea how prophetic those words would be.

One day Scott and Sharla took a spin on Scott's motorcycle, not far from where they lived in the countryside. They approached an intersection at the same time as the driver of a pickup truck. That driver knew that he had the right of way and that a stop sign would signal Scott to stop at the intersection. What that driver didn't realize was that vandals had removed the stop sign. Scott never slowed down. The bike crashed into the truck and slid to a stop under it.

The truck driver saw that Scott had been thrown clear of the vehicles and landed beside the road. He hadn't noticed the woman riding behind Scott on the motorcycle. Without knowing that Sharla was lying unconscious underneath his truck, the driver backed up his pickup to get it off the motorcycle, crushing her pelvis and lower back as he did so.

As soon as my wife called me to tell me about the accident, the two of us rushed to the hospital. Sharla was in intensive care. When Leia and I entered her room, I noticed tubes, needles, and monitors everywhere. Doctors had put her upper body into a pressurized suit as a way to try to increase her blood pressure. Sharla's face was amazingly unscathed and as beautiful as ever.

I glanced around the room and noticed a doctor looking anxiously at one of the monitors. A nurse stood behind him. Sharla's mother, Rose, stood by her daughter's bed, looking hopeless, while Rose's sister, Cindy, held her hand.

The nurse looked at me and frowned. "This is ICU. We can't have all these people in here."

"But, ma'am," Leia said, "this is the girl's pastor." The nurse looked at the doctor. He gave a nod to let her know I could stay.

When she called, Leia had told me that, despite their best efforts, the doctors did not expect Sharla to survive. Rose was most concerned about Sharla's relationship with God.

"Pastor," Rose cried, "you've got to pray with Sharla. You know she was living in sin. I want her to be able to pray, to get right with God before it's too late."

Leia said, "Don, she's unconscious. They do not expect her to regain consciousness. How can she pray? What can we do?"

I approached the doctor.

"Doctor, I'd like to pray with Sharla. Is there any chance she will regain consciousness?"

He pointed at a monitor. "Do you see that? Her heart rate is rising, and her blood pressure is dropping fast. We're losing her right now. The truck's wheels pulverized her pelvis. The sharp points of the pulverized bone probably punctured hundreds of blood vessels. She's bleeding to death internally. Her heart is accelerating, trying to get enough blood to the lungs. But it can't. Eventually her heart will just quit. There is no way we can do surgery; we can't give her enough blood."

I persisted. "What would have to happen for her to regain consciousness for a few minutes?" The doctor looked at me patiently. He spoke kindly and deliberately.

"Pastor, there's nothing you can do. With her blood pressure that low, she will never regain consciousness."

"So you're telling me that what needs to happen is for her blood pressure to go up."

He sighed and shook his head. "Yes, but that would take a miracle. Even if her blood pressure stopped dropping—even if by some miracle it went up—it's still unlikely that she would wake up. The trauma . . ." His voice trailed off.

"If you don't mind," I said, "I'm going to take her hand and pray that her blood pressure will rise."

The doctor shook his head in another gesture of resignation. "Go ahead, Pastor. We've already done all we can do."

I began praying immediately.

Leia, Rose, and Sharla's aunt Cindy, who was also a believer, went to the head of the bed and began to quietly speak to Sharla. Leia took her other hand.

"Sharla," Leia said, "if you can hear me, squeeze my hand." Leia felt a feeble but definite squeeze.

The blood pressure gauge continued to climb. The doctor got up off his stool and moved closer to the blood pressure monitor. He stared at it, and a faint smile touched the corners of his mouth.

Leia and Cindy began to speak to Sharla. They reminded her of the joy and peace she had known as a Christian. They told her that she may have turned her back on God, but he had not turned his back on her. He still loved her. They asked her if she would like to pray to receive God's love and forgiveness. She squeezed our hands firmly. They prayed with her.

Soon Sharla's blood pressure was in normal range, and her heart stopped its racing. Her eyelids fluttered open. She looked around the room in fear and confusion. Then she saw all of us and calmed down. She had been very hostile to me the last time I saw her. She had felt that I was a threat to her Hollywood dreams and her romance with Scott.

Now her eyes smiled peacefully, and she mouthed the words, "I love you, Pastor." Sharla was conscious for almost two hours. She was able to spend time with her sister, Chrystle, as well as with her mother and stepfather. Because of the ventilator tube, she wasn't able to speak audibly, yet she was able to communicate nonverbally with her family.

At the end of the two hours, Sharla simply closed her eyes and was gone.

Meditation on the Miraculous

Physical healing may bring temporary relief and happiness, but only spiritual rebirth leads to unending joy and eternal life.

All praise to God, the Father of our Lord Jesus Christ. It is by his great mercy that we have been born again, because God raised Jesus Christ from the dead. Now we live with great expectation, and we have a priceless inheritance—an inheritance that is kept in heaven for you, pure and undefiled, beyond the reach of change and decay.

1 PETER 1:3-4

CHAPTER 23

MONEY, JOBS, AND MIRACLES

1988

Phoenix, Arizona; and Tecate, Mexico

The church in Moreno Valley was a young church, an exciting place; you could almost feel the electricity in the air. But after only two years there, I was asked by the leadership of our fellowship of churches to become pastor of an older, larger church in Phoenix.

This church had recently been through a difficult and discouraging time. The people were faithful, but faith and expectation was at a low ebb. I did my best to revitalize their passion for God through sound teaching on evangelism, faith, prayer, and miracles.

Early in that Phoenix ministry, several other concerns weighed on me as well. While still at the church in Moreno Valley, I had made a commitment to do an evangelistic crusade in Tecate, Mexico, entirely at my church's expense. In addition, I had promised to make another overseas trip to Malaysia. On top of all this, the Phoenix church was involved in a remodeling project that turned out to be much more expensive than anticipated.

As the time approached when I needed the funds for our Mexico and Malaysia outreaches, I realized that the Phoenix church had no money for these international projects. I knew we needed a financial miracle of our own to meet these obligations. My prayers became a little desperate: "God, I need more money. We have to have more money. Somehow you have to help us." Each morning, this was my prayer. Each day brought me closer to the financial deadline but no closer to having the required finances.

One morning as I cried out, "God, I need more money!" I heard that rare, but now familiar, voice ask, "How much more?"

I realized that my prayers had been pretty vague, even though I often preached to others that prayer should be specific. I got off my knees and retrieved my calculator. I added up the costs of the Mexican campaign and the airfare to Malaysia. The total came to $3,000—I needed an extra $3,000 in less than thirty days. I knew the regular, predictable income stream of our church; no way would we have an extra $3,000 before the end of the month.

I supposed I could ask the people of the church to give more. But I had made both of these commitments while I was in Moreno Valley, and the Tecate crusade was being planned in conjunction with that church. It didn't feel right to put this burden on the people in Phoenix.

I decided to offer a "prayer of faith." I would not worry. I would ask God specifically for $3,000 by the end of the month and would just thank him for it.

This decision lightened my burden. I continued to pray and give thanks. After each service, I looked expectantly at the usher report, hoping to see at least an incremental rise in giving that would signify an answer to my prayers; yet I saw no change.

We approached the last weekend of the month, when offerings are usually the lightest. On Monday, I had to mail checks and pay bills. It was far too late to take an unannounced "special offering." It was too late to think about doing anything but trusting God.

Leia and I took the kids and another couple out to lunch after the Sunday morning service. When we returned home for the afternoon, I sat down, took off my tie and shoes, and got ready to relax. In just an hour or so I would need to go over the message and plan for the evening service. Leia brought me coffee.

"Do you want to know about the statistics from this morning?" she asked.

I did and I didn't.

"Okay, I'll let you tell me." I grimaced into my coffee.

"Hey, you're going to be happy with this." She held out the usher's report.

It was encouraging. The offering was approximately $1,500 more than we would typically expect on the last Sunday morning of the month. We were halfway to the $3,000! My elation quickly dissolved as reality sunk in. Now we were down to the last Sunday evening service. Most people who tithed or gave any substantial offerings did so on Sunday mornings. Sunday evening offerings were a token for most people. Monday was coming, and I was in trouble. I sipped my coffee and prayed silently.

The evening service attendance was lower than normal. Not a good sign.

Back home that evening, Leia and I avoided the bank bag that held the usher's report and offering. She didn't want to be the one to break bad news to me, and I was putting it off as long as I could. We put the kids to bed and sat down with mugs of tea.

"Don, are you going to look at the offering or not? It's getting late. Waiting isn't going to change anything."

"Yes, we'd better do that. Why don't you take a look."

She unzipped the blue canvas bag. She pulled out the slip of paper with the usher's report. "Oh my! You are not going to believe this!"

I put down my tea. "Let me see it."

She laughed. "No, no, you didn't want to look, remember?" She put the paper behind her back. I ignored the paper she held. Instead I grabbed the bag, dumping the contents on the table. There were a few small bills, a few larger bills, and one check.

I unfolded the check. Exactly $1,500!

I almost shouted.

Then I saw it.

My eyes focused on the name on the check. Kevin. Kevin Ross. "Oh, no!"

Kevin was a young man in our church who had come to the Lord from the streets. Before he got saved, he had been so burned out on methamphetamines and other drugs that he couldn't even put a sentence together.

Kevin worked for minimum wage or less at a metal salvage yard. I knew that he planned to marry Terri, a girl in the church, but I had no idea how he could support her. How in the world could Kevin write a check for $1,500?

My heart sank. Too many zeroes, maybe? It could just be a mistake. I reached for the phone.

Leia, ever considerate, cautioned, "Don, it's getting late."

"Yeah, yeah, he's young. He stays up late." I dialed Kevin's number.

"Yes, hello?" Kevin said in his slow drawl.

"Kevin, this is Pastor Don."

"Hey! Pastor!"

"Kevin, I'm looking at this check you wrote tonight. It's for $1,500! Is this a mistake, a joke, or what?" Leia looked at me reprovingly.

"No, Pastor, it's for real."

"Kevin, how in the world—"

"I know, I know. I can't believe it myself. You remember I told you me and Terri are gonna get married soon?"

"Yes, Kevin, we know. That's great."

"Well, you remember how you took an offering pledge about six months ago for our baby churches in Indianapolis and Alabama?"

"Yes, Kevin, I remember. Where's this going?"

"Well, me and Terri decided to take the money from our jobs that we were going to save each week for our wedding and give it instead as a tithe. We can wait another six months to get married."

"But, Kevin, that means you have less money, not more."

"No, no, Pastor. Remember how you've told us that you can't outgive God? Well, a week ago, I got a phone call from an uncle of mine back East. He got my number from my mom. I haven't seen him in years. He is in very poor health. He doesn't want the government to take his money when he dies, and he doesn't want people fighting over it. So he's giving most of the relatives he likes their inheritance in cash. He told me to be looking in the mail. A couple of days ago, I checked my mail, and there was his envelope with a cashier's check for $10,000. We can sure get married now!"

"And the $1,500, Kevin?"

"Yeah, $1,000 is a 10 percent tithe from that inheritance, and we also wanted to give a $500 thanks offering, Pastor."

"Kevin, that is a wonderful story, and as much of a blessing to me as it is to you." I quickly told him of how his gift had met our needs.

God had proven faithful one more time.

The Eyes Have It

My face appeared on banners over traffic intersections, on thousands of colorful flyers that were passed out, and on the posters that were displayed throughout the Mexican border town of Tecate, located about fifty miles southeast of San Diego. This was my first major crusade, and I was nervous.

All the advertising and outreach announced that "international evangelist" Don Schulze would be praying for miracles at the city's main basketball gymnasium. But it wasn't up to me, was it? Just how much responsibility was mine? Had I prayed enough? Were the messages I had prepared really adequate and fitting for the occasion? Should I have prayed with fasting? It was too late now.

The first two evenings of the three-night crusade were a crushing disappointment. The messages I had prepared seemed too long and too dry. I was not Billy Graham. God had, however, graciously moved in a number of people's hearts, and they answered the altar call for salvation. A few people also reported that they had been healed of relatively minor problems after prayer. Both the Mexican and American pastors who had agreed to bring their churches to support the crusade were obviously disappointed with the results and with me.

I was discouraged and depressed. I spent the entire next day in my room. I was praying for a special message, a message from God. It was a difficult day, but finally a message seemed to form in my heart and mind around the theme "The Curse and the Cure!"

This message would show that sin is a universal, always fatal, inherited disease that destroys lives. It would be a message that presented the blood of Jesus as the only antidote and cure. Like AIDS, sin is treatable but incurable. If there were an announcement of a medicine that would clean the body of the AIDS virus, people would be dancing in the streets and the drugstores wouldn't be able to handle the crowds. In Jesus, God has provided just such a remedy for sin. We are announcing the cure! I excitedly scribbled several pages of notes as the time of the service rapidly approached.

Saturday night arrived. The gymnasium was packed, and there was standing room only. The Mexican pastors estimated the crowd at about one thousand people. As the worship team and special music concluded, I approached the podium with my Bible and notes. The pastors on the platform looked bored and dubious.

I began to preach. The message came forth with real power, and you could have heard a pin drop in that large arena as I spoke. Suddenly, disaster struck: the nylon string holding the right lens in my eyeglasses broke. The frame seemed to fall apart, and the lens clattered to the floor. I was unable to see my notes. I hesitated for just a moment, then I dropped them on the lectern and preached from the heart.

When I gave an invitation at the end of the message for people to come and "receive the cure of the fatal disease of sin," my fellow ministers were astounded—and so was I. The people poured out of the bleacher seats. Even without my glasses, I could see that very few people remained in their seats. Hundreds crowded forward toward the platform. The pastors and Christians who made up our team of altar workers struggled to deal with the large response. After praying with all those who responded and connecting them with a local pastor or church, any time we'd set aside to pray for miracles had evaporated.

As the people were about to be dismissed, I made an announcement.

"If anyone came for a miracle of healing tonight, I don't want you to leave without being prayed for. If you need prayer, please stay, and Pastor Sergio and I will pray for you." After the crowd was dismissed, a line of nearly eighty people snaked across the gym floor toward the platform.

Sergio and I prayed for each need individually. There were demonstrable healings of many things, and some unseen things that we took by faith. A family approached us with a little girl of about eight years. She had a patch over one eye. Through the Mexican pastor, I asked the family what the problem was. They said that the little girl had been nearly blinded by measles. An attempt at corrective surgery had resulted in a complete loss of sight in that one eye.

The family had seen the flyer for the services. They told Sergio they believed that Jesus had sent someone to their town to help. I knew that the God who had already given me the privilege of seeing many other miracles could certainly restore the little girl's sight. But *would* he do it?

Pastor Sergio and I laid our hands on the child and prayed. Her parents wept.

Finally, we asked her parents if they would mind removing the patch. They did so. Kids are amazing. She just stood there looking at us. We noticed that her "blind" eye seemed to be focusing on us.

Sergio asked her, "Can you see?"

She looked around the gymnasium. She looked up at her parents. She smiled.

"Yes, yes!" She giggled. After checking thoroughly, there was no doubt that the little one had received a tremendous miracle. Sergio and I prayed with new enthusiasm.

We came to another set of parents—and uncles and aunties and a grandma—and another little girl. She was about the same age as the child who'd received her sight earlier. This little girl also was blind in one eye. However, she didn't wear a patch, and I could see that her bad eye was just one gray mass—with no iris or pupil—looking blindly into space. Her parents told us that she had been born with that unformed eye. They really wanted her to be able to see out of that eye and had come believing that Jesus would help them. The whole family nodded in agreement as her parents told us her story.

Sergio and I looked at each other. All the faith that had welled up with the healing of the other child seemed to flee away. This seemed like an impossible situation. The first little girl had a badly scarred cornea; this girl had no eye.

I tried my limited Spanish on the family, establishing a rapport and asking a few questions. I placed my hand over the malformed eye and began to pray. I asked the family and those standing around to pray with us. Sergio rattled off a string of Spanish supplications that echoed my own desperation. We finished praying.

I slowly took my hand away from the little girl's face.

Sergio was the first to speak. "Look, Pastor Don. Nothing has happened."

I looked. He was confirming the obvious; the eye seemed unchanged.

I closed my eyes and prayed silently. *Lord, what to do? Should we pray again? Should we comfort the family concerning "God's will"?* I had one of those flashes of inspiration. Was that God? *Really? Really? Do I dare?*

"Sergio," I said quite calmly, "how do we know that nothing has happened?"

Sergio looked at me, looked at her eye, looked at the expectant family, and looked back at me. He held his hands up and let them drop to his sides. It was obvious that he thought there was no rational answer to my question.

"No, really, Sergio. We asked God for her to be able to see from that eye. That's what the parents asked for, too, right?" He nodded. I continued, "We didn't ask for a new pupil or iris. Just that she could see. Let's believe God. Let's see what he has done!"

The family understood nothing of our English conversation. Sergio told the mother to place her hand firmly over her daughter's good eye, blocking all sight. Then he told the little girl to look around the gymnasium. All around the gym were brightly colored signs advertising everything from cigars to automobile batteries. "Read, my daughter," he told her. "Read the signs."

The girl began reading, slowly but clearly, and without error. The appearance of her eye was not changed. There was no iris, no pupil, just a gray mass in the middle of her eye—but she could see. There was a collective gasp. No one could believe it. In turn, all the relatives tested her repeatedly. Cover the eye, have her look, have her read, again and again. The little girl was happy, but she quickly got bored and bothered with the repeated questions.

What can we say about this? There is a spiritual reality behind the physical world we see. Jesus said that God *is* Spirit. What *is* spirit? There is so much we don't understand. But we must understand this. There is nothing God cannot do for those with simple faith.

Meditation on the Miraculous

What do you need? Pray! Be specific!

We are confident that he hears us whenever we ask for anything that pleases him. And since we know he hears us when we make our requests, we also know that he will give us what we ask for.
1 JOHN 5:14-15

CHAPTER 24

SWIMMING POOLS, THAI FOOD, AND THE RESURRECTION

1988–1992
Thailand

In the months following the crusade in Tecate, the church in Phoenix began to grow rapidly. The older people were revitalized, the young people were enthusiastic, and new people were filling the building.

We were not rich, but finances were now more than enough. Our family had moved into a modest but lovely Spanish-style home. The built-in swimming pool was shaded by a large, overhanging tree. We should have been satisfied and settled. And we were—until we attended a Bible conference of our fellowship. At the Tuesday evening service, a man who was planting a new church in Kuala Lumpur, Malaysia, preached on the cause of world evangelism.

"The task is not finished," he proclaimed. "The nations of southeast Asia are still largely un-evangelized." Then he began to speak specifically of some of the cities in that region where the need for evangelism was great. Finally, he talked about Bangkok, Thailand.

"Oh my goodness," he nearly cried. "Bangkok is home to ten million people. Young people come there from all over Thailand looking for a change in their lives. What a great opportunity this is for the gospel of Jesus Christ!"

When he spoke those words, I heard no angelic choir or divine voice, but I knew I must go to Bangkok. There were people there

I had to tell about God's Son. I remembered sitting in the service with the Filipino missionaries, Ping and Lina, right after we became Christians and how my heart had been stirred for foreign missions. I thought of the message I had received in my garage in Rialto years before: "Ask, and I will give you the nations."

I dreaded telling my wife. After sacrificing so much, we were finally comfortable and had a satisfying ministry. Leia was the quintessential domestic homemaker, and our "nest" was well feathered. Now God seemed to be calling us into another season that would lead us to tear up the nest yet again.

Leia and I took a short "exploratory" trip to Bangkok together. During that time, Leia came to grips with the reality that this was God's will for us. I was amazed at how stoically she accepted this unexpected turn of events. She loved her home, and she hated moving; but she was willing to follow and obey God's direction as long as she felt that he was in it.

Heidi, our thirteen-year-old daughter, was up for an adventure as always. James, a creature of habit and self-discipline, was—like his mom—very happy and settled in Phoenix. He especially loved the swimming pool in the backyard.

"Dad, I don't want to leave my friends!" he said. "I don't want to leave the swimming pool. In the jungle, we won't have a swimming pool." In James's eleven-year-old mind, all missionaries lived in the jungle.

"James, Bangkok is a huge, modern city."

"Yeah, but still, can missionaries have a swimming pool?" He looked at me reprovingly.

I had to admit that while it was not impossible, it was highly unlikely that we would have a swimming pool in Thailand.

Finally, I said, "James, do you really think swimming pools are the most important thing in life? What about the millions of people in Thailand who have never heard the gospel?" James had a very serious and spiritual side to him even as a child, but the swimming pool was a major issue in his life.

"Dad, remember how God gave me the cowboy hat?"

I nodded. "Yep, I remember."

"Well, if we've got to go, I'm gonna ask him to give me a swimming pool in Thailand!"

I choked up and couldn't reply. James was so sincere and his request seemed so important to him, but I didn't see any way we would have a pool.

A few months later, our family arrived in Bangkok. A "chance" encounter with a waitress in a Thai restaurant in Phoenix had led to an introduction to a pastor in Thailand named Wirachai Kowai. Wirachai gave us much-needed guidance and opened many doors for us. Although we had arrived in Thailand with only some suitcases and boxes, the guesthouse we were staying in soon grew too small for us. In this teeming, confusing city, we needed a place to call home. Where in the world in this megacity should we live? We prayed. We considered. We looked at maps. We called Pastor Wirachai.

"Pastor, we don't speak any Thai yet. We don't know the best way to go about finding housing. Do you know anyone who can help us?"

Wirachai had a friend who was a real estate agent. Most of her clients were very wealthy Thai people. Early one morning we met with the immaculately attired and perfectly coiffed Miss Amporn.

"Miss Amporn, thanks for meeting with us," I said. "We need a residence. We'd like to have a house, not an apartment. Our budget, however, is pretty modest."

Miss Amporn smiled. "Pastor Wirachai told me about you. I've done some looking around and talked to some of my Thai friends. Do you know of the former prime minister Seni Pramot? He's a member of the royal family."

I assured Miss Amporn that we were not personally acquainted with any prime ministers or royalty, unless, of course, you included King Jesus.

"Yes, of course," she smiled politely. "Well, the prime minister has a large compound just off of Sukhumvit Road." (This is pronounced "Sookoomwit Load" by the Thais.) Seeing my lack of comprehension, she continued, "Sukhumvit Road is one of Bangkok's main traffic arteries. And, fortunately for you, it is also the street that has many of the shops that you expatriates like to shop at. Many of my clients live off Sukhumvit because of its conveniences."

I was sure that the well-known and desirable Sukhumvit Road location would prove to be too costly for us, but I didn't want to dampen Miss Amporn's enthusiasm or Leia's obvious hopefulness.

So I pushed ahead with the seemingly futile conversation. "Miss Amporn, I'm sure Sukhumvit is a great location."

She looked pleased. "Well, as I was saying, Mr. Seni Pramot's compound is quite large, almost a city block. On the compound are the homes of several of the Pramot family. Some are artists and actors. It's a fascinating, sophisticated family."

I thought, *I'm sure we would fit right in.*

She continued, "He's also built a small quad-plex for visitors, but that's full of teachers from the International School of Bangkok. Fortunately, there is one small, three-bedroom bungalow that is vacant. It was built for the guests of some of his family members. They are willing to lease it, upon my recommendation, for a year at a very modest price."

The proposed rent exceeded the guidelines from our organization, which had been calculated based on their experiences in the Philippines, where housing costs were lower. Our family needed a home, so I decided that, if I couldn't convince my superiors of the need for an adjustment in our housing allowance, we'd make up the difference from our savings and our salary.

"When can we see it?" I asked.

"Is now okay?" said Miss Amporn, smiling.

We drove through Bangkok's incredibly heavy traffic to Sukhumvit Road. We turned left onto Soi 63 (*soi* means "noodles"; it also means "a small road") and then left again onto the Pramot family compound. We drove past several large houses with beautiful tropical landscaping. On the right, we saw the multiunit house for the expat teachers. Miss Amporn pointed at a small but attractive house on the left surrounded by greenery. "There's the house. I think it's open."

The house was simple but nice. Teakwood floors, concrete walls, gypsum board ceiling—even air-conditioning in the front rooms. This was an unexpected blessing. The house was well appointed, as would be expected since royalty owned it. Leia was enthusiastic and more than ready to begin housekeeping.

"Dad, can Heidi and I go outside?" James asked.

"Sure, but stay right around the house. Don't bother anyone, and don't make any noise."

"Okay, Dad." The door slammed behind them.

But soon I heard the sound of excited screams and the creak of the front door opening again.

"What is it?" I asked.

"Dad, you won't believe it! There's a swimming pool, a real pool, right outside. A pool, Dad." Heidi smiled broadly.

I looked at James, who had a smug look on his face. "Dad, remember the cowboy hat? Well, I got my pool, too!"

Actually, the pool was not ours alone. It was for the use of everyone on the Pramot compound, but during the day our kids were almost the only ones who ever used it. God is good.

Nang and Noi

We rented the ground floor of a dilapidated building in an overpopulated, low-rent district of Bangkok to serve as our new church. The Huay Kwang section of Bangkok was only four kilometers from our house, but in city traffic, it could easily take half an hour to forty-five minutes to get there.

Shortly after leasing the building, our family stood in the middle of the single large room that comprised the ground floor. Concrete stairs along one wall led upstairs to where the building, modeled on Chinese "shophouses," became an apartment complex. The floor was about twelve inches higher along the walls than in the middle of the room, where the concrete floor had sunk into the dirt in an almost perfect concave circle.

The only windows were those fronting the street. The walls were a horrible shade of yellow-orange and streaked with soot, grease, dirt, and other stains. The room had its own unique odor of mildew, dirt, and urine. That aroma was mingled with the heavily concentrated smells of the "fresh market," across the street. The market didn't smell so fresh, though. The stench of decomposing vegetables, overly ripe fruit, fish remnants, buckets full of unmentionable filth, and piles of accumulated garbage was almost overpowering.

Nosy, noisy neighbors and kids in rags stared at my family through the open door. They seemed amazed and curious beyond belief at this very white family standing in the midst of their slum.

"Hey, Leia, look at the bright side," I said. "This place is surrounded by scores of apartments occupied by working-class people and students. What a great opportunity. The building needs some housekeeping, but hey, that's your specialty, right?"

She looked at me in disbelief. She pulled Heidi to her protectively and began to cry. The nosy neighbors kept staring. Weeks later, the grimy walls were painted, the floor had been leveled and covered with ceramic tiles, and Leia had made draperies for the windows.

We were almost ready to start.

There was just one problem. We had looked in vain for a translator. Every young man we interviewed was either already employed or was unsuitable in some way. It would be years before I could preach in Thai; we wanted to get started immediately. What we hoped would be a search of short duration became a disappointing exercise in futility. After more than three months, we still had no translator. I was out of ideas and decided to go to Bangkok's prestigious Chulalongkorn University and just start preaching on the campus. Surely, somebody there would understand English!

Then the phone rang. It was our pastor in the States. "Don, have you found a translator yet?"

"Not yet," I said, trying not to sound too discouraged.

"Well," he chuckled, "looks like God has this under control. There's a Thai family that came into the church that you planted over in Moreno Valley. The new pastor there called me and told me about them. They have a son, about twenty-two; he's having some immigration issues. Seems he has to go back to Thailand to work out some of the problems. His native language is Thai, but he speaks perfect English. I hear he's a good Christian and might make a good translator."

"Wow" was all I could say.

"Anyway, I made a proposal to him. I would pay his airfare back to Thailand, all of his expenses while he works out the immigration deal, and a small salary while he works with you. The deal is he has to stay for one year. He's agreed to that. What do you think?"

"Jack, that's tremendous. When can he get here?"

God had come through again at the last moment.

Less than two weeks later, I was at Bangkok's International Airport picking up Aruphorn Jugsujinda. Aruphorn was all of five feet, five inches tall. He couldn't have weighed more than 120 pounds. His nickname—all Thais have nicknames—was "Big." James and Heidi thought that was hilarious.

Finally, we were ready to start our church. On Saturdays, we went out with flyers and tracts, "street preaching," witnessing to individuals, and inviting the entire neighborhood to hear the Good News.

Nang was the first Buddhist to come to Christ at our church. She was about fifteen. Her black hair was cut in a short bob, and eyebrow-length bangs framed her face. When she first wandered in, she sat quietly and seemed morose. Soon she looked interested and then finally on-the-edge-of-her-seat, captivated by the message.

When we gave the invitation for anyone who wanted to respond to God's message of salvation, Nang literally jumped to her feet. She knelt on the hard tile floor and followed fervently in the simple prayer for forgiveness and salvation. She had come in with a black cloud over her head; now she beamed.

"Oh my!" she exclaimed. "It's real. God is real. This Jesus is real. I feel so happy. So . . . light." I really liked that. So light. Jesus removes our burdens!

Our little congregation grew slowly. The neighbors were suspicious, almost hostile. Thailand is a homogenous society: "To be a Thai is to be a Buddhist!" The king of Thailand is known as the defender of the Buddhist faith. The Buddhist monks in their saffron robes are involved in almost every aspect of Thai culture. Strange foreign doctrines are not welcome.

Nang, however, didn't seem to mind the reproachful stares of the neighbors or the small size of our congregation. She worshipped wholeheartedly and unashamedly carried her new Bible. She was in her seat early each and every time the doors of the church opened. One Wednesday night, however, Nang looked very troubled. "Pastor," she said nervously, "I have a problem. My mom has forbidden me to come to church."

Now I was the one who was troubled. We had grown to love Nang; she was the spark plug in our small group of new Christians.

"But, Nang, you're here tonight."

"Oh, Pastor, don't worry." She brightened slightly. "I just told my mom that I was going to a girlfriend's house to study. She's happy that I'm studying!"

"Nang, Nang, you can't do that. Lying is wrong; it's always wrong. And God teaches us to always honor our parents. You can't disobey and deceive your mom and honor her at the same time, can you?"

Her smile disappeared. She looked down at her dirty tennis shoes. "What can I do then? This is my church. It's like my family, and I meet God here. I must come!"

"Nang, we'll think of something, but it has to be the right thing."

I hit on a simple solution. Nang had, by her own testimony, been suffering with anger and depression almost to the point of suicide. She was now a very happy girl in Jesus. Her mother must see the wonderful difference in Nang's life.

I decided that I would send my daughter, Heidi, along with Duong, a sweet Thai female convert, and Big, our translator, to Nang's home to talk with her mother. They were to make a proposal: Why wouldn't she want to come and see what had so affected her daughter? If she came and observed the church and then still wanted Nang to stay away, we would encourage her to obey her mother.

Noi, the mother, was very negative and suspicious when our little team asked her to visit the church. They reasoned with her, and Nang pleaded. Couldn't she see the tremendous positive difference in her daughter's mind and moods? Wasn't Nang doing much better in school despite all the time she spent in church?

Finally Noi relented and agreed to visit that Sunday.

She came and sat, arms crossed, in a chair at the rear of the room. Finally, just before leaving, she had to admit that she had seen nothing "wicked" in the singing, message, or prayers.

Then we asked if Nang would be able to continue coming. Noi still wasn't convinced. Nang was her little daughter, and she seemed to be mixed up in this strange thing, even if it did look harmless; Noi said she'd have to think about it. The problem was, she said, it was hard for her to think because she was very sick. I had noticed that Noi was thin, even by Thai standards.

"What's wrong, Noi?" Big translated for me.

"I have cancer. A tumor. It's in my throat."

I could see what looked almost like an Adam's apple. I could also see the fear in her eyes.

"It's very serious," she said. "The doctors are going to operate, but they say it could be dangerous. I am very afraid. I don't want to die. Nang needs me."

"Noi, look, come back to church next Sunday. We are going to pray for you between now and then. When you come back, we are going to ask Jesus to heal you. Will you give it a try?"

She looked out of her tired eyes. "Why not?" she said.

Halfway through the service the next Sunday, we stopped to pray for the various needs of our little congregation.

"Noi, can we pray for you?"

She sat alone against the wall in the back of the room. I was already walking toward her with Big and Nang. She nodded in assent and closed her eyes, folding her hands in her lap.

Several other young Thai believers joined us as we surrounded Noi's chair and laid our hands upon her head. We prayed tentatively at first, but then with fervency and boldness. She sat up with a start, straightening her body against the back of the rounded plastic chair. Her eyes grew wide. Our prayer gradually subsided.

"What happened, Noi?" I asked.

She said, "When you were praying, I felt heat all over and something like electricity going through me. Oh, oh." She reached up and put her hand around her throat. She murmured under her breath. Her fingers seemed to clutch at her throat. Her eyes closed.

Big asked her, "What, what is it?"

Finally, Noi relaxed and put her hands back into her lap. "It's gone. Look, it's gone." Sure enough, there was no visible lump in her throat—no sign of the tumor at all. Soon after, the doctors confirmed that her tumor and all signs of cancer had "mysteriously" disappeared!

Noi now joined her daughter in attending church faithfully, worshiping and learning of our wonderful Jesus. Not only that, but Noi soon began helping Leia out with the housekeeping and cooking in our home.

The Resurrection

In Thailand we thanked God that we'd had the foresight to bring all our small kitchen and household appliances with us. The appliances available in Bangkok at that time were either cheap imports or incredibly expensive European goods.

Noi was a good housekeeper and a tremendous cook. She had one little problem, however. She could not seem to remember that all of our American electric appliances needed to be plugged into a step-down transformer, which reduced the voltage from the 240 volts used in most of the world to the 110 volts used in the States.

One by one, over the months, Noi plugged Leia's precious appliances into the 240-volt electricity, frying the circuits and destroying the appliances. Noi was always tearfully sorry, and Leia was always sorrowfully forgiving.

Once, about midday, I came home unexpectedly. I knew that Leia had been struggling lately with culture shock, homesickness, and not a little anxiety and depression. These things are common to women whose husbands take them to a developing foreign nation. So I was a little apprehensive when she met me at the door laughing and repeating something over and over again. What in the world was wrong? Had she finally snapped?

"Leia, please try to calm down and tell me what's wrong."

"Wrong?" she said. "There's nothing wrong." She started laughing again.

"Okay, what's going on?"

She wiped her eyes. "Noi plugged my Moulinex food processor into the 240 electricity today."

She has lost it, I thought. *How can she laugh at that?* I knew how much she valued that food processor and how impossible it would be to replace.

Seeking my stricken face, Leia said, "Don, you don't understand. It's okay. It really is!"

"You mean you're not upset?"

"No, I'm thrilled. Noi was in the kitchen working. I heard her scream. I thought she had cut herself on a knife. When I went into the kitchen, she was very upset. She had plugged the food processor directly into the 240. Smoke was just pouring out of it. She was so panic-stricken; she had just left it plugged in. I yanked the plug. I hoped that it would be okay. Noi ran and got the transformer, and we tried it. We pushed all the buttons; we unplugged it and plugged it in again. Absolutely nothing. It was still smoking. It was dead."

"Yeah, and then?" I was still mystified.

"Well, I told Noi to go home and rest. Then I cried. I told God that this was my last 110-volt appliance. I asked him how he could let this happen. I asked why he sent me to this place. I ranted and raved for a while. Somehow I got the idea to pray for the food processor. We've seen God do so many miracles. I was desperate. So I just put my hands on the food processor and asked God to resurrect it from the dead! After I prayed, I turned it on—and it worked. It just worked.

"You know the funny smell that electrical fires have? Well, it didn't even smell. It was like the story in the book of Daniel where the guys were thrown into the furnace and survived. When they came out, they didn't even smell like smoke! I was so happy to have my food processor back, I told God that I didn't care about all the other appliances. I've been filled with joy since this happened."

Years after we left Thailand, we had the opportunity to contact both Nang and Noi. Their joy and their faith remain intact.

Shortly before we returned to the United States, I was invited to preach at an old and established Pentecostal church in Chiang Mai, located in northern Thailand. This was quite a large church. I prayed before the service and asked God to help me help the people. Was there anything in particular he wanted me to say or do? There was. God spoke by giving me a mental impression that there was a woman who had a problem with her ear and a man who had a problem with his arm. If I would pray for them, he would heal them.

At the conclusion of the service, I announced, "There are two people here whom God wants to heal. One of you has a problem with one of your ears; the other has a problem with one of your arms." That's all I knew, so that's all I could say. I waited. Everyone waited, squirming a bit as the silence continued. I began to understand that even though this was a Pentecostal church, they no longer expected God to perform miracles among them. I waited a little longer, certain that God had showed me these specific needs. My friend, who had invited me, tried to hide his embarrassment.

Just as I was about to try to find some face-saving way out of this predicament, a young woman stood up.

"Do you have a problem with one of your ears?" I asked hopefully. She nodded slightly.

"Then please come to the front where I can pray for you."

As she was nearing the front of the church, an old man stood up in the back.

"Sir, do you have a problem with your arm?" His right arm hung limply at his side. He nodded solemnly.

I turned to the young woman once she and the old man were standing at the front. "Okay, ma'am, exactly what is wrong?"

The pretty Thai woman was a bit embarrassed as she explained. She was a nurse and should have known better. Five years before, while sitting at the nursing station, she had absentmindedly picked up a pen and begun delicately scratching and cleaning the inside of her ear. Just then someone had walked forcefully into her elbow, driving the pen deep into her ear. As a result, her eardrum was destroyed and she was totally deaf in that ear.

This situation seemed a bit daunting, but how could I doubt God? I placed my hands over both her ears and asked God to fulfill his word and heal this young lady. I took my hands away and whispered very quietly into her deaf ear. She smiled broadly, saying, "*Dai, dai lao!* I can, I can hear!"

I tested her hearing in a couple of other ways. There was no doubt: God had either created an eardrum or repaired the damaged one. Who can explain the miraculous? The young woman was all smiles as she returned to her seat.

The older man, at first nervous and hesitant, was now quite eager to be prayed for. Through the translator, we discovered his problem: he had injured his elbow in a motorcycle accident many years ago. Since that time, he had been unable to bend his arm and had little use of his hand.

I grabbed his arm and lifted his hand above his head. "Father, may your will now be done on the earth as it is in heaven." I let go of his arm and motioned with my own arm for him to try to bend his elbow. He complied enthusiastically. He bent it, twisted it, and lifted it up high again and again. He held his arm up and flexed his fingers. He looked around at the ministers and the large congregation like a child who had just won a spelling bee. Whatever he said in his excited Thai went completely past me. I didn't care. I was pretty excited myself.

Sadly, due to some changes in the leadership and direction of the fellowship of churches that were supporting us, we were not able to remain in Thailand. However, the fruit of our time there remains. Big and one of our Thai converts, Nawin, are now pastors preaching to their own people. Nang, Noi, and many others who came into that little church in the slum of Huay Kwang were changed forever.

Meditation on the Miraculous

When we are bold in telling the uninformed about the grace of our Lord Jesus, God is gracious in stretching out his hand to confirm our message.

> [The disciples] stayed there a long time, speaking boldly in the Lord, who was bearing witness to the word of His grace, granting signs and wonders to be done by their hands.
> ACTS 14:3, NKJV

CHAPTER 25

WINDOW GLASS AND BACA FOOD

1992–1995
Casa Grande, Arizona

When we were forced to leave Thailand, Leia and I were crushed. Why had our work ended so abruptly when we knew God had called us there?

Leia was very confused about why we had to leave and what the future would hold. I could rationalize and conjecture with the best of them, but I had no real answers and she knew it.

So she turned to God with the simple question, "What now, Lord?"

One evening we were going over some of the practical details involved in packing up and relocating back to the United States. It was one of several such conversations, which had often deteriorated into "fears and tears" in the past. As we talked on this evening, though, I noticed that my wife seemed to have peace and a certain detachment.

"Leia, are you okay? You seem—I don't know—different somehow." I was concerned that the pressure of our situation might be taking a real emotional and mental toll on her.

"Don, I'm okay. I'm concerned about the future and the way we're leaving here, but God has helped me."

She had my full attention. I was as determined as ever to follow wherever God led us, but I had no real idea of what that was right now.

"Really? Tell me about it."

"Well, it's not very specific, but it's enough for me to have confidence about the future."

"Go on."

"While you and the kids were out, I was feeling sorry for myself and for Nang, Noi, Nawin, and our other spiritual children. I eventually realized that these were God's children, not ours. I would have to entrust them to him. So I asked God to please help me understand where we were going and what we would do. I heard his voice in my spirit, and he said, 'I have called you to be repairers of the breach.' That was all. I thought, what could that mean? I knew those words were in the Bible, but I couldn't remember where. I looked and looked and finally found them in the prophecies of Isaiah."

I reached for my Bible. I knew pretty much where those words were but was eager to see them in context:

And the LORD will continually guide you,
> And satisfy your desire in scorched places,
> And give strength to your bones;
And you will be like a watered garden,
> And like a spring of water whose waters do not fail.
Those from among you will rebuild the ancient ruins;
You will raise up the age-old foundations;
And you will be called the repairer of the breach,
The restorer of the streets in which to dwell.
(Isaiah 58:11-12, NASB)

"Well, Leia, I don't know where we are going, but this looks like a promise that we are going to take a broken-down church, work to rebuild it, and make it a good place for people to live and worship."

Actually, I had been hoping for a big, prosperous, healthy church that would welcome us as heroic missionary pioneers. It was not to be. Both of the US churches we pastored after Thailand were in inhospitable, unprosperous desert communities. Both churches were small and getting smaller. They had been through difficult times that had left them feeling neglected, unimportant, abused, and unloved. They were good people, but the spiritual atmosphere reeked of discouragement and spiritual death. There was nothing promising about either of these "opportunities" except that God had promised that we were to be "repairers of the breach"—those who would rebuild broken-down communities.

The pastoral and spiritual work involved in these situations was difficult and challenging on one hand, but they were also labors of love. We reinforced to God's people the fact that he loved them, we believed in them, and their best days were still ahead of them. These folks gradually shook off the shackles of doubt and discouragement. They began to roll up their sleeves physically and spiritually and got to work in the rebuilding process with us.

While we labored with these churches, our family paid a price. The work required a full-time effort; however, the struggling churches were unable to provide a full-time salary. As a result, both Leia and I worked part-time whenever and however we could. In these minimum-wage towns, finances were tight. Very often we had to pray for our "daily bread" just to survive. Over those four and a half years, God wonderfully provided for our needs innumerable times.

The Sizzler and the Skateboard

Once, during those days, we were driving from Arizona to Los Angeles to visit family. We decided on the spur of the moment to stop off in Moreno Valley, the city where we had planted our first church. One of the first couples to join our church years before had been on our minds. We stopped and telephoned them. The friends we hoped to see, Bob and Elaine, were at home and excited at the chance to meet with us.

It was a timely visit as they were going through some marriage problems and needed to talk. Bob suggested that they buy us dinner at the Sizzler Steakhouse to fortify us for the trip to LA. Everyone thought that was a good idea—everyone, that is, except our son, James.

Since we had mentioned stopping off in Moreno Valley, James had been telling me how important it was for him to be able to see Craig, his best friend from elementary school.

"Dad, I remember where he lives! We could just drive by and I could see him."

I tried to explain to James that there were a lot of people in Moreno Valley we would love to see. The problem was that we had only a couple of hours.

"But, Dad, he was my very best friend. You know I don't have many friends."

Oh, the guilt trip. Our missionary and ministry calling had kept our kids from making lasting friendships. Actually, I really did have great sympathy with that, but I wasn't going to be manipulated by it.

"Dad, I've been praying about this. This is really important."

"James, it's also very important that we talk to Bob and Elaine, and we don't have time to do both."

At the Sizzler, Leia and I visited with our friends, offering some counsel that we hoped would be helpful. As we talked, Heidi and James traded bored looks and waited impatiently. Suddenly James's face brightened.

"Dad!" he interrupted. "Dad!"

"What is it, James? We're about finished here."

"Dad, can I go out front for a while?"

"Why don't you just stay here? We're going soon."

"Dad, I want to go look around to check if I can see Craig."

"James, there are over 100,000 people in this city. Do you think Craig is just outside?"

"Dad, c'mon, I just want to go right out in front of the restaurant and look. Remember the cowboy hat I prayed for? Remember the swimming pool? I've prayed!"

"I remember, son. Go ahead and look."

Bob and Elaine looked on curiously. After James had gone outside, I explained the situation to them, and we all had a good laugh.

The waitress was clearing away the remains of our dinner when James came running down the aisle between the booths.

"James! You know you're not supposed to run indoors," Leia said.

James was breathless with excitement. He jerked his thumb pointing over his shoulder. "Look! It's him! It's him!"

As our eyes followed James's thumb, we saw him. It had been several years, but we recognized Craig right away. James smiled broadly. He went back up the aisle and led his friend to the table. We looked at Craig and then at each other, shaking our heads in amazement.

James, Craig, and Heidi took their own booth for the reunion. Back in the car, James explained his miracle.

"I was sitting in the Sizzler praying the whole time you guys were talking. Then I just felt like I should go outside and look for Craig. I looked around the parking lot and didn't see him. So I walked up to the intersection. I looked and looked and didn't see him. Then, all of a sudden, there he was. He was on his skateboard coming out of the shadows from the freeway underpass. God answered my prayer!"

We added this memory to the miracles of the cowboy hat and the swimming pool.

Broken Glass

One of the hazards of living in the southwest desert is a sandstorm. One day as we were driving home from Los Angeles where we had visited family, we drove right into one. Swirling clouds of sand soon obscured the road ahead. I turned on the headlights and slowed way down.

"Don, do you think we should pull over and wait?" Leia asked. "This looks like one of those serious sandstorms we have been warned about."

"Sweetie, I don't think pulling over is a good idea. I can't even make out the shoulder clearly. What if we stop and someone plows into the back of our car? I think we should just keep moving and try not to run into anything."

As the small grains of sand flew through the air, propelled by high winds, they sounded like hundreds of small rocks hitting our car. Finally the winds slowed and the stars came out in the ink-black sky above us. We instinctively looked back at our kids, who had slept through the whole scary episode. Assured our precious cargo was in good shape, we let out a sigh of relief. Then headlights approaching from the other side of the freeway nearly blinded me.

I realized in sudden dismay that our windshield had been effectively sandblasted by the storm. We barely had money to put gas in the car. How would we pay for a new windshield?

I called our insurance agent the next afternoon and explained what had happened. She gave me the names of two local companies who dealt in auto glass and advised me to get an estimate for replacing the windshield and then call her back.

After checking, both companies told us that a new windshield would cost about $650. I was in shock. I called the insurance lady.

"Oh, Pastor, I'm sorry. That really is an expensive windshield. And, by the way, did you know that your deductible is $500? If you bring me your glass company estimate, I can cut you a check for the balance after the deductible."

I was too embarrassed to admit that I didn't happen to have $500 at that moment.

Now that it was winter, the sky got dark early. It was dangerous to drive after dark because the pitted windshield made visibility very poor. How in the world could I not drive my car?

I prayed, *Dear God, somehow you need to help us here. It is dangerous even to drive back and forth to church in the evening, but we can't walk. Keep us safe until we can do something. Amen.*

A week or so later I sat in my office on a Wednesday evening preparing for our midweek service. James, now fourteen and on a baseball team, was playing catch with a friend in the parking lot.

James came running into my office breathless and near tears. Another boy followed him with a guilty, apprehensive look on his face.

"Dad, Dad, I'm so sorry," James began.

"What is it, James?" He was so upset that I wasn't sure I wanted to know.

"Dad, my friend—Jack, here—threw me a pitch. He threw it real hard. I almost caught it, but it bounced off the tip of my glove and . . ."

"And?"

"And, well, it hit your car in the parking lot."

"Did it make a dent, James?"

"Dad, I think you better come and see."

There was a small crowd of church kids standing around the car, pointing and talking excitedly.

The baseball had crashed through the expansive and expensive rear window of the car. The glass had shattered into something like a million pieces.

Dear God! Can it get worse? No front window and now no rear window? My shoulders slumped as I went in to gather my sermon notes from my desk and head for the platform to preach on faith and victory. God was still God.

The estimate on the rear glass was only slightly less than the windshield. I went to the office of the insurance lady. Perhaps she would have some ideas.

"Well, the good news is we can put both incidents on the claim form, saying they happened at the same time. That way you'll only have to pay the deductible once. That's the best I can do for you."

I was amazed by her proposition.

"You want me to say that while I was driving through a sandstorm, someone threw a baseball through my rear window?" I had to laugh at the absurdity. She laughed too.

"No, no. We'll just say that both your front and rear windows were broken in some small accident. Don't worry, Pastor, this is my business. I can write the claim in a believable fashion."

For a moment I was too amazed to speak. In her "helpfulness," she seemed to be suggesting fraud. How would I handle this tactfully?

"Ma'am, I appreciate the fact that you are willing to do this for me. I don't mean to be critical, but I'm a Christian and I have to tell the truth about what happened."

"You're right, of course. What was I thinking?" She was obviously embarrassed. "I just know you needed some kind of help, but that was a bad idea. I'm sorry. I guess you'll have to be careful not to drive in the rain or in the dark for a while. Fortunately, it doesn't rain here in the desert very often."

"Fortunate," I mumbled. "Well, thanks a lot. I better get home before it clouds up or gets dark."

The next morning my phone rang. It was the insurance lady.

"Pastor, this is a long shot, but I have an idea. The boy who threw the ball—do you know him?"

"He's a friend of my son."

"Well, I was thinking, if his parents have home-owners insurance, their liability portion may at least cover your rear window. I know our company's policy would in such a situation. It's worth a try."

I made some calls and reached the boy's mother.

"Ma'am, I'm Pastor Don Schulze. You don't know me, but our sons play on the same baseball team."

"Yes, and so . . . ?"

"Ma'am, your son accidentally threw a baseball through the rear window of my car."

"Oh yeah, he told me something about that. I'm sorry, but it was an accident. I'm a single mom trying to raise a couple of kids; I can't be responsible for all of these things."

"Ma'am, I'm not asking you to pay for the window. I just wanted to ask you a couple of questions."

"Okay, Pastor. What do you want to know?"

"Well, ma'am, my insurance agent suggested that I ask you if you have a home-owner's policy."

"Pastor, we live in an apartment. I don't even have renter's insurance."

I was defeated. "Okay, I'm sorry to bother you. No problem about the window. Maybe we'll see each other at the boys' games." I started to say good-bye.

"Wait, wait just a minute," she said. "My husband and I are going through a divorce. We both have apartments, but we own a small house that we have rented out until our property settlement. Maybe there's insurance on that house that can help you. I'll call my husband and let you know."

As it turned out, my insurance agent was also the agent for that house! The homeowner's policy covered the full amount of the highest estimate on the rear window. That same day a friend told me about a wholesale glass company that might be able to replace my front windshield for far less than the other estimates I'd gotten.

In the end, that glass company replaced both the front and rear windows for the amount the insurance company gave me. What looked like a disastrous toss of a baseball turned out to be the key to solving the problem of my pitted windshield. God does work in mysterious ways.

BACA Food

According to our long-standing commitment, our family did not tell anyone of our needs. In the small churches we pastored in the desert, the money that came in was often just enough to pay the church bills. For us, paying those bills came before our needs so that the testimony of the church in the community wouldn't suffer.

Leia was an assiduous coupon clipper and knew how to stretch her food dollars. But despite her best efforts, we hit bottom one evening.

"Don, I don't know what to do about dinner. All I have is a chicken back and some rice. I guess I can make a soup. But with two teenagers, that won't go far."

I knew she was right; Heidi had a healthy appetite, and James could eat ten pancakes at a sitting.

"Well, we'll just pray over dinner and believe it to be enough."
It wasn't.

Heidi and James stared at the meager portions in their bowls. "No bread?" James asked.

"James, I'm sorry, son. What you see is what you get."

We ate in silence and went about the evening's business—homework, bookkeeping, and doing the few dishes.

Just as the kids finished cleaning up, I heard a knock at the door.

Pete, a faithful member of our church, stood there looking a little apologetic.

"Pastor, I'm sorry to bother you at this time of the evening."

Pete was in his late forties but looked ten years older. He'd had a rough life. His sandy hair, streaked with gray, was combed in an outdated pompadour. His glasses were perched awkwardly on the end of his nose. His wardrobe was thrift-store chic.

Though Pete was a shy person who didn't talk much, he had an interesting story to tell. After a painful childhood and a disappointing early adulthood, he sunk into severe alcoholism. By his late thirties, he was barely able to hold a job and was plagued by bleeding ulcers and other alcohol-related afflictions.

During one hospital visit for internal bleeding, the doctors made a disturbing discovery. Pete had inoperable cancer. The doctors sent him home to die. But God sent some Christians into his life who offered him the hope of God's love and forgiveness. Pete gave his life to God and asked for his help. Not only did God make a new man out of Pete both spiritually and mentally, but also his doctors were amazed to find no sign of the cancer when they did further tests.

Now Pete was working for low wages at BACA, the acronym for

a county agency that served as a temporary source of meals and shelter to battered wives, indigents, homeless people, and other needy people. Many BACA recipients suffered from addictions like that from which Pete had been rescued. Pete was a highly intelligent and educated man who could have found a better job. However, he felt that the work at BACA gave him the opportunity to share God's love with many needy people.

"Pastor," Pete said, "now that I'm standing here, this idea seems ridiculous."

"Wait, Pete, what is it?" I thought Pete might be coming out of his shell. Perhaps he needed to talk.

My family lived in a very nice home courtesy of the former pastor who rented it to us at a loss while he was overseas. Because of this "nice" house, our mostly poor congregation, including Pete, assumed we had money.

"Well, Pastor, I was getting the leftover food from the BACA kitchen together tonight. I was going to take it to where some homeless guys sleep. Then the idea came to me, *The pastor and his family could use that food.* I thought perhaps God was speaking to me. I'm sorry to bother you."

For just a moment my pride tempted me to thank him for thinking of us and send him away. "Pete, let's take a look at the BACA food! Maybe there's something there that the kids would like."

As if I'd summoned them, the kids suddenly appeared behind me.

"Dad, what's going on? Why is Pete here?"

"Well, Pete just brought some food by, thinking we might like it."

James pushed past me. "Let me see, Pete."

Pete raised a knowing eyebrow and said, "The Lord knows what he's doing, doesn't he?"

I could only nod. I was both embarrassed and filled with gratitude and awe. God does know our needs. The food was wholesome, bland, and generic; we didn't mind. Pete was very discreet and told no one.

On many occasions over the next few months, we would hear Pete's knock on the door. James and Heidi would start laughing and shout, "BACA food! BACA food!" It became a family joke.

For years after that, whenever we had to eat something that didn't really appeal to us, we would all laugh and say, "BACA food!" God is a provider!

Janelle

Our second church assignment after returning from Thailand was in Casa Grande, Arizona, halfway between Phoenix and Tucson. The average temperature in this area is above one hundred degrees throughout the summer. The wind coming off the desert often feels like the heat from a furnace blast or a blow-dryer pointed in your face.

The Casa Grande church was a diverse group of people, making up an interesting kaleidoscope of humanity. The racially and socially dissimilar congregation was comprised of small-business owners and middle-class working people, as well as very poor immigrants and nearly indigent people.

To the credit of this church body, which had been through difficult times, the congregation made everyone feel welcome. I think this is what attracted Janelle. She was a plain-looking woman in her late fifties. Her short, gray hair was cut in an unfashionable, almost masculine style, and she seemed to dress with no thought to fashion. Though her presence was a bit intimidating, the people in our church were kind and treated her graciously.

Leia noticed that Janelle constantly got up and down during church services, which distracted everyone around her. When Leia asked her about it, Janelle explained that she had seriously injured her back while working as a registered nurse. Now she was unable to stand for hours at a time, which a job in nursing required. However, she couldn't sit for long periods either. She had taken a job driving a small ice cream vending truck because it allowed her to frequently shift positions.

From her uncomfortable perch in her non-air-conditioned "tin box on wheels," Janelle dispensed her frozen goods to sweaty children. The only relief from the heat came when she opened the freezer compartment to retrieve some ice cream. And while it helped to be able to constantly get up and down, leaning over to get the ice cream was difficult for her.

When Leia told me Janelle's situation, I immediately thought of Mindy Ehrlinger and her back problems. Janelle's nursing specialty had been working in physical rehab and therapy situations, which involved lifting and supporting patients who could not move around well by themselves. As a result of this heavy lifting, Janelle had compressed a couple of disks in her back.

Later she moved to Israel to live in a kibbutz and volunteered in a large Israeli hospital. She sustained another serious injury while lifting heavy patients. This time she had to have surgery for two ruptured disks. Several discs were fused together and two steel rods were placed in her back to support her spine.

By the time we met her, Janelle was in severe pain every day. She took strong medication for pain and used a TENS (transcutaneous electrical nerve stimulation) device to block pain signals before they reached the brain. This certainly explained why she could not sit for long on our metal folding chairs. We offered to pray for Janelle several times, but she demurred, saying she had been prayed for many times. She was simply happy to be in a church where people loved and accepted her.

After Janelle had been in the church for several months, Vic Eason came to preach during a series of special services. Vic was the pastor in Rancho Cucamonga who invited Leia and me to the Bible conference after our long journey in the van.

Though I didn't tell Vic about Janelle or her issues, I was concerned that her constant getting up and down would annoy him as he preached. For the first two nights, he didn't even seem to notice. On the third night, Vic did spot Janelle. He had just gotten up to preach when he stopped, almost in midsentence. He closed his eyes for a moment and then looked directly at Janelle, who was sitting in one of the back rows of chairs.

"Ma'am. Yes, you in the white blouse and gray pants." Janelle looked around. "Yes, you."

She realized it had to be her. She appeared flustered and didn't say anything as she stood up.

"Ma'am, I feel God has shown me that he wants to heal you tonight. Now, I don't even know what is wrong with you, but if you'll just come up here, I'll pray for you and you'll be well."

Janelle still didn't say anything. She shook her head quickly from side to side. She gripped the back of the metal folding chair in front of her.

"Ma'am, it looks like you're afraid." Vic smiled one of his best, wide, disarming smiles. "Look, I'll meet you halfway."

He stepped down off the platform and took a couple of steps toward her. Janelle stepped into the aisle and took about an equal number of steps in the other direction.

"Ma'am," Vic said softly, "can you at least tell me what's wrong?"

"I know what you want to do," Janelle said. "You want to lay hands on me and pray. Then you're going to try to make me do something to see if I'm healed. My back hurts so badly. I'm afraid I'm gonna be hurt worse." Janelle was obviously observant. She had seen Vic pray with people over the past couple of nights.

She was genuinely afraid. It was sad to see her looking around for a way to escape or for someone who could help her. She stepped back into the seats and again held firmly to the back of the chair.

"Okay, ma'am," Vic said in his friendliest drawl. "I know God wants to help you tonight even if you don't believe it. I can see that you are fearful. I can understand that. I lived with fear for years. Let me make this easy for you. You don't have to come up here. You just stand there and raise your hands, and I'll pray for you from here. How's that?"

Janelle nodded. No one was going to touch her or her painful back.

"Then," Vic continued, "after I pray for you, I want you to go to the ladies' room and check yourself. Just see if you can move without pain."

Janelle nodded her assent; it was a chance to get out of this room, away from the danger. She raised both her hands—not too high, shoulder level. Vic prayed with enthusiasm and authority. When he finished, he told her, "Now, you just go check for yourself. Then you come back and tell us what God has done. Okay?"

Janelle walked as quickly as she could to the hallway exit. My wife caught her eye and indicated that she would go with her. Janelle shook her head, a definite no. She wanted to be alone.

The service continued. Vic preached like a house on fire, and the people loved it. Both Leia and I kept looking for Janelle near the hallway where she'd disappeared. There was no sign of her. Did she leave? Was she upset?

Vic stood in front of the platform at the end of the service. He had prayed for a number of people and was now getting ready to turn the service back to me. Quietly, seemingly out of nowhere, Janelle stood at the sanctuary entrance. Her eyes were wide open and her mouth moved, but nothing came out. She looked as if she had seen the proverbial ghost. One by one, the congregation followed our eyes and looked at her. Without a word, Janelle reached down, bent directly at the waist, and touched both toes! She stood upright and did it again. Women gasped. We all knew Janelle had steel rods in her back. She couldn't bend over. We knew that the slightest sudden motion would send her into a paroxysm of pain. But there she was. She was bending, twisting, and smiling.

Leia, who had taken this lonely, ungainly woman as a friend, approached. "Janelle, look at you. You're healed."

"I know, I know," she blubbered. "Oh God, oh God, thank you, thank you!" Janelle, who was normally shy and avoided human contact, was hugging everyone who came near.

She reached out and smothered Vic Eason's slight frame in a bear hug. "Thank you."

Then she told us that when she had gone into the ladies' room, her first thought was that she had gotten away from that man who wanted her to do things that would hurt. She would simply stay in the bathroom until the service was over; then she would be safe. When she heard the music signaling that the service was coming to a conclusion, she relaxed a little. As she became calmer, it just occurred to her that her back wasn't hurting. Pain had become her world. It was normal. Now it was gone. She stood in front of the mirror and thought, *Why not?* Tentatively at first, she had stretched her fingers toward her knees. No pain. She stretched a little farther. Before long, she realized she could touch her toes without any discomfort at all. She had to tell someone. That was when she came back into the sanctuary, speechless at what had happened.

Leia said, "Janelle, I know you don't have to work tomorrow. In the morning, you're going to the gym with me. We're going to get into shape together, and I'm going to teach you how to play racquetball." We all laughed at the thought of Janelle running after a racquetball.

Bills, Bills, and More Bills

One more story comes to mind from those days in the Arizona desert when part-time work, faithful people, and God's providence kept us going.

The church in Casa Grande had been a merry-go-round for pastors. Several had gotten on and off. Since the pastors' addresses changed so often, all church mail went to a post office box. I always went to the post office in the morning, which was usually a discouraging way to start the day. I disliked going because we were always behind on our financial obligations. Each trip to the post office brought a new batch of bills to add to the stack of already overdue debts.

One Tuesday morning I sat in the post office parking lot on Pinal Boulevard. I cracked the door open, then pulled it shut again. I didn't want to do this. Like a man headed for the gallows, I didn't want to face what I knew was waiting—bills and more bills. Advertising expenses, phone bills, rent payment, electricity, water, insurance bills. Bills that would have to wait; bills that I would have to prioritize and juggle. It was so depressing. I sort of prayed. I actually just "thought in God's general direction."

Dear God! Once, just once, I would like to go into that post office and find that someone had sent me money instead of bills! Just once!

I finally pulled out the post office box key and headed inside. When I opened the box, I saw one solitary envelope. Our address was handwritten on the envelope, and there was no return address. *This is great,* I thought to myself, *probably a letter from some disgruntled church person writing anonymously.*

Back in the car, I tore the end of the envelope off and extracted a sheet of paper. I unfolded the paper and another folded piece of paper fell into my lap. I ignored it and looked at the scrawled note on the paper in my hand. Here is what it said:

> *Don, I went to the water company the other day to have the account taken out of your name and put into mine. It's been quite a while since you left Indio and I took over the church and the house you lived in. Forgive me for taking so long to take care of this. But don't worry, the bill was always paid on time. Anyway, they gave me a refund of your deposit, minus this and that. It's not much, but I thought I should send it over to you.*
>
> *Blessings! Adriaan Zavala*

I picked up the paper in my lap and unfolded it. It was a check. A real check! Adriaan was right; it wasn't much. But as far as I was concerned, it might as well have been a million dollars. I'd received a check, not a bill, that day! God had heard my prayer.

I started thinking about the cosmic implications of this.

I had prayed less than ten minutes ago that I would find a check rather than more bills. Now, here it was. I looked at the postmark—several days old. It seems that God knew about, or had even heard, my prayer in the car and stirred Adriaan to go to the water company before I had even asked. I thought about this Scripture:

I will answer them before they even call to me.
    While they are still talking about their needs,
I will go ahead and answer their prayers! (Isaiah 65:24)

This is all too deep for me. But I know this: God will meet our needs if we ask him. Yes, times were tough in Arizona, but somehow the bills always got paid. The same God who worked small miracles for us in Arizona would keep up his good work in Africa!

Meditation on the Miraculous

Einstein proved that time and space exist only because of the physical laws of our material universe. God is Spirit, not material, so he is limited by neither time nor space.

For I am God, and there is no other;
I am God, and there is none like Me,
Declaring the end from the beginning,
And from ancient times things that are not yet done.
ISAIAH 46:9-10, NKJV

CHAPTER 26

AFRICA

1995–1998
Uganda

In just over two years, the little church in Casa Grande had grown from a feeble, hurting flock of thirty-some adults and kids to a strong congregation of about one hundred. Our finances finally covered all our needs. Whenever I sat on the platform waiting to preach, I realized that although I was very happy with what God had done, I was not satisfied. In my heart I still heard the call to go to the nations.

I knew that Leia was settled and happy. She worked at a bridal shop, where she had become good friends with her boss. She loved her job and the house. She was very content, but she could see that I was not. It amazes me that God gave me a wife who was selfless enough to follow me throughout the world. We prayed and talked together, and we agreed that if the doors opened, we would go back to Thailand to try finishing what we had started. She was willing but not at all enthusiastic, and really, who could blame her? Hadn't we moved enough? Hadn't we risked enough? Hadn't we given up enough?

For all these reasons, Leia could not hide her relief when I told her that our fellowship of churches had made a decision to turn their focus away from Asia for the foreseeable future.

Then one Friday in December 1994, the call came.

"Dad!"

It was my daughter, Heidi, calling my office from our home. "Were you out of the office? Pastor Murphy called here at the house looking for you. He wants you to call him right away."

I immediately called our head office and asked to speak to our missions director.

"Don," he said, "I'll get right to the point. We need someone to go to Uganda to relieve Joe Oberlin and his family. They've been there five years and need to come home."

I took the phone away from my ear and looked at it in disbelief. I finally put the phone back to my ear.

"You know," I began, "I am not really interested in going to that part of the world. I would go back to Asia in a heartbeat. I'd really have to think about this."

"Don, this is a great need and a great opportunity. In addition to the main churches in Kampala, the capital city, we have over forty churches in Uganda. You'd be the national director, a key position. Why don't you take some time and pray about this?"

"Okay, how much time?"

"Get back to me on Monday."

I had three days to make a decision to leave my church, uproot my family, and move to the heart of Africa. Where was Uganda anyhow? I'd heard of it. In those pre-Google days, I had to go to the library to investigate. A recent issue of *National Geographic* had a several-page spread on Uganda. It was worse than I'd imagined.

In 1995 the nation of Uganda was eight years out of a terrible civil war, which finally resulted in victory for the National Resistance Movement. Yoweri Museveni[2] became president, replacing Milton Obote, whose regime had been responsible for approximately a quarter of a million civilian deaths.

Conditions in Uganda were finally improving. Still the country remained racked with poverty, political struggle, rebel guerrilla movements, and a high incidence of violent crime.

Uganda had little in the way of infrastructure or law and order.

The necessities of life were in short supply and very expensive. AIDS had begun in Uganda and other sub-Saharan African nations, and the disease was decimating the population. Villages that had managed to survive the war were now becoming ghost towns because of what was known there as "slim disease." (Infected sufferers got very thin before succumbing to AIDS.)

Looking up from the magazine, I wondered, *What will I tell Leia?* She loved Thailand but really didn't even want to go back there. Now Uganda? Good grief! I knew that I should have told Leia right after I received the call from Rev. Murphy, but I had wanted to have more information before I talked to her. That knowledge would now make things even more difficult.

After dinner that night, Heidi left for work and James headed to wrestling practice. As I walked toward my home office, I thought again how Leia had made our newest home, which we rented from the previous pastor of our church, so personal and comfortable. Even though we had moved so many times, Leia could make any house a home. My eyes clouded over with tears and I felt a great hollowness in my chest as I thought about asking her to pray about uprooting our family once again. After I had been in the office a while, Leia appeared in the doorway with a cup of coffee for me.

We had another one of *those* moments.

"Don, I know you have something on your mind. You might as well tell me now. It had something to do with the phone call, right?" She handed me the coffee as I nodded.

"Okay. What did he want?" Leia asked. "Where does he want us to go?"

"Uganda," I blurted out. "Africa."

Leia slumped against the doorjamb of the office. "What did you tell him?"

"I said we would pray about it."

"How do you pray about something like that?" She seemed to be lost in thought.

"I don't know, but I suppose we had better try." I took her arm and walked with her back to our bedroom. We sat on the bed. We couldn't pray much. Amazingly, though, as soon as we began to pray, we both knew that it was God's will for us to go. We just knew it. We didn't like it. We were not excited about it. We really had so many reasons why it was the wrong move at the wrong time. But we knew we should do it.

"I'll make the call tomorrow," I said.

"No. You better do it now before we get thinking and change our minds."

When I called Pastor Murphy to tell him of our decision, he told me that we would have to be ready to leave by the end of February. We had only a couple of months to make all of our arrangements. I had been very worried about how Leia would cope with this very monumental move. The house in Uganda was furnished, so our mission didn't want to pay to ship our furnishings. That would mean selling or storing everything again. We had grown close to the people in Casa Grande, and Leia had become like a mother to many. Breaking those ties and saying good-bye would be hard. Perhaps most difficult was that Heidi would not be making the trip with us.

Now that the decision had been made, I visited many of our denomination's churches in Arizona and California, preaching on missions and raising the profile of the work we would do in Uganda. Meanwhile, Leia took charge of moving sales and most of our packing. Her stoicism and deliberate efficiency as she prepared for our move made me both sad and proud.

As the days passed, doubts and fears began to nag at our minds. What were we doing? Everyone we told thought we were crazy. When we mentioned where we were going, most people instantly thought of HIV/AIDS or Idi Amin, who'd brutally ruled the country in the 1970s.

Our daughter was to get married before we left. Our close family would be broken up. James, now seventeen, was in love with his future wife and said he would stay in Uganda only until he was eighteen. All of this was almost more than we could bear.

As we were dealing with the turmoil that was precipitated by such a major move, we were invited by a friend of ours to attend a concert at his church.

"Don, they are going to have a children's choir from somewhere in Africa. Maybe you'd enjoy it." The truth was, I didn't think I would. I was going to Africa, but I didn't want to be reminded of it right then. We went anyway.

Leia and I arrived at the church and took our seats. The "children" who made up the Watoto Children's Choir were mostly teenagers, though there was a smattering of little ones as well. We listened to the music and watched the youth perform choreographed songs in their colorful African dress.

Several times the music stopped, and one of the older children would tell how he or she had been made an orphan by war or by AIDS and had found a Father in heaven and a home in the church. Leia and I looked at each other in amazement when we realized they were all from—you guessed it—Uganda. God had brought a children's choir all the way from Uganda to the little desert town of Casa Grande (population 26,000 at the time) just when we were planning to move there. It comforted us greatly to be reminded that God was somehow in this drastic move we were making.

We resumed our packing the next day, encouraged and newly inspired by the stories we'd heard at the concert. A couple of weeks later, I realized that Leia and I needed a break.

"Let's drive up to Phoenix and have a nice dinner and go to a movie," I suggested. "The break will do us good."

"What movie?" Leia knew my proclivity to military and action films. She liked animal movies, musicals, and chick flicks.

"Tell you what. We both enjoy going to the IMAX with that seventy-foot-high screen. They have all kinds of films. Let's just go there and watch whatever is playing. We'll take our chances!" She agreed that seemed fair.

After eating a big steak, we headed for the IMAX theater. Guess what was playing? *Africa: The Serengeti.*

For more than an hour, Leia and I watched in fascination as huge herds of migrating animals crossed over the Mara River. Most made it, though some were devoured by huge crocodiles.

At the time, we had no way of knowing that about six months after our arrival in Uganda, we would take our Land Rover across the Maasai Mara National Reserve in Kenya during the great migration season we had seen at the IMAX. We would drive through what could only be described as a "sea" of wildebeests and zebras, which parted slowly as we tooted the horn. We would stand on the banks of the Mara River on the border of the Tanzanian Serengeti and watch the crocodiles. Who would have ever thought?

After the concert and the movie, we were finally beginning to feel excited about our move to Uganda, or as Winston Churchill referred to it, the "Pearl of Africa." When we saw the Ugandan children, we were powerfully reminded that while the country might be a very "ugly" place in many ways, it was home to many beautiful people who needed the hope and change that only Jesus' gospel can give.

Danger and Disease

After seeing the IMAX movie, Leia was sure that when we got to Uganda, we would live in a mud hut and have to shoo inquisitive lions and baboons off our porch. It was not like that at all. We arrived in Kampala in March. After our flight landed at the Entebbe International Airport, Joe, the missionary we were replacing, picked us up at Entebbe and drove us through Kampala, a city of several hundred thousand people, to our new home.

Joe chose a route through a poor residential area. Piles of burning trash lined much of the road. Children dressed in rags, their stomachs distended by malnutrition, stood by the road, staring and shouting at us. "Hey, *mzungu, mzungu!*" (*Mzungu* is used by East

African Swahili speakers to describe white people.) The red dirt road was almost completely paved with discarded black plastic bags. Goats and chickens roamed freely.

Our first impression of Kampala was that it was crowded, chaotic, poverty ridden, bullet scarred, and dirty.

Leia had been horrified by the trip from the airport and said she would have preferred to live in that mud hut that she had first imagined when she heard we were going to the heart of Africa.

She didn't feel much better when we arrived at our new house. On the one hand, the house itself was fairly nice. Joe had been in housing construction before becoming a missionary. Over several years he had transformed the small, three-bedroom African house into a fair replica of an American home. On the other hand, the security measures seemed a bit extreme. The chain-link fence was topped with razor wire; five-hundred-watt halogen lamps lit up the compound at night; and four pit-bull terriers and a security guard kept watch. Now this compound was going to be our home.

As if to unsettle us even more, later that evening Joe regaled us with horror stories about home invasions and robberies by gangs armed with AK-47s. He brought his short-barreled, Mossberg semiautomatic shotgun out of a closet.

"Here, you might need this," he said, handing it to me. "The first round is birdshot to scare them. The next four are double-ought buckshot in case they don't get the message."

Leia gasped. I stared.

"Yeah," Joe said, clearly enjoying our reaction, "just two weeks ago a gang of thieves broke in. The smallest robber cut through the wrought iron on my daughter's window and crawled inside. Thank God she was at a friend's house. That guy made his way to the front door and signaled for the rest of them to come into the house. I confronted him with this shotgun. I didn't want to shoot him in the house, though, so I just put my head down, screamed, and charged him.

"Man, he got up and flew out of the door. Then I fired the

shotgun a few times in their general direction. Yeah, you might need this thing."

I stared at Joe in disbelief. Why in the world was he telling a story like that in front of my wife and son, who had already been traumatized by the drive from the airport?

Leia spoke with a shaky voice. "What did your wife do?"

Joe laughed. "Well, you notice she's not here! She left on the same plane you all came in on. She couldn't wait to leave."

Leia and I locked eyes across the room. She was appalled, angry, and seemed to be saying, "How could you bring me here?"

I changed the subject.

"Joe, is there any advice you can give us? Anything we need to know right away?"

"Well, malaria is a problem. The mosquitoes are huge here, especially in the rainy season, which is coming up next month. You'll want to get started on a good course of malaria medicine. Of course, some people say that it can destroy your liver." He shrugged dramatically. "I don't know. I guess you can take your chances."

That was enough for Leia. "I'm going to bed now! I can't take any more good news."

"She looks a little distressed," said Joe after she'd left the room.

"Yes, she's upset. I better stay out here for a while."

Later, I tiptoed into the bedroom. *Good, she's asleep*, I thought as I glanced down at Leia. I lay down gently on the thin, bowed, foam mattress and prayed.

"Dear God, you know my wife. If we ever have an armed robber come into this house, she will be headed back to the safety of the USA the next day. I know these things are common here, but I'm asking that as long as we are in Uganda, we never get robbed. And while I'm at it, I came to Uganda to preach the saving, healing power of Jesus Christ. I am not going to preach that and then live on malaria medicine. I am asking you tonight that, as long as we are in Africa, we never get malaria."

We lived on a remote road on top of a hill called Makindye Hill in a Kampala suburb. Many expats lived there because of the view, the beauty, and the fact that the American Club (a recreational center) was at the foot of the hill. Those were the very reasons that Makindye was a favorite target of armed thieves. In one two-week period, eight of our neighbors were robbed at gunpoint.

In fact, violence seemed to be a way of life in Uganda. Heavily armed soldiers manned checkpoints on all the main roads. In Kampala it was not at all unusual to hear gunfire, even machine guns, as army and police units shot it out with gangs of robbers and home invaders. Many civilians in Uganda kept rifles and shotguns for self-defense.

Traveling outside of Kampala could be very dangerous. Gangs of robbers set up their own roadblocks on the highways in the late evenings or early mornings. They would stop trucks, buses, and cars and rob the occupants at gunpoint. The thieves would mercilessly shoot anyone who resisted. For that reason, whenever we had to drive outside the capital city, we timed our travel so that we departed in the safer, midmorning hours, and we made sure to arrive at our destination before dusk.

Even then, driving could be treacherous. Children, old men on bicycles, goats, chickens, and the occasional cow would dart out onto the narrow roads. Trucks heading for the city were often grossly overloaded with mountains of *matooke*, also known as green bananas or plantains. Matooke are one of the staple foods of central Uganda. When an overloaded truck broke down, usually due to a broken axle or an exploded tire, the driver would leave his vehicle in the middle of the road, put a few banana tree branches out to warn approaching drivers, and then crawl under the truck to sleep.

We traveled extensively to carry out my responsibilities of overseeing the development of the Ugandan churches. Leia and I drove from the snowcapped Rwenzori Mountains on the west, which border the Congo, to Mount Elgon, which towers over the eastern border with Kenya. We traveled from the wild, dry, barren north of Uganda, which borders Sudan, to the grassy hills and cow country of Mbarrara, not far from Rwanda and Tanzania. In all our journeys over thousands of miles of dangerous, horrible roads and in every kind of weather, God kept us from any really serious problems.

Not only were we never robbed in our home or on the road, but neither my wife nor I ever got malaria. God had heard my prayer. Years later we would spend seven years in Rwanda, another malaria hotspot. We never took antimalarial medicine there either; again, we never contracted the disease despite being bitten by mosquitoes repeatedly. Everyone else we knew who spent any years in East Africa eventually contracted this tropical plague. They seemed to revel in tales of chills, sweats, shakes, and headaches—how they almost died. We had no such stories; one more example of God's faithfulness expressed through small miracles.

The Church on the Hill

In addition to training pastors and assisting the churches in the Uganda Fellowship, I pastored the church in Kampala, which was located on Kololo Hill, an important part of the city. On the hill above us were the residences of diplomats and government officials. Across the street were some very modest apartments. Just a block to the west of the apartments began the sprawling slum of Tufumbira.

Our church served as a ministry training center, as well as a local congregation. Overseeing the training center and church, as well as traveling to visit our churches scattered around the country, kept Leia and me very busy. A great blessing during our time in Uganda was Pastor Richard Taddwa and his wife, Margaret. Richard, like many other children and teenagers in this war-torn nation, had lived on the streets in Kampala just ten years before Leia and I arrived in Uganda. Missionary Peter Turko, who headed an out-reach to AIDS orphans and street children, had led Richard to Jesus. He had then discipled and trained him to be a village church pastor. Because of Richard's honesty and competency, he was chosen to be our church's assistant pastor and primary administrator when Joe

Oberlin was heading up the Uganda Fellowship. When I assumed leadership, Richard became my guide, interpreter, assistant pastor, cultural liaison, and generally my right-hand man. By 2002, he was the national leader of a strong fellowship of churches in Uganda.

Every weekday morning Richard and I led a prayer meeting and Bible study. I conducted training classes many weeknights and led three services each week. The church also held regular evangelistic outreaches of many kinds.

We held Jesus Marches fairly frequently. Anywhere from thirty to sixty church members and ministers in training would meet at the church. Then we would walk or take minivan taxis to a certain area of Kampala. We formed two columns and marched around the neighborhood singing upbeat worship choruses in Luganda, the national language. After a short time we would have a crowd of neighborhood people following us around. Then we would stop, and using a battery-powered PA, various people from our church would talk about what Jesus had done in their lives. Other marchers distributed written invitations to church, talked about the gospel, and prayed with many people.

The majority of our church members lived in the Tufumbira slum and were part of the lowest strata of Ugandan society. They had little dignity or self-esteem. We also had a sprinkling of middle-class professionals and businesspeople, government officials, and military officers. John Ssjemba, the lieutenant in the Presidential Guard who experienced the dramatic healing from AIDS, fell into that category. One of the reasons these "upper-class" Ugandans came to our church was because I was a not a Ugandan and, therefore, free of tribal preference. Uganda is made up of many distinct tribal groups, and unfortunately, many churches tend to show favoritism and prejudice along tribal lines.

When we first arrived in Kampala, our church met in a large, tattered tent. A long green dumpster overflowing with uncollected and fermenting rubbish sat on the corner nearby. A tall tree on the east side of the church was full of large, ugly marabou storks that picked at the garbage in and around the dumpster. These birds left their white droppings everywhere. A tree on the other corner was home to hundreds of fruit bats. Before our evening services we would see the bats swarming out like a black cloud.

Although we were in the city, we also saw our share of "wild animals." Wild or stray dogs, goats, and chickens wandered the neighborhood. These animals easily passed under or through our barbed-wire fence and wandered around on our property.

Snowballs on the Equator

Leia and I were the only missionaries in Uganda from our American fellowship of churches. All our forty-plus churches in Uganda were led by native pastors whom Joe Oberlin and his predecessor had trained. This made us a bit lonely at times. We were not really looking forward to our first Christmas in Africa. Considering the tropical climate of Uganda and the fact that Heidi wasn't with us for the first time, it didn't seem much like the holiday season.

There was one bright spot. Our good friends, whom I'll call Mitch and Sallie Stone, had gone to Kisumu, Kenya, as missionaries at the same time we went to Uganda, and they invited us to their home. The drive from Kampala to Kisumu should have taken about four hours. Because of the random police checkpoints, huge potholes, and slow-moving trucks on the two-lane highway, the trip seemed to take forever. As I navigated the dangers and difficulties, Leia held on to the dash-mounted handgrip most of the way.

As we approached the international border, we saw a line of trucks and private vehicles a half-mile long waiting to cross. We took our place in line, rolling up the windows to keep the beggars, curious faces, and little hands out of the car. *No problem*, I thought. *While we're waiting, I'll get out the paperwork and take care of that.* I knew we had to get several papers signed by government officials before we'd be allowed across the Kenya-Uganda border. "Leia, whenever the line moves, please move our vehicle up." She agreed.

When I returned, paperwork finished, a half hour later, the Land Rover was right where I'd left it.

"I see you didn't have to move the car," I joked. The midday equatorial sun was beating down on the roof, and Leia was in no mood for joking.

"No, we haven't moved an inch."

Now that I had all the paperwork in order, I was impatient to get across the border. I got in and started the engine. Ten minutes later I turned it off again. After another ten minutes in what was beginning to feel like an oven, I had to find out why our car had been sitting in the same spot for an hour. Straddling the traffic lanes that went into and out of Kenya was a small, primitive tin-roofed building, its windows broken or missing. On either side of the building were simple gates made of crudely welded galvanized pipe.

I watched as the gate leading from Kenya into Uganda swung open and shut every minute or so, admitting vehicles into Uganda. The gate on the other side, allowing vehicles to enter Kenya was firmly locked; a chain and padlock held it closed. Obviously no one had opened that padlock in nearly an hour. *Good grief*, I thought, *this is an international border*. I looked for someone who might be able to unlock the gate and break the logjam. The Kenyan police and customs people standing around studiously ignored me.

I approached a man in uniform who looked responsible.

"*Jambo, bwana!*" I said. [Hello, sir!]

The officer rolled his eyes and replied in perfect British English, "How may I help you, sir?"

"Well, we have been sitting in our car for nearly an hour now, along with all these other people." My hand swept toward the line of vehicles now a mile long. "When do you think they might let us go across?"

The big Kenyan policeman smiled and said, "Anytime from now." I had not been in Africa long, but I knew what that meant. "Anytime from now" means just that—*any time* from now. It could be five minutes, five hours, or five days.

Now he looked over my shoulder at the long line of waiting vehicles. He avoided my inquiring gaze. "The man with the key is gone," he said. He made it sound so . . . normal, so reasonable. I was new to Africa; I would learn that he was right. At that moment, however, his answer seemed absolutely preposterous.

"The man with the key is gone!" I echoed incredulously.

Why would the official with the key just walk off and leave people stranded at an international border? I later learned that Dr. Ian Clark, who labored for many years in a dangerous and distressed area of Uganda called the Luwero Triangle, had written a book full of wonderful human-interest stories. The book, which details many adventures and sacrifices made at his clinic, is called *The Man with the Key Has Gone.* You really would have to live and work in East Africa to understand.

I started to ask more questions of the immigration officer, but the Kenyan had no more to say to me. "Please return to your vehicle, sir," he said. "The gate will open anytime from now."

I returned to the car. Leia was relieved to see me; beggars had begun pounding on the window as soon as they noticed a woman sitting alone in the car.

"Don, what took you so long? Why aren't we moving?" She was obviously steaming, physically and emotionally.

"I could explain it to you, but it wouldn't make any more sense to you than it does to me. We just have to wait." And we did.

After nearly another hour, the "man with the key" returned, and the long line began its slow stop-and-go through the border.

Late that afternoon we passed through the granite formations that signaled the approach to Kisumu on the northeastern shores of Lake Victoria, colloquially known as the malaria capital of the world. We arrived at the home of the Stones and eagerly got out of the Land Rover under their carport. Thank God, shade; and tomorrow was Christmas.

The Stones' fifteen-year-old daughter, Rhia, greeted us excitedly.

"Hey, welcome! It's so good to see you guys. Guess what? We're going to have a white Christmas!"

Oh man, I wondered, *what has happened to Rhia? Snow? In Kenya?* Maybe it would snow on seventeen-thousand-foot high Mount Kenya, but certainly not in subtropical Kisumu. I decided she had to be kidding and ignored that part of her greeting. Soon we were seated around the Stones' dining room table, catching up and comparing our impressions about our first few months in Africa. During a lull in the conversation, Sallie laughed and asked, "Did Rhia tell you about her plans for a white Christmas?"

I replied, "Well, she joked about that when we first got here."

"I was not joking!" Rhia interjected. She leaned forward and folded her hands on the table. "My dad says we can pray for anything. Well, I love snow at Christmas. I believe God can give me a white Christmas. Right, Dad?"

An embarrassed silence from the Stone parents.

Sallie got up and began to clear the serving dishes from the table. "Why don't we move into the other room where we can be more comfortable?" she asked. She obviously was hoping to change the topic before Michael had to explain the extent of his faith or contradict that of his daughter.

We moved into their living room. Leia and Sallie began sharing their mutual experiences in the months since they had arrived in Africa. Mitch and I compared notes on how different ministry in Africa was from what we had expected.

Our conversation was interrupted by what sounded like a hundred hammers pounding on the tin roofs of the carport and the verandah. Then it got louder! We rushed immediately to the windows to see what in the world was going on. In just a few minutes, the Stones' lawn was covered several inches deep with mothball-sized hail. It *was* a white Christmas. Rhia gloated and gave thanks to God. We debated as to whether our lack of faith was more reasonable than Rhia's unreasonable prayer. We decided that the faith of a child and the love of God trump human reason.

Meditation on the Miraculous

You may be enjoying life right where you are and still feel unsettled because you know in your soul that God is readying you for a new assignment.

> *One of the things I always pray for is the opportunity, God willing, to come at last to see you. For I long to visit you so I can bring you some spiritual gift that will help you grow strong in the Lord. . . . I want you to know, dear brothers and sisters, that I planned many times to visit you, but I was prevented until now.*
> ROMANS 1:10-11, 13

CHAPTER 27

AUF WIEDERSEHEN

1998–1999
Germany

Leaving Uganda came about almost as suddenly and unexpectedly as going there. After more than three difficult but rewarding years in Uganda, the work was well organized and moving ahead slowly but steadily. I was very pleased with the young Ugandan leaders who were emerging, but because of their youth and inexperience, I knew many years of development were necessary. This development needed to occur at a much slower, methodical, and deliberate pace than the exhausting and exhilarating schedule I had been keeping.

I felt I needed a break before I broke. The almost nonstop traveling and ministering under always-stressful circumstances were producing signs of exhaustion in both Leia and myself. I needed rest and also time to evaluate my place in the mission. After all of our experiences over the years, Leia and I recognized that our ministry strengths were in pioneering, evangelizing, and trouble-shooting—not maintaining a continuous, steady course. The work in Uganda needed someone who could be content to make a long-term commitment. I needed time and space to pray about that.

In what seemed like an answer to my prayers and needs, my good friend, Pastor Peter Vandervalk from the Netherlands, called me on the phone. Peter was the national leader of a powerful fellowship of churches. We talked for a while, and then he offered to fly Leia and me to Europe for a "working vacation." He would arrange for me to preach at several churches in Holland, as well as have plenty of opportunity to rest.

When we arrived in Holland, Peter jokingly told me, "Since your name is Schulze, I've also arranged for you to preach in Germany."

As we visited and worked in Germany for about a week, I felt that God was telling me that he had something for us to do there and that it was imminent. I told Leia that I felt we should call our mission director and tell him how we felt. Reverend Murphy said he would pray about it but that he would prefer we stay in Uganda for another year unless there was some compelling reason to go to Germany.

About a month after we returned to Uganda, Pastor Peter contacted me again. "Don, Helge Schmidt, a man from Augsburg, Germany, near Munich, came all the way to Holland to ask me to send someone to help him start a church in Augsburg. He is sincere and seems like a very sound and spiritual person. I told him about you. He said that is exactly what he wants—an experienced church planter to help him. He's willing to interpret for you while you learn German and to work under your authority. I have talked to him several times now. I think we should respond to this, and I think God may have arranged this for you—or maybe he's arranged *you* for this."

There was the compelling reason to go to Germany. Leaving the young men I had worked with so closely in Uganda was difficult. Yet I felt confident that the young national leaders were sufficiently established and trained to progress with whomever replaced me.

By May of 1998, Leia and I were living just south of Augsburg, Germany, at No. 7, Gartenstrasse in the small town of Koenigsbrunn, about forty-five minutes northwest of Munich. Helge and Frauke Schmidt and their three children gave us a wonderful welcome, helping us in every way possible. They were faithful, tireless workers for the gospel.

I think Bavaria is one of the most beautiful places in the world. Each season has its own physical attraction. The yellow fields of flowers in summer stand waving in front of the distant, snow-covered Alps. In the winter, the barren branches are decorated with multitudes of glimmering icicles. Everything looks like a scene from a postcard. God's wonderful creation is on continuous and magnificent display.

We also saw God exhibit his love and power in Germany. It all began when we invited Rudolf, our postman, to a weeknight Bible study that we were holding at our house as part of our church-planting strategy. The postman, in turn, gave our phone number to Janie Stutzel, a woman who lived on his mail route. Janie was the American wife of Otto, a German pilot for Lufthansa Airlines. Janie was in her late forties. She had lived in Germany for twenty years yet spoke limited German. Except when going shopping or making small talk, she rarely used it. The presence of a large American army base in nearby Augsburg provided her with plenty of English-speaking companions.

After Rudolf told Janie about the new Americans on his postal route, Janie called Leia and welcomed her to Germany. She then asked if Leia would like to come by for fresh bread, jam, and coffee. Janie's husband was gone much of the time, flying around Europe. They had two beautiful teenage daughters, Kim and Pam, and Jennie, a ten-year-old. The older girls, too, were gone most of the time, busy with school and friends.

Leia enjoyed her time at Janie's house and was happy to meet another American. "Oh, Janie," she said, "I'm glad you are so nearby and that you're a Christian. It would be wonderful to have you with us at our Bible study tomorrow night."

Janie told her that it would be absolutely impossible for her to come. Leia looked at her, surprised. "Janie, it's only a couple of blocks. If you need a ride, I would be more than happy to come get you."

"Well, I guess you'll find out sooner or later. I can't *come* because

I might *go*." Janie laughed a kind of sad and hopeless laugh as she saw Leia's bewildered look.

Sighing, Janie said, "That was a joke, but I guess it's not really funny. The reason I can't come is that I can't go anywhere. Really. Two and half years ago I had a hysterectomy. The doctors made a horrible mistake; they damaged the nerves that control my rectal sphincter. Now I have very little control of my bowels. They did another surgery, but that only made the problem worse. Now I am completely incontinent. Oh, Leia, it's so embarrassing to have to tell this to someone I have just met."

"Well," Leia took her hand, "at least now I get your joke. What's life like for you now? Two years, oh my, that's . . ." Leia was at a loss for words.

"Life is terrible," Janie admitted. "Otto's gone most of the time; the older girls are great, but they're busy. I have little Jennie, but she doesn't want me fussing over her much. I'm pretty bored. Like I said, I can't go anywhere. I never know when I'll have an accident. That would be so embarrassing that I just don't go anywhere. Well, I get on my bicycle and go around the corner to the bakery sometimes in the morning. That's about it; I'm just stuck here." She began to cry.

In her tenderhearted way, Leia said, "Janie, I just can't believe that our God wants to leave you in this condition. Why don't you come to the Bible study tomorrow and let us pray for you? My husband and I have seen so many wonderful miracles over the years. I'm sure God will do something to help you. Just say the word, and I'll be here to pick you up."

"You don't understand," Janie said, shaking her head. "The doctors actually cut the nerves. They say it is impossible to fix this problem. Nerves like this can't be repaired, and they don't grow back. I've been a Christian many years. I've heard stories of modern-day healing and miracles, but frankly, I have my doubts. Do these things really happen?"

Leia smiled gently. "Look, Janie, we've seen blind eyes healed, crippled people healed, and even a man and his family healed of

AIDS! I'm sure God can help you. Please, let me pick you up tomorrow evening."

"Leia, what if I had an accident in your car? That would be terrible." She continued to cry softly, then seemed to calm herself. Looking at Leia, she said, "Look, here's my idea. Maybe my daughter Kimmy and I will come on our bicycles. It's close enough. That way if I have to, I can jump up and leave. Now I'm not promising anything, but we'll try to make it. Okay?"

The next evening only a few people came for the study in our living room. When Leia ushered Janie and Kim into the sitting room, Rudolf gave Janie a surprised look. We supposed he knew her secret and was surprised to see her out of the house. Janie sat perched nervously on the edge of the sofa as we began. After just a few minutes, she lifted her chin toward Kim and the two of them moved quickly and silently toward the door.

Leia followed them to their bicycles. "Janie, is there . . . is there something wrong?"

"No, but I'm just so afraid. I'm afraid something will happen because of those destroyed nerves. Just let me go home. I'll call you tomorrow."

The maternal instincts came out in Leia. She took hold of the handlebars.

"Janie, please come back in. I won't embarrass you, but I'll ask Don and the others to pray for you in a general way. After they pray, if you still want to leave that's fine. But, please, please don't leave before we have the opportunity to pray. I just know God wants to help you."

Janie dismounted. "Okay, but I really can't stay. You understand."

When they walked back into the living room, Leia, using a great deal of discretion, asked the group to pray for Janie. She simply told them that Janie had an injury and physical condition that kept her home most of the time. Then we gathered around her place on the couch. At first she looked like a trapped animal as we put our hands upon her and began to pray. Her conservative upbringing had not prepared her for this kind of intercession. We asked God to do a miracle so Janie could live a normal life. As we finished praying, Janie said she had a feeling of great peace. All the anxiety she had felt about being away from home was gone. She and Kim stayed for the rest of the evening.

As they mounted their bikes for the short trip home, Janie said to my wife, "Leia, thanks for your insistence. I know you care. I will call you tomorrow and let you know how I'm doing. It was so nice to get out and be around people; I hope God really has healed me."

Early the next morning a very excited Janie called a very sleepy Leia. "Leia! I can't believe it. Well, wait—that's not right. I do believe! Anyway, I'm sorry to call so early but I just had to tell you. I'm healed. I really believe—no, I know I am. I woke up this morning and realized I needed to use the bathroom. For two years, I had not had that feeling. My body has just gone without any warning! I was able to lie there and control it till I felt like getting up. I'm just like a normal person again. . . ." Janie was so excited she could hardly get the words out.

Janie was indeed completely healed by the power and the goodness of God. Now that she was liberated from the confines of her house, she started to attend the German language school with us. She and Leia went shopping and touring on their bicycles. For the entire year we were in Germany, we stayed in close touch with her family.

Back Where It All Began

When we left Germany, God blessed us with the opportunity to pastor another "broken" church, this time in Southern California. Though we'd had past success in helping restore discouraged congregations, this particular church seemed almost beyond hope. God encouraged us by healing Raquel Rodriguez, a fiftysomething woman, of a debilitating and advanced case of lupus. She was so weak that she could not stand and had to use a motorized wheelchair even to get around her house. Her eyes were so sensitive to light that she wore dark sunglasses indoors. A visiting pastor and evangelist prayed for her in our church, and the next morning she was *completely* and, as far as we know, permanently healed. The greatest miracles, of course, were seeing how God gradually brought spiritual vitality, healing, and growth to that congregation.

Despite the challenges that came with pastoring a struggling church, Leia and I had been ready to settle down in Southern California where our adventures had started so many years before. One more time, God allowed us to buy a home and pastor a wonderful church. I was fifty-three years old and had two beautiful grandchildren in addition to our kids. It seems that God is not impressed with our chronological age or our material comfort. He has greater things in mind for us.

In January 2003, the Holy Spirit began to help me understand that our work in that place was finished and that I should start seeking God's direction. Offering your life to God, without reservation, can have unexpected consequences. As I gave early mornings and late nights to prayer, God began to direct my heart back to Africa, which was strange in a way because we had never really wanted to go to Africa in the first place.

When we had left Uganda, we were sad to leave our friends and disciples, but we felt almost guilty about our relief at leaving behind the multitude of difficulties, dangers, privations, inconveniences, and cultural dissonance that were our daily experience there. So in retrospect it seems remarkable that, as I felt the Holy Spirit begin to direct us back into foreign missions, I knew without doubt that the African continent was where we should go. I also just knew that God wanted us to pioneer and build a new work from the ground up. I prayed and considered the various nations in which our fellowship of churches had no missionaries or churches.

I considered the Central African Republic, but it was too chaotic and dangerous, not to mention likely to be more primitive than what I could subject my now "grandmotherly" wife to. I also thought about the eastern Congo, where a devastating volcano and recent civil war had left the people in desperate need of God's help. I felt strongly attracted to that opportunity but wasn't sure it was God's direction. Then I turned my attention to Rwanda, which I knew little about except that it was the one of the poorest, smallest, and most densely populated countries in Africa.

I flew to Rwanda and went to Goma, eastern Congo, by car. Because of the ongoing guerilla warfare, the lack of infrastructure, and very primitive conditions in Congo, I didn't feel I could ask Leia to move there. While traveling through Rwanda, I spent a few days in the capital of Kigali. The country had been devastated by the Hutu genocide of the Tutsi tribe just nine years earlier. However, under the leadership of President Paul Kagame, Rwanda was making great strides toward recovery and seemed to be a truly "developing nation." Electricity, water, and fuel were sometimes in short supply and housing was scarce and expensive, but I sensed excitement in the air. By the time my airplane landed in Los Angeles in May 2003, I felt certain that God was directing us there.

I expected that the leadership of our denomination would not be open to me pioneering a new field at my age. Starting a church in a difficult place like Rwanda would be a difficult, risky, and costly venture. I decided to talk with our missions' leader, who would ultimately make the decision. Certain that he would turn me down, I was prepared to go home and tell God, "See? I tried; I must have misunderstood what you were saying. Now can I pastor my church and watch my grandchildren grow up?"

When I met this leader for lunch, I explained how God seemed to be directing me. The older man looked me in the eye for a long moment. Our forks were suspended over our meals. Finally he spoke. "Don, you need to fly over there, check some things out, and be ready to leave by July." I *had* heard correctly from God.

Leia was not so easily convinced. When she took the matter to God, he told her, simply and gently, "I have called you to be as

Sarah, who left all to follow Abraham, so follow and support your husband." So for the next seven years, we made Rwanda our home.

Although recounting the adventures we experienced there would take another book, I hope that *this book* has done what I set out to do: encourage you to believe in the great love God has for you and the wonderful life he has planned for you—if only you step out in faith and obedience to do his will.

Promising God that we'll go wherever he sends us has made life challenging at times, yet Leia and I can't imagine a more rewarding way to live. We do not spend a lot of time looking backward. Like Paul said, we forget the things that are behind and press forward toward the goal of the high calling of Christ. But when we do look back, there is no second-guessing and no regrets—only wonder that God in his sovereign purposes chose two weak, ordinary people to serve and know him.

Meditation on the Miraculous

Living without regrets means abandoning your own desires and comfort to follow God where he is at work—and where he seems to be moving you.

> *Everything else is worthless when compared with the infinite value of knowing Christ Jesus my Lord. For his sake I have discarded everything else, counting it all as garbage, so that I could gain Christ and become one with him.*
> PHILIPPIANS 3:8-9

Epilogue

In July 2011, Leia and I left Rwanda for the last time. The most difficult part was leaving the precious spiritual children God had given us during our seven years of evangelism and church planting there. Although we are separated physically, through the wonder of technology, Facebook, and Skype, we are able to stay in touch with many of them.

Since returning to the United States, Leia and I have been able to spend precious time with our children and grandchildren in San Diego. It is amazing that even though we were separated from them by years of time and thousands of miles, we are an incredibly close and loving family. We kept the faith, and God kept our children. Knowing that we will spend eternity together is always sufficient comfort for the years we missed with them here.

Over the last year and half, we have been rebuilding our lives and giving no thought to retirement. No, rather we are getting ready for our second half. As I write this, we are praying about exactly how to return to the work of evangelizing, making disciples, and church planting here in the States.

I have long wanted to write down for my own posterity a record of God's love, power, faithfulness, and how Jesus Christ is, indeed, the same yesterday, today, and forever.[3] No one is more amazed than I am that God has allowed Leia and me to do what we have done and see what we have seen. It is my hope that those who read this book will be in awe of God's miracles, particularly in light of the weakness and humanity of his servants.

I believe that Christians have been coached into thinking that the things you read about in this book only happen to Christian celebrities. That's why I have tried to be honest and transparent. I want you to understand that God does not do wonders for those who are strong or holy, or worthy or fearless, but rather for those who simply try to believe and obey him—for those who love him and want to see him glorified.

Remember that Philip was just a deacon, waiting on tables and distributing food, when he went to Samaria and shared his faith, prayed for the sick, cast out demons, and saw a whole city affected (see Acts 8). This was the normal Christian life.

Faith and obedience are two sides of the same coin. It is hard, if not impossible, to step out in faith if you won't obey God; it is also difficult to obey God completely without faith. Jesus said, "These miraculous signs will accompany those who believe: They will cast out demons in my name, and they will speak in new languages. They will be able to handle snakes with safety [have authority through Christ over the devil], and if they drink anything poisonous, it won't hurt them."[4] Notice he did not say that the apostles would do these things; he did not say that "Christians living in the first century" would do these things. What he said was "those who believe" will do these things. If you believe the life and the words of Jesus, you *will*, when the occasion or opportunity arises, do these things.

Think of how our world and our lives would be impacted if every Christian decided to obey, follow, and imitate Jesus in the context of the place God has them. We would all be missionaries and please him who said, "As the Father has sent Me, I also send you"[5] and "he who believes in Me, the works that I do he will do also; and greater works than these he will do."[6] It is time to simply believe that Jesus meant what he said and has not changed his mind. Then, with an intentional dependence on the Holy Spirit, we will step out in obedience and follow his leading—whether that means giving sacrificially, laying hands on a neighbor and praying for healing, boldly sharing the Word with a relative, or forgiving the unforgivable.

The only alternative is to rationalize the example and commandments of Christ, as well as the mighty works and teachings of the apostles in the book of Acts. Because many of Jesus' teachings are so radical, so foreign to human logic and worldly wisdom, and so dependent on the reality and immediacy of the supernatural, we may be tempted to decide that Jesus couldn't have actually meant what he said. Yet when we do so, we leave the will of God undone and the glory of God unseen. God is glorified when we simply believe and obey.

I truly hope you have found the stories in this book entertaining and encouraging. More than that, however, I hope the fact that God used simple people like Leia and me will help you realize the tremendous potential in your life that will be released by simple faith and obedience.

Acknowledgments

Thanks to my sweetheart and companion, Leia, for her endless encouragement and hours and hours of patient proofreading. Thanks to my mother-in-law, Patricia Jennings, who provided encouragement, proofreading, and a comfortable place to finish the work on this book. Thanks to Ms. Tara Merrill who spent much valuable time in editing and corrections and to Mr. J. Robert Lee of Charlotte, North Carolina, who in the midst of his own sorrow did so much to encourage us to push forward with this project. Thanks to all of our friends over the years who kept saying, "You *really* ought to write a book." A big note of gratitude to Mrs. Pat Johnson of Charlotte for proofreading and editing and to author Robert Whitlow for his advice and encouragement.

I owe a debt of gratitude to Pastor Alex Wilson who, along with the people of his church in Rancho Cucamonga, California, took a big gamble on us and financed us in pioneering our first church.

Leia and I owe very much to Pastor Vic and Wilma Eason and Marcia Regan who prayed for us and helped us enter our destiny. A big thank-you to Edwin B. Corley who was an early mentor and is still my good friend.

I want to express my gratitude to my mother, Kathy Collette (1929–2005), who often worked from morning until night as she, a single mom, sacrificed the best years of her life to focus on raising my brother and me. I want to thank James D. Schulze, my dad, who died in 2004, and his wife, our "adopted mom," Louise Schulze, who died in 2013. They always supported us and encouraged us in our foreign mission work, though they wanted us to be nearby.

There are innumerable people in the churches we have pastored and in the mission communities we have led who have supported, encouraged, and helped to make all these things possible. Thanks to you all!

Endnotes

1. Neither the idea nor the survey itself was completely original. I used materials and ideas from Campus Crusade, Dr. James Kennedy's *Evangelism Explosion*, and Dr. Bill Bright's "Here's Life" campaign.
2. At the time this book was written, Museveni remained the president of Uganda.
3. See Hebrews 13:8.
4. Mark 16:17-18
5. John 20:21, NKJV
6. John 14:12, NKJV

About the Author

Don in Vietnam

Don Schulze considers himself a "trophy" of God's redemption and grace. The family Don grew up in was shattered by divorce, and he and his brother were raised by a devoted mother who endured great difficulty in the days before food stamps, housing assistance, or other public aid.

Don enlisted in the United States Marine Corps immediately after high school and was sent to Vietnam in 1968. He married Leia in 1971 and became a sales representative for Southern California manufacturers and a sales manager in

Don, Leia, Heidi, and James

the western United States for a Canadian manufacturer. He also started a small contracting business in related fields.

After coming to Christ, Don felt a call to full-time Christian ministry. His first pastorate was a church

Don and friends in Africa

in Moreno Valley, California, which Don and Leia started in 1986. By 1988 they were leading a church-planting effort in Bangkok, Thailand. Over the years they served as church planters in Uganda and Germany as well. In addition, Don has spent time ministering in Mexico, the Philippines, Malaysia, the Netherlands, England, Zambia, Kenya, South Africa, Madagascar, and Fiji.

Don and Leia

Don and Leia lived and served in Rwanda from 2003 to 2010. During that time they began working closely with the Anglican Church of Rwanda in Gahini and neighboring Tanzania. In 2010 Don was ordained first as a deacon and then as a presbyter in the Anglican Province of Rwanda.

James & his wife, Karina

Today Don lives in northeast Florida and is a priest in the Anglican Church of North America. Don's passion is to share the reality of God's love and power with as many people as possible. He pursues this through speaking, teaching, writing, and maintaining a new web-based teaching ministry, www.imana.info.

Heidi & her husband, Malcolm

Online Discussion *guide*

TAKE *your* TYNDALE READING EXPERIENCE *to the* NEXT LEVEL

A FREE discussion guide for this book is available at bookclubhub.net, perfect for sparking conversations in your book group or for digging deeper into the text on your own.

www.bookclubhub.net

You'll also find free discussion guides for other Tyndale books, e-newsletters, e-mail devotionals, virtual book tours, and more!

DISCOVER HOW ONE PARENT,

desperate to get everything right,
lost control—and regained his family.

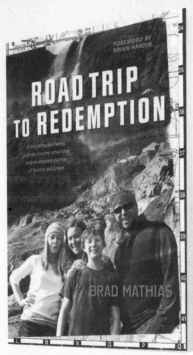

ISBN 978-1-4143-6394-3

Brad Mathias thought everything in his family was fine . . . until
he and his wife learned a secret, one that rocked their family to
the core. In a last-ditch attempt to reconnect as a family, Brad
and his wife piled their three children into the car and embarked
on a wild, crazy, seven-thousand-mile trip across the country.
As they drove, they realized how far apart they'd drifted, found
unexpected blessings—and journeyed together from pain and
loss to recovery and healing.

CP0755